ECONOMIC SURVEY 1919–1939

by the same author

DEVELOPMENT PLANNING

THE PRINCIPLES OF ECONOMIC PLANNING
A Study Prepared for the Fabian Society

THE THEORY OF ECONOMIC GROWTH

OVERHEAD COSTS
Essays in Economic Analysis

SOME ASPECTS OF ECONOMIC DEVELOPMENT

POLITICS IN WEST AFRICA

TROPICAL DEVELOPMENT 1880–1913
Studies in Economic Progress

GROWTH AND FLUCTUATIONS 1870–1913

ECONOMIC SURVEY

1919-1939

by

W. ARTHUR LEWIS

London
GEORGE ALLEN AND UNWIN
Boston Sydney

FIRST PUBLISHED IN 1949
EIGHTH IMPRESSION 1978

ISBN 0 04 330049 9 Paperback

PRINTED IN GREAT BRITAIN
BY UNWIN BROTHERS LIMITED
THE GRESHAM PRESS, OLD WOKING, SURREY

CONTENTS

TABLES

CHARTS

PREFACE

THIS book is the substance of a course of lectures given at the London School of Economics in the sessions 1944–47. The original purpose of the lectures was to give students a brief idea of what happened between the two wars as background knowledge needed in interpreting the literature of the period; but out of this has grown, as the reader will see for himself, an over-ambitious attempt to interpret the inter-war years in the setting of world economic history.

The humble origin of the project is given in explanation of its form. First, the book is not an attempt to settle definitively for professional economists any of the major controversial issues. It is not intended for professional economists at all. It is intended for students of about second year level, and for the interested lay public. Reference is made to theoretical controversy where such controversy is relevant, but the present intention is only to provide a background against which such controversy may be set.

Secondly, the material is highly condensed so that problems may stand out in framework rather than in detail. The book is meant as a starting point; copious source references and a bibliography are the means by which the reader is intended to acquire detailed knowledge, and to check for himself the accuracy of digest statements and conclusions. The writer confesses to having himself been startled on finishing the book and discovering how short it is for so large a theme, but he has resisted the temptation to expand by adding detail. There are already plenty of large books full of detail in which any student who so desires can easily lose himself; there seems greater need for a book that establishes a framework into which the detail can easily be fitted later.

It is particularly necessary to draw attention to the limited purpose of the chapters in Part II devoted to individual countries. None of these is meant to give a chronological history of the country with which it deals. The object is not to write a history of countries, but only to select some of the more interesting experiments made by governments in the inter-war period, and to examine their results. There is no intention to give a complete account of individual countries.

Footnotes are as disturbing as they are unsightly, and have

been banned. Notes to the text have been collected together at the end of the book. With few exceptions they are mainly references to sources, and they can all be ignored by the general reader.

W.A.I.

CHAPTER I

INTRODUCTION

IN November 1918 the first world war terminated; in September 1939 the second world war began. To future historians the twenty-one years which intervened will appear at the same time among the saddest, the most exciting and the most formative in human history. To take the social changes only—there were new techniques of government, communism, fascism, a League of Nations; there was unprecedented mass unemployment, and vast experiments designed to eliminate it; there were marked shifts in the balance of political and economic power, from Western Europe eastwards and westwards; and these are only the more spectacular features which spring to mind. Of course, the philosopher sees nothing new under the sun; everything that happened in this period had its roots in the years before 1918, and its parallel in some previous civilisation; but there can have been few periods of twenty-one years into which so much experience has been packed, and most of us will hope that at any rate we and our children shall not have the privilege of seeing such exciting times again.

This book is confined to the economic history of the period. Its purpose is to record events, and to seek their causes and their lessons. The obstacles to achieving so large a purpose are so obvious that they need hardly be recorded. Any newspaper which appeared throughout this period will have published over six thousand issues, nearly every one recording some event in some part of the world with some economic significance. What shall we exclude? What was cause and what effect? What was, or was not "economic"? We are too close to what has happened to understand it, or even to agree about it. And yet we must make the effort, for we need the past in order to shape the future. This book is offered only as a preliminary essay; doubtless soon to be displaced by others as time recedes into clearer perspective.

Whatever the mellowing of history may reveal, two features stand out to characterise the period. It was an age of dislocation, and an age of experiment.

The dislocation stands out clearly. In all these twenty-one years there were not more than five, the five which ended the twenties, that men felt to be years of normal prosperity. Taking the period as a whole, many of the prosperous pre-war trends continued; productivity increased; the standard of living was materially higher in 1939 than it had been in 1914; the people's houses were better and they contained more comforts. But still it was an age of dislocation. The first half of the twenties was dominated by attempts to recover from war, by inflations and deflations, by violent boom and violent slump, by low production and high unemployment, and by a general feeling of insecurity. Then came the five good years, in which men breathed freely, only to be followed swiftly by descent into the greatest trade depression ever recorded, whose gloom hung over the whole decade of the thirties. The world was richer after the 1914 war than it had been before; but it seemed also much less secure.

The answer of governments to this insecurity was greater experimentation in economic affairs. No period is so rich in plans for prosperity. Democracies and dictatorships alike resolved that society should no longer be at the mercy of economic events, and sought gropingly, and in conflicting and contradictory ways, to control events by government agency. There is a harvest of experience to be reaped in analysing the nature and results of all these plans.

But behind all the dislocation and experiment lurks the fundamental question: why, bye and large, was the inter-war period so much less favourable in its economic experience than the decades before the war? The sixty years before 1914 witnessed an astonishing expansion of the world economy, in area, in production, in interdependence, and in complexity. Why did progress reduce, not indeed to a halt, but to a much slower pace after 1918? Was this change only the temporary consequence of the war, or were there more fundamental causes of disequilibrium? Could a return to pre-war rates of progress have been expected, in the normal course of events, or has the world entered an era of relative economic stagnation? No confident answer can be given to these questions; but they are vital questions, and an attempt to answer them must constitute the major object of any survey of the period.

PLAN OF THE BOOK

The task has been divided into three parts. In the first part of the book there is given a brief chronological survey of the events of the twenty-one years. The emphasis is on cyclical movements. This is not a history of industrial relations, or of economic organisation, or of public finance, or of anything but the ebb and flow of economic activity. Labour relations, monopolisation, and so on are mentioned, in so far as they throw light upon the ebb and flow, but they are not our main concern in this book. Our task is not to write a complete economic history of the inter-war period, but merely to seek light on the fundamental determinants of growth.

Part II is a brief account of some national experiments. Here again there is no attempt to give a twenty-one year economic history of any of the countries included. The emphasis is solely on experiments and their lessons, and there is not even any attempt to include all the experiments which any country made. Thus the German chapter is concerned mainly with the first four years of the thirties, whose lessons seem more useful than those of later years. The French chapter is focussed on the Blum experiment, the American chapter on the New Deal, the Japanese chapter on the first half of the thirties, and so on. A complete history of all these countries for all these twenty-one years is beyond the competence of any writer and of any book.

Then finally in Part III, having surveyed the events of the period, we try to put them into their setting. The pre-war world is brought in for comparison with its successor, and we come at last to grips with the fundamental movements. The tentativeness of our conclusions calls for no excuse. It emphasises rather how little we know about the causes of economic progress and of stagnation. The result of the book is to present a challenge to the students of today and of tomorrow; that their researches may shine a clearer light on matters which now rest largely in obscurity.

PART I

THE CYCLE

CHAPTER II

1918–1925

CONDITIONS at the end of World War I were so much like those with which we have become familiar at the end of World War II that we need no detailed picture to bring them home to us. On the whole, they were not so bad as conditions in 1946, although of course to their contemporaries they seemed quite catastrophic. The French, for example, were appalled by the physical destruction in their country. They estimated that 2,700,000 people had been driven from their homes; that 285,000 houses had been destroyed and 411,000 houses damaged; that 22,000 factories, 4,800 kilometres of railways, 1,600 kilometres of canals, 59,000 kilometres of roads and 3,337,000 hectares of arable land had been rendered useless; and so on.[1] But the world destruction done by the 1914 war was small compared with that done by the war of 1939; it was more or less confined to a gash five miles wide across France and Belgium, and it was made good with astonishing speed. There are closer parallels in other spheres. The collapse of Germany as an economic unit on this occasion compares with the collapse last time of Russia and of the Austro-Hungarian empire, with the hunger, exhaustion, bewilderment and economic and moral disintegration, which on both occasions made the organisation of relief measures so urgent a task. There was also, in the political arena, the same sense of hopelessness produced by the immediate outbreak of quarrelling and suspicion between the victors over the fate of the vanquished, with the additional complication last time that war continued in various parts of Europe for some years after the main conflict was over.

RELIEF

Then as now, relief seemed the most urgent task. In its later stages the Allied blockade had done its work well. By the end of 1918, and even before the end of the war, the peoples of Central Europe were starving, and agricultural output was so low that there was no prospect of their being able to feed themselves for a long time. Russia, also, was in an exhausted state owing to the civil war and the decline of production. The first task of the Allies was thus to bring food to the peoples of Europe, allied, neutral and ex-enemy.

The organisation and finance of relief is an important study, but one which we need not now pursue in detail.[2] The work was done mostly by the American Relief Administration, which was created early in 1919 by the United States Government and which served also as the executive arm of the section of the Allied Supreme Council responsible for relief, until with the signing of the Peace Treaty in June 1919, the Council ceased to exist. Thereafter the American Relief Administration remained an official American body for some months, and then became unofficial. There were also many other private relief agencies in the field, but their work was overshadowed in volume by that of the A.R.A.

By June 1919, relief deliveries to Europe reached the sum of $1,214,000,000 and in the next four years a further $201,000,000 brought the grand total to $1,415,000,000. For most of this the receiving countries were expected to pay; 29 per cent was sold for cash, and 63 per cent on credit; only 8 per cent was given away.[3]

Magnificent work was done by the A.R.A., and without it the plight of Europe would have been beyond description. The fact that most of its deliveries were on a business footing—for cash or credit—proved of little consequence, as credits were freely granted, and, as things turned out, were mostly never repaid, being merged with war debts ten years later. A much graver deficiency was the fact that relief deliveries were confined to foodstuffs and excluded raw materials. Most of Europe was completely denuded of raw materials by the war, and economic life could not be re-established until raw materials were made available to the factories. But the end of the war was followed by a boom, and an acute shortage of raw materials; in the ensuing scramble America, Great Britain and other countries with sound financial resources, got the lion's share, and it was not until the slump that the countries of Central Europe were able to get the raw materials they needed to reconstruct their economies.

Raw materials was one of the problems discussed at the first post war International Conference (also the first League of Nations conference) held in Brussels in October 1920, when a scheme of international credits was agreed; but by this time the boom was over, and the Ter Meulen plan (as it was called after its proposer) was never actually brought into effect. It was this difficulty over raw materials which caused the relief organisation of our times, the United Nations Relief and Rehabilitation Administration to be instructed not to confine itself to food, but to give equal priority to the materials needed for reconstruction.

BOOM AND SLUMP

In Western Europe and the United States there was no such acute distress as in Central Europe. Here the problem was simply that of reconversion from war to peace. Millions of men were anxious to be released from military forces, and to be reabsorbed into industry; and factories which had been engaged on munitions had to be converted to civilian needs. As the war neared its end considerable apprehension had been felt lest the process of reconversion should prove prolonged and painful. Many persons expected that the curtailment of war demands would produce a slump, and in this context there was considerable discussion of the future of wartime controls. For in the first world war, as in the second, a whole network of controls had been built up and in a number of industries, e.g. railway transport, coal and munitions in Great Britain, the Government itself was actively engaged.

Fears of a slump proved to be unfounded. For a month or two after the Armistice there was uncertainty, and a slight recession, but by March 1919 this gave way to a boom of astonishing dimensions. In Great Britain prices had risen during the war at a more or less even rate; as Chart I shows, they shot up in the next few months to heights which would not have been thought possible. This was unfortunate in many ways; but the favourable effect of the boom was to simplify immensely the switch over from war to peace. Factories were deluged with orders, and in turn absorbed labour rapidly. Demobilisation was thus speeded up; within five months of the Armistice Britain had demobilised two million men; four million were out by the end of the year, and there was virtually full employment. The experience of the U.S.A. was similar. Both countries also, in this atmosphere, grew impatient of restraints. Business men demanded the end of controls, and the process of decontrol was greatly accelerated.

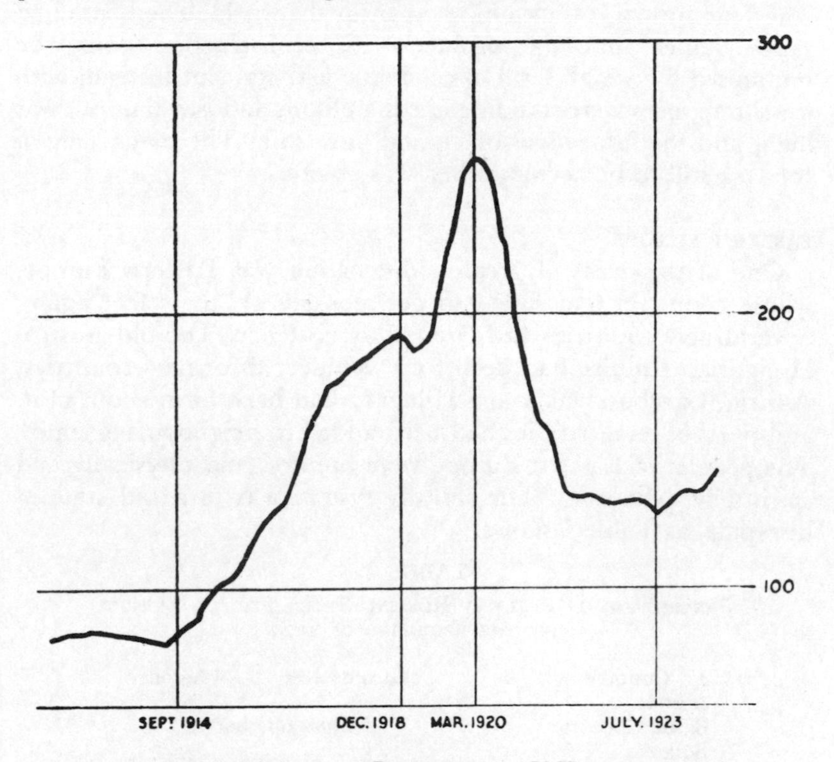

CHART I. WHOLESALE PRICES IN THE U.K., 1912–1923.

The main cause of the boom seems to have been a universal desire to replenish stocks. All over the world larders, wardrobes, and shops were empty; all over the world, too, purchasing power had accumulated. The rush to replenish drove prices up. Moreover, additional purchasing power continued to be created, as Governments were still maintaining expenditure at high levels, retaining wartime practices of deficit budgeting. Governments were also anxious to keep interest rates low so that short term debts could be converted to long on favourable terms. The boom collapsed when raw materials and foodstuffs, which had accumulated overseas during the war for lack of shipping, began to arrive in Europe; when factories began to meet the accumulated demand; and when financial authorities, desiring to check the speculative inflation, took steps to restrict credit. Prices began to fall in March 1920, and within the next two years, were halved.[4] The year 1921 was thus a bitter year for the world. The boom had raised hopes that the problems of reconstruction could be minimised by a high level of economic activity. But instead, with the slump, men were standing idle in millions, industrial unrest was high, and the future was black and uncertain. The magnitude of the task still to be accomplished was obvious.

EASTERN EUROPE

One of the areas of greatest dislocation was Eastern Europe, whose countries had failed to get securely on their feet again. Several new countries had come into existence. The old Austro-Hungarian Empire had been torn asunder; three new countries, Austria, Czechoslovakia and Hungary had been formed out of it, and parts of its territories had been added to neighbouring states. The peoples of Eastern Europe were hungry, and physically and spiritually exhausted. The railway system was in a sad state of disrepair, as Table I shows.[5]

TABLE I

PERCENTAGE OF RAILWAY ROLLING STOCK FIT FOR SERVICE AT THE BEGINNING OF 1920

Country	Locomotives	Wagons
Austria	63	67
Baltic Countries	"situation chaotic"	
Bulgaria	37	56
Czechoslovakia	62	88
Greece	76	86
Hungary	27	76
Poland	70	90
Roumania	29	57
Russia	15	20

Governments and administrative systems were in chaos, having in many cases to be created virtually from nothing.

To all this was added the consequences of a fierce nationalism. Austria and Hungary were disliked by the peoples liberated from their rule, and these peoples set out to make their economies as independent of these two countries as they could. New currencies were adopted to replace the Austrian crown. The Austro-Hungarian railway system was disintegrated; each country seized the fixed equipment and rolling stock within its borders, and as for some time no country was willing to allow rolling stock to cross its border, fearing that it would be seized, goods had to be unloaded and reloaded at frontier stations, this adding greatly to cost and inconvenience. In any case, for some time, trade was virtually prohibited. In each country imports and exports were prohibited except under licence, and as food and raw materials were so scarce, very little was allowed to cross frontiers until the boom was over.

The Austro-Hungarian empire had been a single economic unit covering a large free trade area. Now it was split into a number of countries each with its own currency and tariffs. The railways had been constructed with Vienna and Budapest as centres. Now each country remodelled its communications, to turn upon its own capital. Industries in one part depended on raw materials from another. Now the raw materials were kept, and efforts made to foster local industries, while men and materials stood idle in what was now a different country. For example, "Austria was left with sufficient spinning mills and finishing works, but with too few looms. At the same time Czechoslovakia, where the weaving mills were located, gave protection to an infant spinning industry, and so cut off the natural outlet for Austrian yarn. Austria's famous tanneries lost their sources of skins and tanning materials; her Alpine iron works lost their coal—about half of the old coal fields having gone to Czechoslovakia and Poland. Czechoslovakia contained a high proportion of the old Austrian industries, but not a population large enough to absorb their products. Hungary's great flour mills lost both their sources of supply and the market for their products. The industries in Slovakia decayed because the favours and support they used to receive from Budapest dried up."[6]

The strangulation of trade by import and export prohibitions was felt to be one of the most serious obstacles to economic recovery, and attracted international attention at an early stage. Most countries in Europe, including Great Britain, emerged from the war with trade prohibitions, but they were soon relaxed in most places, except in Central and South-east Europe, where they were incorporated into the nationalist policy. In 1920 the Brussels Conference recommended that trade should be freed from such restrictions. In 1921 the Central European States signed a protocol at Portorose engaging themselves to abolish import and export prohibitions, but the protocol was never ratified. A further international conference, at Genoa in 1922, similarly pronounced against prohibitions, but without much effect. The Central European States gradually abolished some prohibitions, replacing them by high tariffs, but many remained, and the subject was to come up again at international conferences until the end of the 1920's, when the hope of abolishing prohibitions was finally abandoned.

In the meantime, the effect of the nationalism of the new states was to make untenable the economic position of Austria and of Hungary.

Austria collapsed first. Vienna had been the administrative capital of an empire. When that empire disappeared, a vast number of civil servants became superfluous; and their numbers were swollen as the new states dismissed and repatriated the Austrian civil servants in their territories. Vienna had been also a financial and business centre for the empire, and the same thing happened to thousands of commercial employees whose services were no longer required. 1919 saw a high level of unemployment and no prospect of putting people to work. The government had to provide relief, and had in addition, to find money to try to establish itself, and the country. Unable to balance the budget, it borrowed, and printed paper money, and soon a substantial inflation was under weigh. Prices rose phenomenally, and the exchange value of the crown dropped until the end of August 1922 when the dollar exchanged for 83,600 crowns instead of the par rate of a little under 5 crowns.

A good part of the depreciation of the external value of the crown was due to the heavy adverse balance of payments. Austria needed food, raw materials and manufactures, and had little to offer in exchange. As early as 1919 Austria appealed to the Supreme Economic Council for assistance. Various credits were granted, but they were insufficient to meet the needs of the country. Eventually in 1922, when the crown was virtually worthless, the League of Nations arranged an international loan on condition that Austria's finances be subject to international control.

The League of Nations regime lasted until 1926. The budget was balanced, by severe cuts in expenditure and increases in taxation. This forced the Austrian economy to begin to adjust itself to the new situation in Central Europe, a painful process, as a fairly high level of unemployment bore witness. However, prices and the external value of the currency were stabilised, and a new currency unit, the schilling introduced. By 1926 conditions were stable though not prosperous, and League of Nations control was withdrawn.

The same fate attended Hungary. Here, in addition to the dislocation of losing its share of an empire, there was revolution in 1919, a communist government for a few months, counter-revolution and a short war. There followed an inflation of the same magnitude as that of Austria, the external value of the currency falling to one-hundreth of one per cent of par. Eventually early in 1924, the Austrian plan having proved successful, the League of Nations arranged a loan, and its Commissioner took over Hungary's finances, balancing the budget and restoring stability. His regime lasted until 1926.

THE GERMAN INFLATION

Austria and Hungary were not the only two countries with whirlwind inflations, reducing the value of the currency almost to zero, and necessitating the establishment eventually of a new unit. Russia, Poland and Germany also had the same experience. At the end of the inflation prices had risen in Austria 14,000 times, compared with their pre-war level; in Hungary 23,000 times; in Poland 2,500,000 times; in Russia 4,000 million times; and in Germany one million million times. The German case is an instructive example of the process.

A runaway inflation may derive from three sources. First it may be due to upward adjustments of wages, e.g. under trade union pressure. As wages rise, prices rise. The advantage of the increased money wage is thus largely offset, and a further wage increase is demanded. This leads to a further rise in prices, and the cycle may continue unchecked. Secondly, it may be set in motion by the depreciation of the foreign exchange value of the currency, e.g. because of an adverse balance of payments. This raises the cost of imports, and therefore the cost of living. Wages then rise, if linked to the cost of living, prices rise further, and the foreign exchange value falls still more, setting the cycle in motion. Thirdly it may be due to a budget deficit financed by increasing the amount of money in circulation. If money increases faster than the volume of goods (and this is inevitable after full employment is reached), prices rise. This makes the government need more money, the issue of which causes prices to rise still more. It also causes trade unions to press for higher wages, and the foreign exchange value of the currency to fall, each of which enforces the inflationary trend.

The German inflation had some of all these elements.[7] Its genesis was the creation of money by the Government to meet its expenses. This had started during the war. After the war the budget deficits were greater than ever, and prices rose even faster. To help things along, there was also an adverse balance of payments because Germany could not export enough to pay for her imports. This gap caused the exchange value of the mark to fall, and the fall was especially great in September 1921 after a particularly heavy reparation payment. Budget deficits, an adverse balance of payments, and rising money wages all contributed to make the greatest inflation in history. Taking average wholesale prices in 1913 as 100, the following prices for December of each year show what happened (Table II):

TABLE II

Wholesale Prices in Germany, 1918–1923

Dec. 1918	245
Dec. 1919	800
Dec. 1920	1,400
Dec. 1921	3,500
Dec. 1922	147,500
Dec. 1923	126,000,000,000,000

In the early stages of the inflation, the rise of prices does not seem to have stimulated as much protest as one might have expected. This was partly because inflation creates its own vested interests. The Government, beset with its problems, and having a very uncertain basis—the defeat was followed by attempts at revolution, much social unrest, and uneasy coalitions—found it easier to carry on by creating new money than to face the unpopularity of raising taxation. The industrial and mercantile classes also benefited from rising prices, because, by the time they came to sell what they had bought, the further price increase had added to their profits. And, so long as production was so profitable, there was an unsatisfied demand for labour, and unemployment virtually disappeared; the trade unionists occupied themselves with trying to secure that wages should rise as rapidly as prices, and did not, in the early stages, view the price increase with great alarm.

The final blow came in 1923. In January of that year the French Government, which had long been disputing with the Allies over the amount to be extracted from Germany, claimed that one of the reparation payments was in arrear, and sent troops to occupy the Ruhr. The German Government's reaction was passive resistance; the inhabitants of the Ruhr were urged to strike, and to support them the Government was forced to print ever increasing quantities of money. By the end of 1923 prices had risen to such fantastic heights—e.g. the price of a newspaper rose to 200,000,000,000 marks, the par value of a mark being about one shilling—that the mark was practically valueless and people were ceasing to use it.

An inflation of this magnitude has a number of interesting features which are worth recording.

(a) One feature was that prices were affected in different degrees. Some prices are more flexible than others. For example, as railway charges were adjusted less rapidly than many tramway charges, it was frequently cheaper to travel from one town to another than from one street to another. Rents moved very slowly, and so did salaries. Wages moved slowly at first, and the workers lost through inflation; but after a while wage rates were tied to changes in prices. Bye and large wage earners lost a little from the inflation, and manufacturers and traders gained considerably. The heavy losers were pensioners and the middle classes, who lost both because pensions and salaries were left lagging far behind prices, and also because their savings were virtually wiped out.

(b) Middle class savings were wiped out because they were usually invested in loans which could be repaid at their nominal value, and that value became negligible. Creditors benefited at the expense of debtors. In fact for all practical purposes debt disappeared. This wreaked great hardship on persons dependent on their savings, including retired persons, and on institutions like philanthropic societies dependent on endowments. After the inflation legislation was passed to write up the value of debts; but only some debts were affected, and the writing up still left them at only a fraction of their real pre-inflation value.

(c) One result of the profitability of commercial enterprise was to make capital extensions profitable. Farmers bought machinery; industrialists built factories, and so on. So great was the boom in investment that labour was attracted out of the industries producing consumers' goods into those producing investment goods, which were accordingly swollen. Many business men also invested their profits in trying to create commercial empires by buying up other concerns and forming combines. When the inflation ceased this in due course produced a crisis; the swollen investment goods industries lost part of their market, and many unsound firms went bankrupt. The increase in capital construction was associated with the shift of income tc the entrepreneurial classes. Savings increased and consumption declined.

(d) Side by side with the increase of fixed capital there was a decrease of working capital, i.e. of stocks and of work-in-progress. Goods were snapped up as soon as they reached the market. For the economic system as a whole stocks remained the same, or increased, but the share of the stocks held by users increased, and the share held available centrally to all buyers, whether in shops or in the hands of wholesalers, diminished. There were many complaints that this exhaustion of stocks hindered the smooth flow of production.

(e) In the early stages foreigners noticed how cheap the cost of living in Germany became for them. Many went to Germany at this stage and bought valuable property for very little, causing some Germans to complain that foreigners were "buying up the country." The reason for this was that the external value of the mark, its value in terms of sterling or dollars, fell more rapidly than internal prices rose. This was due partly to the passive balance of payments, including reparations, and partly to the fact that foreigners and German financiers realised what was happening sooner than the German public in general (not because of greater intelligence, but because the people who deal in foreign currencies understand these matters better than the man in the street). As soon as the German people themselves realised what was happening, the gap between internal and external values decreased. Prices rose as fast as new money was printed and even faster.

(f) Prices rose faster than the quantity of money in the later stages because people expected the value of money to go on falling and got rid of it as fast as they could—its velocity of circulation rose. In the latest stages prices rose faster than the quantity of money and the velocity of circulation together; prices rose so fast that there was not enough money to buy goods with. It is one of the paradoxes of an inflation that, although it is due to printing too much, it ends with the emergence of an acute shortage of money! The printing presses were working full time, but were unable to print all the money that people needed to buy goods at the inflated prices. The smaller denominations ceased to be issued; at the end mark notes were being printed bearing the stamp 100,000,000,000,000 marks, which at par should have been worth five million million pounds, but which in fact were enough to buy only about 2,000 loaves of bread.

(g) The shortage of money caused firms to start issuing their own money in payment of wages. This was preferred because it was issued in stable terms; its value was expressed not as so many marks, but as so many dollars, or grains of gold, or kilogrammes of wheat or rye. This was the last stage in the life of the mark. People began to refuse to accept it, or to use it for contracts. Foreign currencies came into circulation, and prices ceased to be expressed in terms of marks. The currency was simply rejected.

(h) It is this that explains how stabilisation became possible. Prices were not stabilised by drawing money out of circulation; on the contrary, still more money was put into circulation, but it was money which people were willing to accept, and for which there was therefore a great demand.

The mark was stablilised by announcing that a new mark, the rentenmark, would be issued. To encourage confidence people were told that this mark was to be backed by an internal loan founded on the real assets of the country, its land and other property. What mattered however, was that it was to be strictly limited in supply. Once people believed that the wild issue of paper money was to cease, they believed that prices would not rise any more, and they were therefore willing to hold money. The Government was therefore able to issue this money, using it to meet its obligations, and knowing that it would be readily accepted and held. This gave it a breathing space in which to balance its budget. The new rentenmark, valued at one million million of the old marks, was first issued in November 1923, and the Government set about drastically reducing expenditure and increasing taxation. The experiment was successful.

Part of its success was due to the German Government's receiving an international loan in 1924, which marked the beginning of a flood of loans to that country. For the origins of this we must trace in outline the history of reparations.

The Treaty of Versailles did not fix the amount of reparations, although it provided for some interim payments in cash and in kind. It established the principle that Germany should indemnify the Allies for their losses, and created a Reparations Commission to assess the amount. In 1921 the Commission assessed the damages at a sum equal to 6,600 million pounds sterling and laid down a time schedule of payments. It soon became clear, however, that Germany could pay nothing approaching this sum, and indeed, by 1922, with the inflation well on the way, was so disorganised that for the time being she could pay very little, and rather needed assistance. British proposals for a moratorium were fiercely resisted by the French, who were depending on reparation payments to help reconstruct their devastated areas, and in the general deterioration of international relations which ensued, France in January 1923 occupied the Ruhr.

With the collapse of the mark, which this occupation then stimulated, it became quite obvious that Germany could pay very little. Emphasis shifted from arguing about what she ought to pay, to estimating what she could pay, and a Committee under the American General Dawes was appointed to report on this. On its recommendation, Germany was required to pay a sum rising in five years from 50 million to 125 million pounds per annum, the number of years of payment being left undetermined. The first payment was facilitated by raising an international loan of 40 million pounds (the Dawes Loan) whose proceeds went towards it. After this loan foreign countries began to be interested in the reconstruction of Germany, and for the rest of the 1920's both the Government and private firms were able to borrow large sums abroad. Comparative stability had returned.

Stabilisation, however, had its costs. So long as money was continually injected into the system, economic activity was maintained at a feverish level. When credit began to be curtailed, to ensure stabilisation, the boom conditions of inflation collapsed. The reaction was, actually, delayed. Towards the end of the inflation economic conditions had deteriorated because of the virtual uselessness of money, and 1924 brought renewed confidence. Factories reopened, and unemployment declined. Readjustment did not begin until the second half of 1925. When it came, the heavy industries were affected most. We saw earlier that the inflation had caused the producers' goods industries to expand at the expense of the consumers' goods industries, because of the anxiety of profit makers to convert cash into fixed capital. This desire lost its *raison d'être* when prices ceased to rise, and pressure on these industries relaxed, with a consequent increase in unemployment. It was here too that the biggest combines had been created. Many of these proved to be unsound. The liquidation of "inflation" businesses began in 1925 and continued in 1926. Germany did not really begin to recover from the inflation until the middle of 1926.

RUSSIA

The economic collapse of Russia was even more spectacular than that of Germany or Austria or of any of the other countries with whirlwind inflations, for in other countries it was principally the currency which collapsed, whereas in Russia it was production as well.

The economic history of Russia since the Revolution falls into distinct phases, and much confusion is caused by thinking of communism as a simple well defined type of economic organisation. The form which communist economic organisation should take had never been specified by Marx, and neither Lenin nor Stalin ever attempted to give it detailed finality. The single objective of the Russian Government has been to make Russia a strong, economically developed country, without private ownership of the means of production, and the economic forms have been changed whenever circumstances seemed to require change.

At the time of the Revolution in 1917, Lenin seems to have intended the process of nationalisation to be gradual. Circumstances, however, forced his hand. Civil war broke out almost at once, and continued for three years, with foreign countries intervening to assist the counter-revolutionary elements. The Red Army was at first driven back on all fronts, and Lenin was compelled to take more drastic steps to control the economy than he had intended. The first three years of the Revolution have therefore come to be known as the period of "War Communism."

The war produced a violent inflation. Prices had been rising before the Revolution; they were already eight times the pre-war level when the communists took over. As the civil war proceeded the government issued more and more money to meet its expenses, and production declined; the price index rose from 100 in 1913 to 1,680,000 in January 1921, 13,800,000 in December 1921, and 1,644,000,000 in December 1922, and was not checked until February 1924, when stabilisation was introduced at the rate of 50,000,000 old roubles for one of the new.

In this background of war and inflation nationalisation was pressed ahead. All factories and credit institutions and internal and external trade were nationalised. Labour was conscripted and equality of earnings adopted. Money values were ignored, and requisitioning and rationing took the place of trade. A more thorough form of communism was achieved than had ever been intended, or has ever since been attempted.

Despite the feeling of some communists that this was the ideal state, this form of organisation had to be abandoned. The greatest troubles were with the land. The peasants took over the large estates and redistributed them, output falling somewhat in the process. The government needed food for the towns, but the prices it was willing to pay were well below the inflation level, and the peasants were unwilling to deliver. A vicious circle set in. The government tried to requisition grain; the peasants reduced their sowings; the towns got more short of food and agricultural raw materials; workers returned to their villages in search of food, and factory output declined; the peasants were then even less willing to part with their crops, as the industrial products offered in exchange got smaller and smaller. Rationing had to be introduced in the towns, and famine made its appearance. The official figures tell the story plainly.[8]

	1913	1920
Industrial Production	100	20
Gross yield of crops (1909–13)	100	54

The number of livestock was also greatly reduced. By the end of the war in November 1920, it was clear that there must be a new beginning, as industrial production had virtually collapsed, and with agricultural output getting smaller and smaller the country was unable to feed itself. Accordingly in March 1921 Lenin announced that there was to be a New Economic Policy.

The distinguishing feature of the New Economic Policy was the restoration of private trading. The state retained a monopoly of production in all the most important industries, while allowing small private factories to operate in not so important ones. But it relaxed almost completely its interest in trade, state factories selling their output to private traders, through whom it reached the consumer. Grain requisitioning was also stopped; the peasants sold their grain in the open market, and taxes in money were eventually substituted for deliveries in kind.

A determined effort was made to stop inflation. A new rouble, the chervonetz was introduced in 1922. At first it circulated with the old, its value being kept stable by careful limitation while the old depreciated all the faster. Eventually in 1924 the chervonetz rouble became the sole currency unit; the budget was balanced, and relative stability of prices was attained.

Private enterprise seized its chance, and certainly achieved results. Production increased rapidly. The peasants once more increased their sowings, and food and raw materials became more plentiful in the towns. Factory wheels started to turn once more. By 1926 industrial production was back to the level of 1913, and if agricultural production was still below the pre-war level, this was because the yield had declined; the area sown was already somewhat larger. The share of private enterprise in this recovery was, however, restricted to restoring the market. Industry and credit continued to be primarily state enterprises; and even the market was gradually being taken over as more cooperative and state trading associations were organised; the share of private traders in retail trade fell from 75 per cent in 1922–3 to 22 per cent in 1927–8.

Our aim at this stage is not to describe the Soviet economic system but rather to consider its impact on the world economy. Here, the spectacular feature was the virtual disappearance of Russia from the international economic scene. Russian exports fell from 1,520 million roubles in 1913 to 1 million roubles in 1920. Thereafter they recovered very slowly, and even by 1929 had not reached two-thirds of the pre-war level. This collapse was due to several features; to the great decline of Russian production in the first four years after the Revolution; to the fact that several countries refused to recognise Russia in the early 1920's or to trade with her; and to the fact that the Russians were unable to obtain foreign loans. Whatever the cause, the principal impact on the international economy was the disappearance of Russian grain from the market at a time when many European countries were short of food, and the failure of Russia to import.

THE "MINOR" INFLATIONS

Austria, Hungary, Poland, Germany and Russia were the five countries where such violent inflations occurred that the currency became valueless and new units had to be introduced. There were, however, quite a number of "minor" inflations, not only in Europe, but also in other continents, resulting in the foreign exchange value of the currency being eventually formally devalued. The principal European countries which eventually stabilised their currencies below par were the following: the figures in brackets showing the ratio of the dollar value of their currencies in December 1925 to its par value: Roumania (2.4 per cent), Bulgaria (3.8 per cent), Portugal (4.7 per cent), Greece (6.7 per cent), Jugoslavia (9.2 per cent), Finland (13.1 per cent), Czechoslovakia (14.6 per cent), France (19.4 per cent), and Belgium (23.3 per cent). The only European countries which finally returned to parity with the dollar were Britain, Switzerland, Sweden, Norway, Denmark and Holland.

The experience of France illustrates a "minor" inflation. Taking wholesale prices in 1914 as 100, December prices were as follows, 1921, 333; 1922, 370; 1923, 468; 1924, 518; 1925, 646; 1926, 640. The main cause was the need to finance reconstruction of the devasted regions. Until 1923 it was assumed that the cost would be met by Germany, and the Government borrowed freely instead of increasing taxation. The desired result was certainly achieved; reconstruction was pushed forward rapidly, and after a short recession in 1921, due to the post-war slump, French production forged ahead in a minor boom which continued throughout the 1920's. By 1924 it was clear that Germany would contribute only a part of the cost of reconstruction, and as a result, in 1924 the French public grew afraid of the continued Government borrowing, and the Government found itself suddenly unable to meet its obligations either from taxation or by borrowing. The resultant crisis showed itself in politics and in the foreign exchanges rather than in production. In politics there was a rapid succession of Governments, six ministries in 18 months. And in the foreign exchanges, lack of confidence (to which the fact that these were "left" governments contributed) caused Frenchmen to convert their holdings of francs into foreign monies, and the franc fell heavily, to levels in no way justified either by internal prices or by the economic situation. Eventually in 1926 a "right wing" ministry under M. Poincaré took stern measures to balance the budget. Confidence returned; refugee capital returned home; the dollar value of the franc rose rapidly, and at the end of the year the Government decided to hold it stable. Formal return to the Gold Standard followed in 1928. The rate chosen undervalued the franc. Compared with 1913 French prices in 1927 had risen four and a half times more than U.S. prices, but the franc had been devalued to one-fifth of its value, and French exports were accordingly stimulated.

The experience of Great Britain and of other countries which returned to parity was very different from this. Their prices had risen during and after the war more than American prices, and after the boom of 1919–20, they found it necessary to deflate in order to get back to parity. Compare wholesale prices in the U.S.A. with wholesale prices in some of these countries (Table III).

TABLE III

Wholesale Prices, 1913–1927

	1913	1920	1921	1922	1923	1924	1925	1926	1927
U.S.A.	100	221	140	139	144	141	148	143	137
U.K.	100	307	197	159	159	166	159	148	142
Sweden	100	359	222	173	163	162	161	149	146
Holland	100	292	182	160	151	156	155	145	148

As their prices had risen to much higher levels than U.S. prices, the required deflation was also greater. Some of them were not able to get their prices right back into line with U.S. prices before returning to the Gold Standard, and they therefore started upon the second half of the 1920's with their currencies somewhat overvalued.

The relative stagnation of Great Britain at a time when several other countries were forging ahead, occasioned particular comment. In the United States a constructional boom got going as early as 1922, and in that country all the years from 1922 to 1929 are counted as a boom period. So also in France, where the expenditure on restoring war areas brought a high level of employment from 1922 onwards, and in Japan, where the earthquake of 1923 was followed by a reconstruction boom.

The slow recovery of Great Britain after the 1920 slump is attributable to two main factors. First, deflation. The decision to return to the Gold Standard at the pre-war rate was taken as early as 1919, and the fairly stringent credit conditions which obtained from the end of 1920 hindered recovery. There was not much deliberate deflation; a budget surplus used for debt redemption, was the principal instrument, and set the general tone.[9] Secondly, although there was a housing shortage there was no housing boom such as occurred in the United States, and this has been attributed partly to the ineffectiveness of local authorities, who then as now were the "chosen instrument", but even more to the joint effect of rent restriction and high building costs, which made new building unprofitable.[10] And thirdly it was due to the changed international position of Great Britain which was to become even more obvious later, and to which we shall refer in the next chapter.

CONCLUSION

The year 1925 is usually taken as the end of the period of reconstruction after the war. It is an apt date, in politics no less than in economics. Up to 1925, in the political sphere, the Allies were still wrangling with each other over the treatment of Germany, and the international atmosphere was as clouded as it is now as these words are being written (October 1946). Not until the acceptance of the Dawes Reparation Plan (1924) and the signing of the Locarno pact (1925) did the atmosphere of mutual suspicion and recrimination disperse. In 1925, Europe seemed at last to close its ranks once more; men ceased to look back to the war and its consequences, and looked forward to a new era of peaceful cooperation.

1925 was just as much a turning point in economic affairs. It was the first year in which the volume of world trade passed its pre-war level, though some of the countries in Western Europe and overseas had passed that level earlier. 1925 was also the first year in which European primary production reached and exceeded the level of 1913; and the year Great Britain returned to the Gold Standard, leaving few important currencies still in a state of fluctuation. Not all countries had fully recovered from the war by 1925, and indeed their fortunes differed considerably in that year. But in economics, as in politics, it was a cheerful year. The dark days of post-war dislocation seemed to have been left behind, and the prospects for progress seemed good.

Naturally the war had altered the balance of economic power. We have a good pointer to the change in the index of manufacturing.[11] Taking 1913 as 100, the index for the world as a whole stood in 1925 at 121, while individual countries stood in the following order:

Japan	222	France	114
Italy	157	Sweden	113
U.S.A.	148	Belgium	100
Holland	142	Austria	95
Australia	141	Germany	95
Czechoslovakia	136	Roumania	92
New Zealand	136	U.K.	86
India	132	Hungary	77
Norway	117	Russia	70
Canada	117	Poland	63

Bye and large, the overseas countries had naturally fared best; not only their manufactures but also their primary production had grown relatively to European production, and so had their participation in world trade. The countries of Eastern Europe share the bottom of the list with the U.K., which was adversely affected by shifting trends of world trade, and with Germany, adversely affected by inflation.

Looking backwards from 1925 one must enquire why recovery was so slow and painful. Why did it take six years to return to an atmosphere of normality?

The physical destruction caused by the war, or other capital depreciation, is not the main answer. In agriculture wartime deterioration was quite important; so much land went out of cultivation, and what remained had so deteriorated in yield that European production did not return to the pre-war level until 1923[12]. But destruction and deterioration of other property was not very large, all told, and recovery was indeed quite rapid in the country where that destruction was greatest, namely in France.

Three factors seem to have predominated—the slump, the shortage of capital in most European countries, and the hindrances to trade.

The slump was the most important. It came too soon after the end of the war—within 18 months, and set back the incipient recovery. The boom had been a commodity boom, based on local rather than on total shortages; it collapsed when stocks of foodstuffs and raw materials locked up in distant countries started to move to the consuming centres. This is not to say that the preceding boom was in itself desirable; it was the boom that caused the slump, and if the world could have returned to peace with neither speculative boom nor slump, its progress would have been more rapid. But, given that this is a world of ebb and flow, it would have been better if the boom had been less wild and longer, which might have been the case if inflationary financial policies had not pushed prices far beyond what the fundamental demand and supply conditions justified.

Secondly, recovery would have been swifter if appropriate action had been taken to finance the needs of European countries. Their restoration was greatly delayed by shortage of raw materials and by lack of foreign reserves with which to purchase them. Had they received loans sooner than they did, their demand would have been sustained, and the collapse of 1920 might have been delayed, just as the export surplus from the U.S.A. is now playing so large a part in keeping economic activity high. They would also not have had such pressure on their budgets, and the wild inflations might have been avoided. Inflation banished unemployment while it lasted, but when it ended the country experiencing it was in worse straits than it had been before. Foreign loans would have facilitated sound recovery.

International lending would also have diminished the barriers to trade. It would have reduced the pressure on the foreign exchanges and the wide fluctuations which were such a deterrent to trade. It would also, by maintaining production, have diminished the incentive to keep such high tariffs. The war had damaged the pre-war network of trade, and to repair it was more difficult than to repair the physical damage. Factories stood ready to produce, but in many cases either their pre-war markets or their sources of supply had disappeared, and a new trade network had slowly and painfully to be woven. There was full agreement that obstacles to trade, both tariffs and currency fluctuations, should be reduced; international conferences at Brussels in 1920, at Portorose in 1921 and at Genoa in 1922 all recommended to this effect; but without positive help from abroad few countries felt able to relax the controls which each required to protect its internal market.

The need for international lending was widely recognised. The United States and the United Kingdom made fairly substantial loans, but they went mostly to the countries which were strong and good borrowers rather than to those which were weak and needed loans most; and the League of Nations Reconstruction Loans (Austria 1922, Greece 1923, Hungary 1924, Bulgaria and Estonia 1926, Danzig 1927) were too long delayed. There were many good resolutions passed at international conferences, but good resolutions are not an adequate substitute for financial assistance. The speed of our recovery from World War II will probably depend more than anything else on the measures which the stronger countries take to help in restoring their more unfortunate brethren.

CHAPTER III

1925–1929

FROM 1925 to 1929 the clouds seemed to roll away. The political atmosphere was much better. The Locarno pact signalised the return of international confidence. The suspicions of the war were banished and men looked forward lightheartedly to peace. The economic atmosphere was no less confident. Between 1925 and 1929 world production of foodstuffs and raw materials was increased by 11 per cent and world trade by 19 per cent; world manufacture proved particularly buoyant, increasing by as much as 26 per cent. The times felt prosperous, and so indeed they were.

THE UNITED STATES

The pattern was set by the United States of America. There the boom which had begun in 1922 went gaily on until 1929. There were minor setbacks in 1924 and again in 1927, but on each occasion the recession was mild and short, and recovery swift; 1922 to 1929 can be taken as one fairly continuous boom.

There were several contributory elements. Residential construction started the boom. A housing shortage had been inherited from the war, and construction started with a swing in 1921, aided by a fall in building costs relatively to rents. Factory construction soon followed, to cope with a series of innovations in American industry. In the year when the volume of construction was at its peak, 1927, the expenditure on private and public building was as large as 12 per cent of the gross national income.[1]

The innovations were of two kinds. First, there were many new products to be exploited. Of these the motor car was the most outstanding. The expansion of motors (annual production increased by 33 per cent between 1923 and 1929) gave the lead to many ancillary industries; to petroleum, to rubber, to steel and to tin; to road construction; and to road transport—to mention only the more obvious. But electricity, with its associated industries of generation (the output of electric power doubled between 1923 and 1929), and the production of a whole range of new industrial and domestic electrical appliances, also made an important contribution.

Apart from new products, however, this was also a period of notable increase in the application of new inventions to old products; there was a considerable increase in the use of capital and of power. Between 1923 and 1929 productivity per man hour increased in manufacturing by 32 per cent, in electricity generation by 39 per cent, on the railways by 18 per cent, and in agriculture by 15 per cent.

Given these opportunities investment maintained a high level. Gross capital formation was as high as 21 per cent of gross national income in 1923, and expanded steadily, keeping this ratio throughout the twenties. Easy credit conditions also kept investment high. Bank deposits increased by 33 per cent and their turnover velocity by another 44 per cent; and the rate of interest declined. A good deal of this money seems to have gone into speculation rather than into increasing output, but the ease with which money was available certainly facilitated the growth of production.

In these circumstances gross national income increased (1923–29) by 23 per cent, compared with an increase in population of only 9 per cent and in the labour force of only 11 per cent. The output of manufactures increased by 30 per cent, and of agriculture by 9 per cent. Unemployment was negligible. In the bad year 1924 it was as high as two millions, or 4.5 per cent of the labour force, but in most other years it was less than 2 per cent. Gross income per head of the population increased by 13 per cent.

Prosperity in a country as important as the United States is bound to spread itself over the world. American imports increased, especially imports of raw materials, and their producers were buoyant. And American loans helped the rest of the world to reconstruct its industry. Between 1925 and 1929 the U.S.A. lent abroad, on long and short term, 2,912 million dollars net, an achievement all the more remarkable because up to 1913 the U.S.A. had been a debtor country.

The indices show that only two major countries did not share in this prosperity. The index of manufacturing (1913 = 100) for the world as a whole rose from 121 in 1925 to 153 in 1929; in Germany it rose from 95 to 117, and in the United Kingdom from 86 to 100.

GERMANY

The "stabilisation" crisis in Germany lasted from mid-1925 to mid-1926, and was followed by comparative prosperity until 1928. Towards the end of 1928 prosperity began to diminish, and from 1929 a steep decline merged into the worldwide depression.

The prosperity of 1926–1928 was based on reconstruction, financed largely by foreign borrowing. This reconstruction was both private and public. Private industrialists borrowed to reconstruct their plant, on a "rationalised" basis. The word "rationalisation" became very popular in all countries. It referred to two separate processes. One was the building of up-to-date plants, usually of enormous size, to secure the fullest economies of scale; whatever the long run advantage of this, it was to prove very costly when the slump came and German industry found itself burdened with heavy overhead costs. The other process was the elimination of competition by market sharing and similar arrangements. This was designed to eliminate the costs of competitive marketing; at the same time it eliminated one of the incentives to efficient production, and some of the experts who have investigated the German economy since the end of the second world war have concluded that the latter effect was more important than the former. Added to this private industrial reconstruction there was considerable expenditure by public authorities, much of which was strongly criticised because it was "unproductive", i.e. mostly on public buildings, theatres and other social amenities which do not yield an exportable surplus.

This phase of German economic history has not yet received considered appraisal. The general tenor of foreign comment is that there was too much capital investment for a country so short of capital. Net investment was running very high. In 1927 and 1928 it averaged 11.8 per cent. of the national income.[2] This was greatly in excess of what the German people themselves were willing to save, and was possible without renewed inflation only because foreign countries were willing to lend freely to Germany; nearly a half of the net investment was in fact done with foreign funds. The ease with which Germany was borrowing is shown by the fact that she was able to raise much more than she really needed to finance her adverse balance of payments. According to the official estimate she borrowed abroad between 1924 and 1931 about 30 milliard reichmarks, and according to another estimate[3] as much as 9 milliard reichmarks of this accumulated abroad. But though money was easy to get, it was expensive; short term rates of interest as high as 8 per cent and 9 per cent and more had to be paid. These high rates of interest were bad for the economy, burdening it with debt, and the form of the foreign borrowing was also specially unfortunate in that more than 40 per cent of it was short term borrowing, both industry and the banking system thus becoming dependent on a form of credit which could very easily be withdrawn, and the disappearance of which would cause economic contraction.

This is, in fact, what happened. In 1928 Americans began to withdraw their short term funds for investment at home, where stock exchange speculation had become very profitable, and these withdrawals continued throughout the first months of 1929. After the collapse in Wall Street some money returned. But political confidence in Germany was shaken for various reasons in 1930 and 1931, and heavy withdrawals started again. The result, from 1928, was further contraction of domestic credit; employment declined rapidly and the ensuing depression proved to be worse in Germany than in any other country except the United States.

GREAT BRITAIN

The British experience was different. Here there was not even an interlude of prosperity; throughout there was a high level of unemployment, averaging between 10 per cent and 11 per cent. The causes of this high level, which was between two and three times as high as the pre-war expectation of "normal", provoked considerable discussion. The concensus of opinion among economists was that in returning to the Gold Standard at the pre-war parity in 1925, sterling was over-valued about 10 per cent.

It is true that the depression was centred in the export trades, and that most of the unemployment was concentrated there. And it is also true that exports of these staple industries would probably not have been much higher if the pound had been devalued 10 per cent. Different staple export industries were depressed for different reasons. The coal industry was depressed principally because new mines had been opened elsewhere, and water power developed, depriving it of export markets. Cotton lost its export markets because of the growth of Indian domestic production and of Japanese competition in the Far East. Iron and steel, shipbuilding and metal trades generally were suffering from wartime over-expansion in Great Britain and elsewhere. In all these staple industries prices were low, and it is doubtful whether devaluation would have helped their exports much.

But the important point is that it might have helped the new industries to expand more rapidly, both by making competing imports dearer, and so reserving the home market, and also by increasing exports. Prices of British manufactures were too high, compared with foreign prices, and the result was to make it difficult for the country to adjust to lost markets by developing new ones rapidly. The need for adjustment was not new. The British share of world trade had been diminishing steadily for several decades before the war, but the absolute volume of British exports had nevertheless been growing all the time. The new phenomenon was that British exports should have lost ground in absolute terms, so that while world trade after 1925 exceeded the pre-war level, British exports remained smaller than before the war. This can partly be attributed to the war, which, by cutting off British exports, caused industrial development in overseas countries to be concentrated on those products which had figured most largely in British exports. But it is also to be attributed to over-valuation, which restricted the adjustment process by restricting the growth of new industries and new exports. This is clear if we compare British experience with that of France, Italy and Switzerland. Taking 1913 as 100, the average of export prices[4] for 1927–29 was France 101, Italy 123, Switzerland 149, and U.K. 162; and the average quantum of exports was France 147, Italy 136, Switzerland 101, and U.K. 85. This leaves no room for doubt that British prices were too high.

Was this also the explanation of the other problem that gave so much concern, namely the difficulty experienced in keeping on the Gold Standard? For most of this period the exchange value of the pound was slightly below par, and the Bank of England experienced difficulty in preventing an outflow of gold. This difficulty was not in the first instance due to an unfavourable balance on income account; exports and earnings from invisible items were more than enough to meet current liabilities. The cause of the difficulty was excessive lending, in the sense that the sums lent exceeded the current balance available. Monetary institutions in London had been geared to a high level of foreign investment before 1913. After 1925 Britain could not really afford to lend as much as she had been lending before 1913, but the machinery continued as before. More was lent than was possessed. The difference was met by attracting short-term funds to London for re-investment abroad, and this short term borrowing was destined to cause trouble in 1931, when money was suddenly recalled. Nevertheless, this too can be attributed to the over-valuation; for we can say that the trouble was not that Britain lent too much but rather that she had too little to lend. This is merely a difference of formulation. If the price level had been lower she could have lent more without difficulty; but given her price level, she was lending too much.

Meanwhile, the attention of the authorities was concentrated on the over-valuation of the pound, for which they considered that the remedy was not to devalue the pound but to reduce the British price level. Prices were to be reduced not so much by deliberate credit restriction, of which there was very little, but rather by reducing money wages. The attempt to put this policy into practice produced a major social crisis.

Money wages followed more or less the course of the boom, slump and recovery. Taking December 1924 as 100, the index of average weekly wages in the United Kingdom[5] was 115 in January 1919, rose to 155 in January 1921 and fell to 97 in January 1924, after which it rose again. These changes were accompanied by violent labour disputes; the "labour offensive" in 1919 continued long after the boom had broken and in the face of falling prices in 1920, and the disputes, strikes and lock-outs associated with it and with the subsequent "capitalist offensive" which began to be successful in 1921, were extraordinarily bitter and prolonged, and destined to poison industrial relations for another twenty years. The statistics of disputes[6] tell their own story (Table IV):

TABLE IV

U.K. INDUSTRIAL DISPUTES, 1919–1929

Year	Number of Disputes	Working days lost (millions)	Av. Weekly Wages (Dec. 1924=100)	Wholesale Prices (1913=100)
1919	1,352	35.0	119	242
1920	1,607	26.6	143	295
1921	763	85.9	142	182
1922	576	19.9	109	154
1923	628	10.7	98	152
1924	710	8.4	99	165
1925	603	8.0	101	160
1926	323	162.2	101	150
1927	308	1.2	101	144
1928	302	1.4	100	142
1929	420	8.3	100	134

1921 was the bitterest year; as prices had been falling steadily from the second quarter of 1920, whereas money wages had continued to rise, and were not successfully attacked until the beginning of 1921. Gradually the deflation of prices came to an end, and with it the attack on wages; prices began to move up in 1923, and money wages in 1924, and 1924 and 1925 were relatively peaceful years. In 1925, however, Britain returned to the Gold Standard at too high a parity, and the need for lowering wages and prices to secure equilibrium in the exchanges began once more to be widely canvassed. Matters came to a head in the coal industry, which was one of the staple export industries which showed no signs of returning to its pre-war level, and was accordingly carrying a great deal of unemployment. The demand of the mineowners that wages should be reduced was rejected by the union. The mineowners then "locked out" the miners, who called on their comrades in other trade unions to come out in sympathy. There was an enthusiastic response. For nine days, from May 4th, 1926, there was virtually a complete strike of manual workers. The leaders of the Trades Union Council, however, urged the miners' leaders to accept a compromise, and when this was rejected, called off the "general strike." The miners held on for six months, but were eventually defeated. The occasion was spectacular, and the temper of the British Labour Movement cannot be appreciated by anyone who has not studied the events leading up to 1926. But the immediate affect on the general level of wages was small; miners' wages were severely cut, but neither the general level of wages nor the general level of prices was much affected by this dispute.

The movement of real wages was much less spectacular than the movement of money wages. In 1921 prices fell faster than wages and real wages rose (as did also unemployment). Soon, however, money wages were driven down correspondingly. From 1922 real wages increased slightly, reaching in 1929 a level about 9 per cent above that of 1913. This was due to a fall in the cost of living while money wages remained constant.

PRICES

The fall in the price level was one of the notable features of this period. The wholesale price index fell in Great Britain from 160 in 1925 to 134 in 1929; and in the United States from 148 to 138. It is unusual for the price level to be falling during a boom of such magnitude as was occurring in the United States, and the fact that prices were falling helped at the time to conceal the magnitude of the expansion that was occurring. The basic reason for the fall of prices was the great increase in productivity; prices would have fallen even more in the United States but for the fact that money wages were rising—from 217 in 1921 to 237 in 1929 (hourly wages).

Also specially notable was the downward trend in agricultural prices. Some prices were in fact very buoyant, especially those of raw materials and of animal products. Wheat and sugar were the two which were declining most markedly, and the countries in which these commodities were important became increasingly anxious as the twenties drew to a close. The indices for the U.S.A.[7] (1909–14=100) show the general position:

	1925	1926	1927	1928	1929
Prices paid by Farmers	156	155	153	155	154
Prices received by Farmers	156	146	142	151	149
Prices of Food Grains	171	152	135	128	116

It will be observed that while prices paid by farmers moves down very little, prices received by farmers falls more, and the fall in prices of food grains is spectacular. In the United States the agricultural economy is variegated, and as the general index of prices received shows, the fall in the price of wheat was offset by an increase of other agricultural prices. But in countries where wheat is more dominant, as for instance in Germany, the whole of this period is regarded as one of growing agricultural crisis.

Both wheat and sugar suffered from the same processes. First, during the war output contracted in Europe and expanded overseas, especially in the American continent. The overseas acreage of wheat and of sugar continued to expand after the war, while European production was climbing back to its pre-war level. By 1925 European production had been restored, while the overseas acreage was greatly in excess of the pre-war level. And secondly there was an increase in yield per acre, and a reduction of costs; in wheat due to breeding and the wide adoption of mechanical methods, and in sugar due also to new breeds and to improved methods of extraction. Production outran consumption, and stocks increased steadily throughout the second half of the twenties, with depressing effects on prices.

Many people attributed the world depression, when it came, to effects of the agricultural overproduction. Farmers, they argued, had less to spend and so industrial producers received less; they therefore bought still less from farmers, and depression proceeded in a spiral. This view is unacceptable. In the first place, while the fall in prices gave farmers smaller incomes, it left consumers with more free cash in their pockets, and there is no evidence to suggest that they did not spend on other things what they saved on agricultural products. And secondly, the slump started in the United States; but there on the average the prices received by farmers did not fall very much in comparison with their payments, and if their incomes were smaller, bearing in mind the increase in production, they cannot really have been so much smaller as to create a slump. The relevance of falling agricultural prices was not in initiating the slump but in aggravating it when it came. When once the slump had started, the collapse of agricultural prices, the insolvency of rural banks and the burden of rural debt all proved to be highly deflationary factors.

THE INTERNATIONAL ECONOMY

Thoughts of a major slump were however far from people's minds. The international economy seemed to have settled down. Currencies were stabilised, trade was growing, and there was a large flow of international investment.

Great Britain's return to the Gold Standard in 1925 signalised the re-establishment of stable exchanges; there were still a few countries to comply, but they came in one by one, the most important late comers being (*de facto*) France in 1926, Belgium in 1927, and Italy in 1928. The new Gold Standard, however was different from the old in that a large number of countries held as reserves foreign exchange in place of or in addition to gold. This increased the importance of London and of New York, the two centres in which most of the foreign exchange reserves were held; at the same time it increased these two countries' need to hold gold, which they needed now not only for their own purposes but also as cover for other countries' reserves. London, unfortunately, was not equal to this strain. For reasons we have already examined her own international exchange position was weak; she was having difficulty in preventing an outflow of gold, and was not able to acquire sufficient gold to hold in reserve. This was to have drastic consequences later when a temporary loss of confidence in London caused foreign creditors to withdraw their reserves, demanding gold in payment, and reduced the gold stocks in London so severely that Great Britain was forced to abandon the Gold Standard.

There was yet another source of weakness in the new "Gold Exchange" Standard, as it was called. A number of the countries which returned to it acquired their reserves of gold or foreign exchange not by means of an export surplus, or of long term borrowing, but through short-term loans. This made their position precarious, for if a loss of confidence initiated a withdrawal of these short-term loans, they would be denuded of reserves and unable to remain on the standard. The fact that the new standard was so vulnerable made it in fact an unsuitable monetary mechanism. Its ultimate collapse was destined to add greatly to the deflationary forces.

In a situation so unstable as this, movements of French balances which occurred were unhelpful. During the French crisis from 1924 to 1926 the French people exported capital, by the process of selling abroad more than they bought and holding the difference in foreign exchange. After the stabilisation they sold their foreign exchange to the banks, and thus the Bank of France acquired considerable foreign holdings. In 1928 the Bank of France decided to convert these holdings into gold. There followed a drain of gold from other countries to France, which was aggravated by the undervaluation of the franc giving rise to an export surplus which also was paid for in gold. The gold reserves of the Bank of France increased (in equivalent) from 954 million U.S. dollars at the end of 1927 to 1,633 million at the end of 1929 and 3,257 million at the end of 1932. This put an extra strain on all debtor countries, and was one of the factors that eventually caused the system to collapse.

The instability of the Gold Exchange Standard was not however realised at the time. There was more anxiety about the continued growth of obstacles to international trade. International conferences at Brussels in 1920, at Portorose in 1921 and at Genoa in 1922 had all recommended in favour of reducing these obstacles, but in the atmosphere of falling prices produced by the slump of 1920 they had met with no response. By 1925, however, the atmosphere had improved sufficiently for it to be felt that new preparations should be made for international conferences on trade restriction. A League of Nations calculation[8] (Table V) showed how tariffs had grown since 1913.

TABLE V

AVERAGE TARIFF LEVELS, 1913 AND 1925

	1913 %	1925 %	Increase %
Spain	33	44	11
U.S.A.	33	29	−4
Argentine	26	26	0
Australia	17	25	8
Hungary	18	23	5
Czechoslovakia	18	19	1
Italy	17	17	0
Canada	18	16	−2
India	4	14	10
Sweden	16	13	−3
Austria	18	12	−6
France	18	12	−6
Germany	12	12	0
Switzerland	7	11	4
Belgium	6	8	2
Denmark	9	6	−3
Netherlands	3	4	1
U.K.	0	4	4

Two conferences were held at Geneva in 1927. The first dealt with absolute prohibitions on trade, and the second with tariffs. From the first (and subsequent conferences on this subject) emerged a convention agreeing to abolish all absolute prohibitions, which nearly secured enough ratifications to come into force, but which failed owing to German and Polish reservations. The second produced recommendations in favour of tariff reductions. It was followed by some months during which the flow of tariff increases was greatly curtailed, and there was also some reduction of tariffs. Hopes, however, diminished as news of proposed tariff increases in America began to crystallise, from the end of 1928; and the onset of the slump in 1929, followed by the American "biggest ever" Hawley-Smoot tariff in 1930, made agreement impossible. Tariff increases after 1929 were bigger than ever.

The increase of world trade between 1925 and 1929 was assisted by the maintenance of a high level of foreign investment. The following estimates[9] for 1928 show the principal lenders and borrowers:

Lenders	$000,000	*Borrowers*	$000,000
U.S.A.	1,099	Germany	1,007
U.K.	569	Australia	193
France	237	Argentine	181
Czechoslovakia	61	Canada	164
		Poland	124

The supreme importance of the United States as a lender stands out and so does the predominance of Germany as a borrower. In relation to world trade as a whole the total sums involved in foreign investment were small, in the neighbourhood of 6 per cent, but they were large elements in the economies of the countries specially involved, and as these were important countries, the importance of capital movements in the flow of trade was greater than this figure indicates.

The methods of financing foreign investment caused some disquiet. A large proportion, as we have already seen, was short term lending and its volatility was liable to do mischief. But even the long term lending was not well proportioned as between fixed interest loans and equities, and between government bonds and industrials. Thus in the year 1928 American long term investment[10] was divided as follows: Government and municipal loans 45 per cent, industrial bonds and notes 47 per cent, preference shares 3 per cent, and ordinary shares 5 per cent. A good deal of the money lent to governments was just wasted; and in any case even where the money was well used, it imposed a fixed interest payment without always adding even indirectly to the exportable surplus from which this payment could be made. The low proportion of equities also meant that, as trade diminished, fixed interest payments would absorb a constantly increasing proportion of the disposable surplus. So long as the upward movement continued, all was well; but as soon as conditions began to deteriorate, weak policies would stand revealed. The fact that New York had not adequate machinery for foreign lending was also unfortunate. There were no specialised houses with a long tradition; the cost of issues was very high; and the investing public fickle, shifting its interest too easily between foreign and domestic capital issues. This added to instability; the suddenness with which the flow of foreign loans contracted did much eventually to increase the difficulties of overseas countries.

CONCLUSION

It is easier now to assess the second half of the twenties than it was at the time. The current view was dominated by rising prosperity, so largely associated with American expansion and American lending. The war and its strains were being forgotten. But we can see now that if 1919–25 was a period obviously dominated by the effects of the war, 1925–1929 was just as much a period of readjustment to the effects of the war, though these effects were no longer visible on the surface. Problems left by the war remained unsolved, especially the creation of a stable international currency system, the adjustment of the size of the agricultural economy, and the reorientation of Britain, of Germany and of France in the post-war world. So soon as America ceased to expand and to lend, then underlying maladjustments were to come out and to take charge.

CHAPTER IV

1929–1939

COLLAPSE

SUCH had been the expansion of prosperity in the United States since 1922 that many people had come to believe that the country had found the secret of permanent prosperity, and would never again be submerged in depression. This, however, was not the opinion of economists, nor of the monetary and other authorities. On the contrary they were expecting a slump sooner and were surprised that it was so long delayed.[1]

The reason for this expectation was that the country was recognised to be in the grip of a speculative fever, which could not last. After a slight recession in 1926, the prices of stock exchange securities had begun to rise, and this rise had continued with accelerating speed to levels out of all relation to real values. The index[2] had risen from 100 in 1926 to 216 in September 1929. The boom was based not primarily on an increase in profits, but rather on a process which can only be described as "a dog chasing its own tail": since prices were rising it was profitable to buy to resell, irrespective of the yield of the securities, and even of whether they were paying any dividends or not; all sorts of persons who knew very little about securities were drawn into the market, and prices soared gaily upwards.

The monetary authorities knew that this process could not last and that if prices rose too far the shock of their collapse would surely damage the economy. From the beginning of 1928 they tried to check the boom, by trying to restrict the sums available for stock exchange speculation, but they were unsuccessful. They resigned themselves therefore to an inevitable collapse. Indeed in many quarters the collapse was eagerly awaited, since it was expected to bring prices back into reasonable relation with each other, and so to strengthen the economy.

Stock exchange prices collapsed in October 1929. The news was received with some relief by the authorities, and a mild recession was expected to give place rapidly to continued expansion. In the first half of 1930 a rally did occur, but to everyone's surprise it gave way in the second half of the year. The slump that started in 1929 was not a mild recession, but the biggest in recent history, both for its length and for its severity. The bottom was not reached until 1932, and the estimate of the number of people unemployed in the world when conditions were at their worst is thirty millions.

It is clear that the centre of the depression was the United States of America, in the sense that most of what happened elsewhere has to be explained in terms of the American contraction, while that contraction is hardly explicable in any but internal terms. The slump was also worse in the United States than anywhere else (with the possible exception of Germany, whose severe contraction was a direct result of American events). Between 1929 and 1932 the American national income contracted by 38 per cent, and the unemployment figure increased to fifteen millions. An analysis of the causes of the slump must therefore start with the United States.

The stock exchange collapse was the signal for the slump, but not its cause. It was not even its beginning as other indices had already begun to fall, especially industrial production earlier in 1929, and building in 1928. The spectacular fall of security prices drew attention to underlying troubles; its importance lay mainly in altering business psychology from expansion to recession.

The relative importance of the underlying maladjustments in the United States remains disputed to this day, but it is possible to enumerate the principal factors.

We can begin by dismissing two of the suggested causes. One school of thought, more popular with the public than with professional economists, saw the origins of the slump in a shortage of gold. This clearly cannot have been the case. It is true that gold production was declining in the 1920's. But the United States, in which the slump was generated, and where it proved most severe, had not a shortage but an excess of gold; it was also less dependent on international trade than almost any other country in the world, and not greatly susceptible to international movements. It is clear that the United States slump did not start because of adverse movements in international trade or because of any shortage of gold. To a second school the slump, or at least its severity, was to be attributed to a growing rigidity of the economic system, resulting from increased monopolisation and the rise of trade unions, which made wages, costs, and prices less flexible, and so prevented the economic system from adjusting itself to adverse changes as easily as before. Such statistical evidence as exists has been examined,[3] and it does not support the belief that prices were less flexible in 1929 than they had been before the war. Trade unions were still only a minor element in the U.S. economy at the time of the slump, and the prices subject to monopoly control do not seem to have been noticeably more rigid than before the war.

The relative importance of other suggested causes is a matter of opinion. In the earliest analyses the boom and slump were seen primarily as a phenomenon of credit inflation[4], but this is primarily because the importance of more fundamental maladjustments was not yet clear. How much real credit inflation occurred in the United States in the twenties is still a subject of controversy, but there seems no room for doubt that the volume of money increased much more than the volume of trade; and in addition the velocity of circulation of money also increased.

Then there is the view that the slump was due to "underconsumption", i.e. to failure of consumption to rise sufficiently to make profitable the high level of investment which had been maintained for so many years. There are many variations on this theme, which cannot be analysed here. The evidence suggests that the rate of growth of consumption was slowing down in 1929, but the change does not seem to be great enough to bear all the weight that has been attached to it.[5]

Next comes the argument that there was in 1929 a temporary exhaustion of investment opportunities. The slump came at the end of seven years of active construction. The housing shortage, in particular, had been met, and the decline of building activity from 1928 was a deflationary factor. There had also been much factory construction and re-equipment. It is not necessary to believe that investment opportunities were exhausted in any permanent sense—as some writers suggest—to see that after seven years of new investment, further investment must become highly sensitive to the general outlook. Falling stock exchange and primary prices from 1929 made the general outlook unfavourable; business men held off investment, and this very holding off made the depression worse. The decline of investment is the most prominent feature of the American slump. It is reflected in the national income figures; net investment became negative in 1931, i.e. capital depreciation was not made good, fell to *minus* 5.8 billion dollars in 1932 (in 1929 prices) and did not again become positive until 1936. Indices of industrial production tell the same story:

	1929	1930	1931	1932	1933	1934
Consumer goods	100	90	85	75	85	87
Investment goods	100	74	51	31	41	50

The low level to which investment fell, and its failure to recover is the most important feature of the slump, and the fact that 1922 to 1929 had seen such a high level of investment is without doubt an important reason why investment was so small in the 1930's.

Another contributory factor was the banking crisis. 5,096 banks[6] suspended payment in the years 1930, 1931 and 1932, principally because the fall of agricultural prices and of security prices reduced the value of their assets. The United States is a country not of a few large banks with branches all over the country, but rather of thousands of small independent banks; nearly 24,000 banks of all kinds at the beginning of 1929. Half the failures were of banks in villages with less than a thousand inhabitants; the fall of agricultural prices, bankruptcy of farmers, and the fall in real estate values being the most important factors in bank failures. A bank failure destroys money, and also saps confidence, encouraging hoarding; it is therefore highly deflationary.

Equally deflationary was the high level of indebtedness. If debt is repaid in a boom, the creditor looks around for new ways to invest; if it is repaid in a slump he holds his money waiting for prosperity, and debt repayment becomes deflationary. Moreover, as prices fall, the real burden of debt grows correspondingly, bankruptcies increase, and the general atmosphere is gloomy. Now the United States entered the slump with a very high debt burden. Farmers had been borrowing to buy land and invest in machinery; manufacturers to build new plants and new machines; consumers to buy houses, and new consumers' goods on the instalment plan. This pressing weight of debt helped to make the depression more severe; its mitigation became one of the major objects of the New Deal.

And finally the wage policy pursued made matters worse. The government and the business men took the view that wages should be maintained despite falling prices in order to maintain purchasing power; when, however, it was seen that the slump was not just a minor recession, wages began to drop steadily. Maintaining wages in consumer goods industries probably had no effect on the economy, positive or negative. Maintaining them in investment goods industries probably had a negative effect, since industrialists might have been willing to invest more if there had been a sharp fall in construction costs, and the total incomes generated in investment goods industries would probably have been greater at low than at high wages. Certainly the policy eventually pursued after 1930, of allowing wages to fall gradually, was deflationary; since once it was seen that wages were coming down, business men waited for them to reach their lowest point before embarking on new investments.

In the light of all this it is not difficult to explain why the slump occurred. There was some credit inflation, some underconsumption, some temporary exhaustion of investment opportunities, and excessive speculation on the stock exchange, any one of which could have started a downward spiral; and this spiral, once started, would have been accelerated by the fall of agricultural prices, by bank failures, by the high level of indebtedness, and by the wage policy pursed. In 1929 what without doubt gave the kick-off was the stock exchange speculation. From at least as early as March business men knew that it had got out of hand and must bring a crash, and many of them started reducing their commitments in preparation for the crash.

But it is not enough to explain why a slump occurred in 1929. Slumps had occurred before, with regular frequency. What has to be explained is why the slump was so severe and dragged on so long. None of the factors so far mentioned can explain this. The credit inflation of the 1920's was no greater than previous credit inflations, which had not had this severe result. The underconsumption was no greater, as far as we know, than it had been before; there is no evidence that the distribution of income in the United States had become more uneven over the course of the previous sixty years; the evidence on the contrary suggests less inequality[7], and suggests also that the proportion of the national income being devoted to consumption was about the same in the twenties as it had been before the war.[8] Neither was the rate of growth of production greater in the twenties than it had been before; on the contrary, pre-war rates of growth had often been higher.[9] Comparing the origins of the 1929 slump with the origins of earlier slumps, none of the factors so far mentioned, and not even the coincidence of all these factors can tell us why the slump was so severe.

What was probably the most important factor emerges if one concentrates attention on the year 1930. In the earlier part of that year there was some revival, and the experts announced that the recession was over; conditions on the contrary deteriorated rapidly in the second half of the year. The principal cause seems to have been the surprisingly rapid fall of agricultural and other raw material prices, which checked confidence in recovery, and persuaded business men to "wait and see" rather than to make new investments. Next year confidence was further shattered by the collapse of the international monetary mechanism, and it was not until 1932 that recovery began.

The decline of primary product prices was so decisive in checking the incipient recovery because it was so unusually severe. From 1929 to 1930 the average price of wheat[10] fell 19 per cent, cotton 27 per cent, wool 46 per cent, silk 30 per cent, rubber 42 per cent, sugar 20 per cent, coffee 43 per cent, copper 26 per cent, tin 29 per cent; the index of prices of commodities entering world trade fell from 1929 to 1932 by 56 per cent for raw materials, 48 per cent for foodstuffs and 37 per cent for manufactures. In most of these commodities the collapse was due to over-investment. Wheat and sugar were war casualties; but others, notably tin, rubber, and coffee had expanded in the 1920's beyond the level justified by demand even at the height of the boom, and the fact that their position was already shaky before 1929 made the collapse of prices all the greater.

The collapse of primary product prices was decisive because its ramifications were so wide. The fact that prices were falling itself checked confidence, causing business men to be more cautious in investment. Also, it provoked a crop of bank failures, with their trebly deflationary effects in destroying money, in encouraging hoarding of currency, and in discouraging further investment. And in the international sphere, primary producing countries were placed in difficulty; some were driven off the Gold Standard in 1930, or forced to take other measures to curtail their international payments, measures which started a train of restrictions on international trade, and harmed industrial producers as well, If primary prices had not fallen so severely in 1930 the slump in industrial production would not have been so great.

INTERNATIONAL CRISIS

A slump in the United States was bound to affect the rest of the world profoundly. In 1929 United States industrial production represented 46 per cent of the total industrial production of the 24 most important producers in the world;[11] United States consumption of nine principal primary products was in 1927 and 1928 39 per cent of the total of the 15 most important nations.[12] A fall in American buying could not but profoundly affect world markets. So also a fall in American lending, which had contributed so much to world prosperity in the 1920's. In 1929 the U.S.A. made available to the rest of the world through imports and investments the sum of 7,400 million dollars (world imports amounted to 35,601 dollars); this sum contracted in 1932 by 5,000 million dollars to as little as 32 per cent of what was made available in 1929.[13] It is hardly necessary to look much further for the causes of world-wide depression. This loss of American dollars produced, through a multiplier process, a contraction of output several times larger in the rest of the world.

The sequence of events in the international sphere is the contraction of lending, the fall of prices, the contraction of trade, and the monetary crisis.

Lending began to contract in 1928, when the stock exchange boom diverted American funds from foreign investment to domestic speculation, and there was even some withdrawal of short-term funds. Germany, as the biggest borrower, was also the greatest sufferer. The monetary authorities could have expanded domestic credit somewhat as foreign credits were withdrawn, but for reasons we have already considered they did not. The German decline which began in 1928 with these withdrawals was never checked, After the stock exchange collapse in 1929, American foreign investment revived, but it fell off again in the latter half of 1930 as the crisis deepened (the large number of votes for Hitler in the 1930 elections also discouraging investment in Germany), and eventually disappeared. From 1934 the movement of capital into America exceeded outward movements. The contraction of foreign investment caused a sharp curtailment in the imports of borrowing countries. Germany, for instance, having reparations and interest commitments to meet, had suddenly to convert an import surplus into an export surplus, which it did by slightly increasing exports and sharply curtailing imports, its net merchandise balance altering from minus 1,250 in 1929 to plus 31 in 1929 and plus 1,644 in 1930 (in millions of reichmarks). Other debtors felt the same strain: the net export surplus of five countries—Argentine, Australia, Austria, India and New Zealand—increased from plus 119 in 1929 to plus 239 in 1931 (in millions of dollars).[14] Correspondingly creditors exported less, the United States export surplus diminishing from plus 1,037 in 1928, to plus 842 in 1929, plus 782 in 1930 and plus 333 in 1931 (in millions of dollars).

Most of the debtor countries were primary producers, and they suffered also from the fall in primary prices, which like the decline in investment, had begun before the American slump, but which moved much more swiftly after October 1929. These countries found increasing difficulty in balancing their international accounts, especially as part of the proceeds of exports was required for fixed interest payments. Four of them were unable to maintain their currencies at par in 1929—Hungary, Argentina, Paraguay and Brazil—and four more—Australia, New Zealand, Venezuela and Bolivia—were driven off in 1930.

What with the slump in America, curtailing the demand for primary products (and to a lesser extent manufactures) and what with the decline of foreign lending and the difficulties of primary producers curtailing the demand for manufactures, world trade was bound to contract; the index shows what happened:

TABLE VI

PRODUCTION AND TRADE, 1929–1937

	1929	1932	1937
Foodstuffs			
World trade	100	89	93.5
World production	100	100	108
Raw materials			
World trade	100	81.5	108
World production	100	74	116
Manufactures			
World trade	100	59.5	87
World production	100	70	120

The decline of world trade was, however, greater than the decline of production, except in the case of raw materials; and again in the recovery to 1937 production surpassed trade.

The principal reason for this is that trade contracted, not only because of the slump and the decline of foreign investment, but also because the reaction of most countries to the depression was to increase the barriers to trade. Restrictions were applied especially to imports of food and imports of manufactures.

The reasons why tariff barriers were increased were various. The debtor countries and the primary producing countries—mostly the same—were compelled to take special measures to reduce their imports, in order to be able to meet their obligations. To these countries the burden of fixed debts was very onerous, as it increased in proportion to their disposable funds as those funds (proceeds of exports) diminished. Tariffs, quotas and exchange control spread as weapons of defence. This in turn reacted on industrial exporters, whose exports were curtailed. Industrial countries benefited from the fall in primary prices, and though their exports fell, in some cases the effects on the balance of trade cancelled out. Nevertheless these countries also increased their obstacles to imports; in some cases trying to protect their farmers, hit by the fall of agricultural prices, and in others trying to extend domestic production at the expense of imports, in order to find employment for persons in the export trades. Whatever the cause, the results were the same. Tariffs moved sharply upwards from 1930, following the lead of America's Hawley-Smoot tariff, which became effective in June of that year. By 1932 world trade was well tied up.

This uprush of restrictions on trade proved very controversial. At the time economists almost unanimously disapproved. They conceded that it is often possible for a country to improve its position by reducing imports and thus increasing both employment and its national income, provided that it is acting alone; but they argued that when all countries are cutting imports at the same time possible benefits of this sort cancel out because each inflicts unemployment on the export trades of the others. The rapid decline of the export trades is deflationary; export employment contracts faster than domestic employment expands to replace imports, and the general air of depression helps to check investment and to increase the severity of the slump. So while admitting that it was the slump that caused international trade to contract, they argued that it was also, in no less important a sense, the sharp contraction of trade through restrictions that helped to aggravate the slump.

This conclusion is not now so easily accepted, because we understand better the way in which a slump transmits itself from country to country. When there is a slump in one country (call this country A) it transmits itself to other countries in the first place by reducing their exports. If these countries take no evasive action *two* multiplier processes are set in motion which aggravate the original disturbance. In the first place, each country is forced to cut its imports by the amount by which its exports have fallen. If it could cut imports from country A only while continuing to trade as much with all others, the slump might be isolated. International trade would fall only by the amount by which A's trade was reduced, and there would be no multiplier effects, except such as might flow from a redistribution of trade between the other countries. But A's trade cannot be cut like this without violating the rules of non-discrimination. A country must treat all others alike, according to these rules; so, unless A's currency appreciates in terms of all others (which cannot happen without its consent) countries wishing to eliminate a deficit of A's currency must cut their trade by a multiple of this deficit. But this is not all. For, unless special measures are taken, a cut in imports will be achieved only through a fall in income that is several times greater. So, to take arbitrary figures, if A's imports fall by one unit, other countries may have to cut their imports by 6 units, and in order to do this, may experience a cut in income and production of 30 units. The first multiplication can be avoided by discrimination against A, by general currency depreciation or by discriminatory tariffs or licences. The second multiplication is avoided if imports are cut directly by tariff or by licensing instead of waiting for them to be cut by the natural multiplier process that spreads from the fall of exports. On this analysis, therefore, the general increase of tariffs that occurred after 1929 may have been beneficial; by cutting trade directly these tariffs arrested the second multiplier, and so prevented production from falling in the same proportion as trade and to a much greater absolute extent. It would have been better if these tariffs had been raised exclusively against the U.S.A., and had thus isolated the slump without any multiplier effects at all; but even non-discriminatory tariffs were better than none.

The same argument calls for a reduction of tariffs in the upswing. If one country starts to increase its production, employment and imports, other countries will benefit; their employment and production grows by a multiple of the increase of exports, and they import more from each other in an upward spiral which expands their total trade by several times the initial increase, until the country initiating the upswing is itself exporting as much more as it is importing. If, however, restrictive licensing of imports prevents this second multiplier from coming into effect, international trade will not expand spirally; the country initiating the upswing will not be able to continue its increased importing, and other countries will get no benefit. The case for raising tariffs when the slump starts is also a case for lowering them when the bottom is reached. The mistake that countries made was not the raising of tariffs in 1930, but the failure to lower them again from 1933 onwards, as production increased.

The impact of the slump on different countries was very different. Taking industrial production in 1929 as 100, the figures for 1932 are:

U.S.S.R.	183	France	72
Japan	98	Belgium	69
Norway	93	Italy	67
Sweden	89	Czechoslovakia	64
Holland	84	Poland	63
U.K.	84	Canada	58
Roumania	82	Germany	53
Hungary	82	U.S.A.	53

The U.S.S.R. was insulated from the world economy, and little affected by the slump. Japan, as we shall see, attacked it at once with measures of an inflationary character (including war and war preparation) and so experienced very little decline in industrial production, though both in standard of living and in its balance of payments, Japan suffered greatly as a primary producer, because of the collapse of the demand for silk. The Scandinavian countries are exporters of raw materials of a kind for which the demand was maintained fairly well during the slump, and they did not suffer as badly as others. The countries which suffered worst were in two geographical areas, the United States and Canada, and Germany and the countries adjacent to it, especially Austria, Poland, Czechoslovakia and Italy, France and Belgium. Broadly we can say that the two great centres of depression were the U.S.A. and Germany.

Industrial production fell as much in Germany as it did in the United States. The superficial explanation of the German collapse is the American collapse, in the sense that Germany had been buoyed up during the 1920's by American loans, and it was the drying up and recall of these loans which set the country on the downward path from 1928. This, however, is the superficial explanation in the sense that Germany would not have been so dependent on foreign loans if its policies had been different. The dependence on foreign loans was due to the desire to invest more than the country was willing to save. This was good sense so long as the loans were available, because it increased productive power; in the second half of the 1920's all the indices were moving favourably—unemployment was low, production and exports were increasing swiftly, and the gap in the balance of payments was contracting. The fundamental error was the decision to do nothing to counteract the effects of the drying up of foreign investment, and the withdrawal of foreign credits. The drying up of foreign investment meant necessarily that imports must be curtailed. But the process through which this was brought about, namely a much greater deflation of the national income, was unnecessary. Foreign imports could have been curtailed directly by controlling imports at such level as German earnings abroad (and reduced borrowing) could afford. At the same time national income could have been maintained by expanding domestic credit in place of foreign credit. And at the same time, investment could have been cut to the level of what the country was willing to save, and resources diverted instead towards producing exports and substitutes for imports. Repercussions of the slump elsewhere could not have been avoided entirely, but they could have been reduced to much smaller proportions. However, such a policy was not feasible in the Germany of 1929; the runaway inflation was too recent a memory for the authorities or the public to be willing to contemplate credit expansion not backed by foreign assets or by gold; there might well have been a panic. Three years later, when the desperation of deep depression made any policy worth trying, this very policy was at last adopted. But by then the social and political atmosphere was already vastly changed, and monetary policy soon became the instrument of militarism. Much of the misfortune of Germany can be laid at the door of bad monetary policies; too easy credit conditions up to 1923 and too severe restrictions after 1928. If there had been more restriction up to 1923 and more inflation after 1928 in Germany, the conditions which brought Hitler to power would not have been created, and the world's history would have been different.

As it was, Germany contributed also to the "crisis within the crisis" which prolonged the slump. Following the American collapse and the collapse of primary prices, world economic conditions deteriorated in 1929 and 1930. Then in 1931 came another crisis, the international monetary crisis, which added another year to the depression.

Strictly the crisis began in Austria. Early in 1931 Germany and Austria announced that they wished to form a customs union. This proposal was resented by the ex-Allied nations, and particularly by France, which exerted pressure by withdrawing short-term funds. The withdrawal exposed the weakness of Austria. The largest bank in Austria, the Creditanstalt, was found to be insolvent in May 1931. The Austrian Government undertook to guarantee its liabilities, an international loan was raised, and foreign creditors agreed to cease withdrawals. But this failure served to draw attention to the financial weakness of Central Europe. A new run developed on German foreign reserves; the Reichsbank lost gold heavily, and one of the biggest commercial banks, the Danat bank, was suspended in July. The run on Germany continued until an international moratorium was agreed in August. Austria and Germany having succumbed, confidence was lower than ever, and attention shifted to London. Two recent reports had disturbed confidence; the "Macmillan Report", drawing attention to the weakness of British gold reserves, and the "May Report" predicting a substantial budget deficit unless the Labour Government curtailed its expenditures. London's short-term obligations were large, for reasons we have already seen; she was also owed large short-term sums but much of these were tied up by moratoria in Austria and Germany. The Bank of England had therefore to pay in gold, and withdrawals proceeded so rapidly that in September 1931 gold payments were suspended. Great Britain was off the Gold Standard and the pound was allowed to depreciate.

The psychological repercussions of the abandonment of the Gold Standard by Great Britain were immense; the "fall of the pound" heralded the collapse of the international monetary mechanism which had been painfully rebuilt during the 1920's. Any chance that the slump might have ended in 1931 was now definitely postponed.

The depreciation of sterling was followed at once by a number of other countries. Almost immediately, Canada, India, Iceland, Denmark, Egypt, Norway and Sweden left the Gold Standard, and by the end of 1932 the number of currencies which had depreciated in relation to gold since the beginning of 1929 had risen to 32. Some of these countries decided to keep their currencies stable in relation to sterling. Thus by the end of 1931 countries were in three groups; those which were still on the Gold Standard, those which were depreciating freely, and those which were linked to sterling.

With so many countries now off the Gold Standard, the fact that others remained on the Standard was a further hindrance to international trade. As the free currencies had depreciated substantially, the price levels of these countries were now much below those of the Gold Standard countries. The exports of the "gold bloc" countries contracted and their balances of payments became more passive. The most important countries remaining on the Gold Standard were the United States, Germany, France, Belgium, Holland, Italy and Poland. The United States was strong enough to stand the strain. The depreciation of sterling in September 1931 was followed immediately by a run on New York, and much gold was withdrawn; but America had a great deal of gold, and the withdrawals soon ceased. France also had large gold reserves; but the depreciation of so many currencies left her price level too high. Her exports declined, and imports threatened to increase. The French alternative to devaluation was to increase the tariff and extend import quotas. Germany had such large obligations payable in gold that she was unwilling to depreciate, and so raise their burden in terms of marks; also the inflationary experience of the first half of the twenties made the monetary authorities unwilling to leave hold of something apparently so stable as the Gold Standard. Instead, exchange control was applied to keep imports low, and at the end of 1931 wages and prices were reduced all round by decree, in an effort to get the German price level nearer to that of Great Britain and other depreciated countries. Nearly all the countries which remained on the Gold Standard were driven to desperate measures to keep their imports and exports in line; exchange control with or without increases in tariffs, or the extension of import quotas became the order of the day. Many countries which had depreciated their currencies also adopted these measures. At the end of 1931 foreign exchange controls were in force in Portugal, Turkey, Spain, Brazil, Germany, Hungary, Chile, Colombia, Czechoslovakia, Greece, Uruguay, Bolivia, Austria, Argentina, Jugoslovia, Latvia, Bulgaria, Nicaragua, Estonia and Denmark with many others to follow in 1932. General licensing of imports had been adopted in Brazil, Latvia, Denmark, Turkey, Estonia, France, Japan, Holland and Spain; and the list of countries which had increased their tariffs is much longer.

INTERNATIONAL EFFORTS

The decline of international trade caused considerable apprehension, and many international conferences were summoned to discuss what might be done. Attention focused on the following points—on the possibility of securing a tariff truce, on the special problems of Eastern Europe, on the possibilities of customs unions, on the burden of debts and reparations, and, after 1931, on the collapse of the Gold Standard.

Concern over tariff barriers was not special to the slump; international conferences had been passing resolutions on this subject since 1919, and when the slump came governments were still actively considering how to bring into effect the resolutions of the conference of 1927. A conference summoned in February 1930 actually resulted in a tariff truce convention, its 18 signatories, including the chief countries of Europe, agreeing to prolong all existing commercial agreements until April 1931, and not to raise duties during the period without first consulting interested parties. But further conferences in 1930 and 1931 failed to achieve any positive results.

Meanwhile, the plight of the agricultural countries of Eastern Europe attracted attention. Conferences held in 1930 and in 1931 resulted in the suggestion that European importers should give preferential treatment to cereals coming from Eastern Europe.

This proposal was however rejected by some of the countries, especially the United Kingdom and the United States, as involving a violation of the Most Favoured Nation Clause, and nothing came of it. A Conference held at Stresa in 1932 further proposed that the return of these countries to free exchange dealings should be facilitated by the creation of a "currency normalisation fund", contributed to internationally, which would support their currencies during the transition. But nothing came of this either. Nevertheless, for political reasons (to thwart proposals for union with Germany), Austria was singled out in 1933 for further international assistance, under League of Nations supervision.

The Most Favoured Nation Clause wrecked also proposals for customs unions, which were made by Austria and Germany in March 1931, and by the Netherlands, Belgium and Luxembourg in the Ouchy Convention of July 1932. The opposition of Great Britain to these unions was all the more resented because she was already receiving preferential treatment in the markets of the Dominions and of various colonies, a system which was greatly extended by the Ottawa agreements of 1932. Foreign countries found it difficult to reconcile her attitude that the Dominions were independent nations each entitled to a vote in international conferences, with her claim that in economic matters they should count as one with Great Britain. In face of this opposition proposals for customs unions made no headway. There was, nevertheless, increased regional cooperation, as exemplified by the Oslo Convention between Norway, Sweden, Finland, Denmark, Holland and Belgium in 1930, various Balkan conventions, and the Montevideo resolutions for Pan-American cooperation.

In 1931 the run on Austrian, German and Hungarian reserves brought the burden of international debt into urgent discussion. On an American initiative the immediate crisis was met by moratoria for six months, which were again extended early in 1932. Some countries did not wait for international action; they simply declared their inability to meet the service of external debts, whether public (e.g. Brazil) or commercial (e.g. Uruguay), and in many others exchange control was operated in such a way as to withhold foreign exchange for this purpose. The burden of debts had been greatly increased first by the fall of prices, and secondly, where debts were payable in gold, by currency depreciation.

The effort to get rid of war debts was again renewed,

and coupled with the reparations problem. The Dawes Plan had been succeeded in 1929 by the Young Plan. Germany in 1929 was still comparatively prosperous. The reparations payments were reduced from 125 million pounds to 100 million pounds, and fixed for 37 years. (At the same time the Bank for International Settlements was created to facilitate the transfers; there was much hope that this would grow eventually into the Central Bank of Central Banks, able to control and coordinate financial policy on the world level, but the Bank had no such powers, and the collapse of the Gold Standard soon rendered it unimportant.) Both inter-allied war debts and reparations were covered by the moratorium on inter-governmental debt accepted on Mr. Hoover's initiative for 12 months from August 1931. A conference was then summoned at Lausanne in June 1932 to consider the future of these obligations. Eventually the European nations present agreed to wipe out most of the German reparations and their own war debts on condition that the United States also agreed to waive its own claims. This the United States refused to do; but after a while countries just ceased paying. By the end of 1933 the only country still making war debt payments was Finland.

The Lausanne conference also recommended that there should be a World Economic Conference, which was duly summoned for June 1933 in London. Great hopes were fastened upon this conference, which was to be the summit of international efforts to cope with the depression. Its agenda was carefully prepared by preliminary meetings of "experts". Their emphasis was mainly on what was needed to revive international trade; tariffs should be reduced, the Gold Standard restored, and international lending resumed. How these reforms were to be initiated did not emerge, and when the delegates met to discuss them, their general agreement on objectives was matched by equal disagreement on methods. It is doubtful whether any more could have come out of this conference than came out of the conference of 1927 and its predecessors, namely resolutions in favour of good international behaviour with little practical effect. But the event was never tested.

In April 1933 the U.S.A. left the Gold Standard. The newly elected President had decided to try to eliminate the slump by raising prices. He had been advised that if the U.S.A. did this on the Gold Standard, U.S. prices would get out of line with world prices, and gold would flow out; and also that one of the quickest ways to raise commodity prices would be to raise the price of gold. Accordingly the Gold Standard was abandoned, and the dollar left to fluctuate wildly in the foreign exchanges. When the World Economic Conference met in June, the delegates hoped that the President would decide to stabilise the value of the dollar; no one was willing to enter into commitments without knowing what level the dollar would ultimately reach. Discussions proceeded in the conference, but most of the delegates were waiting all the time for the President to declare his mind. On July 3rd he announced that he was unwilling to stabilise the dollar. Desultory committee work continued, but eventually at the end of July the conference disbanded without reaching any important conclusions.

The failure of the World Economic Conference marks in a minor sense, the end of an era. It was the last international economic conference before the war; the last major effort to cope with economic problems internationally. From 1933 countries abandon hopes of international revival and concentrate on stimulating domestic demand, if necessary at the expense of still greater restrictions on international trade. From 1933 the divergent domestic policies of the nations become more important than the international economy, to the extent even that the world market disintegrates into many different markets with different price levels and restricted interchange. Indeed the whole climate of economic opinion alters; up to 1933 world statesmen and economists focus their attention on international trade and investment; after 1933 this interest diminishes and economists hardly less than statesmen are preoccupied with domestic policies. Neither is the change confined to economic affairs. By 1933 the political situation had already begun to deteriorate. In 1931 Japan invaded Manchuria; in 1933 Hitler came to power; in 1935 Italy attacked Abyssinia. Already in 1933 the world was clearly moving towards war, and discussion of economic cooperation gave way to increased political tension.

REVIVAL

Fortunately revival did not wait on international action. Towards the end of 1932 the economic indices began to move upward. Production and trade increased and unemployment declined. The upward movement continued until 1937, when a short boom was followed by further recession. 1937 is therefore taken for comparisons in measuring the extent of recovery.

Just as the slump was greater in some countries than in others so also some countries recovered to a higher level than did others. Comparison of the indices of industrial production for 1932 and 1937 (1929=100) shows this:

	1932	1937
Sweden	89	149
U.K.	84	124
France	72	82
Germany	53	117
U.S.A.	53	103

The recovery was not complete, except in a few countries. In Germany unemployment almost disappeared, the rearmament boom dominating everything. In France, also, curiously, unemployment disappeared—curiously because production was still nearly 20 per cent below the level of 1929; the reasons were that some of the foreign workers in France, whose numbers had increased to three millions after the war, were repatriated during the slump, that many nationals returned to their farms, and that hours of work were reduced, so that the reserve of industrial unemployed was small even though production was so low. Elsewhere there was still a great deal of unemployment in 1937, so much so that the fact that a boom was occurring escaped the attention of all but the keenest observers; thus at the height of the boom there were over 5,000,000 unemployed in the U.S.A., and over 1,000,000 in the U.K.

As so many different domestic policies were pursued in the thirties, the revival has been claimed by different schools of thought as proving the success of their own policies. In fact it is doubtful whether recovery is to be attributed to any particular national policy. The economic system usually recovers from slumps. During the depression prices fall, marginal firms go bankrupt, investment is curtailed, and confidence recedes. After a while it is felt that prices have fallen too low; depreciation has accumulated, confidence returns, and reinvestment begins. There would have been recovery in Germany or the United States without Hitler or Roosevelt or their spectacular policies; and indeed the indices show that recovery had begun before such policies were initiated.

The puzzle is not that there was recovery, but that it was so incomplete. This is particularly puzzling in the United States, because in that country the Federal Government incurred large budget deficits every year, in its effort to reflate. The object of policy was to stimulate private investment, and the indices show its limited success.

U.S. INDICES OF INDUSTRIAL PRODUCTION

	1929	1932	1933	1934	1935	1936	1937
Consumption Goods	100	75	85	87	97	108	114
Investment Goods	100	31	41	50	63	81	92

Consumption revived, but investment lagged behind. There seem to have been two principal reasons for this. One was the fact that the slump had been so severe—worse there than anywhere else. A large stock of capital equipment had accumulated, which hung over the investment market. Measured from 1932 the American recovery looks much more spectacular than it does when measured from 1929. Taking 1932 as 100, the indices of industrial production for 1937 are France 114, Sweden 169, U.K. 171, U.S.A. 194, Germany 221. If the U.S.A. hardly surpassed the 1929 level, it was because it had so far to go to get there. The other reason to which some importance is attached is the political atmosphere in the U.S.A. after 1933. As we shall see in a later chapter, American capitalists as a class were hostile to the New Deal administration, and this may have reduced their willingness to make investment commitments. This, however, seems the less important explanation.[15]

In the United Kingdom there had not been a boom in the years before 1929; there was more obvious reason for investment, and as the collapse was not so great as in the United States, there was less distance to go in order to overtake the levels of 1929. The leader in recovery was the building industry; the building boom which the U.S.A. had experienced from 1922 was delayed in the U.K. until 1932 and after. But there was also an expansion of other industries catering for domestic consumption, notably electricity, rayon, and motor cars and also service industries. The fact that recovery was in domestic demand was noticeable; the quantum of exports,[16] taking 1927 as 100, was 106 in 1929, 66 in 1932 and only 88 in 1937.

The disintegration of world trade remained. In previous recoveries world trade had always been a leader; on this occasion it moved behind production, at a low level.

The abandonment of the Gold Standard by the U.S.A. in 1933 was a blow to the remaining "gold bloc" countries. It was generally expected that they would have to follow suit sooner or later, as they could not permanently retain price levels above those of the rest of the world, and accordingly it paid holders of their currencies to convert them into other currencies which could retain a stable value. Investment in the gold bloc countries was thus reduced, and deflationary pressures kept unemployment high. The export of capital was marked by an outflow of gold, particularly to London and New York. Thus while the French gold reserves[17] fell from 3,022 million dollars at the end of 1933 to 1,529 million dollars at the end of 1938, those of Great Britain increased in the same terms from 928 to 1,587 and those of the U.S.A. from 4,012 to 8,609. Eventually in 1936, the gold bloc could no longer stand the strain, and its principal members devalued their currencies.

Meanwhile some order had begun to be established. In January 1934 the dollar was stabilised; the U.S.A. was virtually back on the Gold Standard at 59 per cent of its former parity. The pound was then loosely linked with the dollar, at about the previous dollar parity, and most other countries began to try to keep their exchange values stable. When in 1936 France decided to leave the Gold Standard, Britain, France and the United States signed a tripartite agreement not to alter exchange rates without consultation. The Gold Standard had not been restored, but the intentions and the practical consequences of the new arrangements were similar.

As recovery proceeded, restrictions on imports were also relaxed. The lead was given by the United States, which from 1934 negotiated a series of trade treaties, each providing for reciprocal reduction of duties. As the prices of primary products revived, the balance of payments position of several countries improved, and they felt able to relax their import licensing and exchange controls. What was most notably missing was any revival of international investment; the creditor countries had in the thirties a net inflow in place of a net outflow of capital.

BOOM AND COLLAPSE

Prices moved upward with recovery, gradually from 1932 to 1936, and then with sudden violence early in 1937. But in the second half of 1937 they started to drop again, continuing their decline in 1938, and with them went also a decline in industrial activity. The boom and collapse of 1937 awaits satisfactory analysis for the phenomenon is unusual when unemployment is as large as it still was in 1937. For explanation one must turn again to the United States in which the movements originated.

One of the principal elements in the circulation of money in the United States had come to be the Federal Government's deficit. As recovery proceeded the Government began to hope that having "primed the pump" it could withdraw and leave the economy to support itself; continued increases in the public debt were beginning to cause some alarm. In 1936, however, owing to political pressure the Government was forced to have a larger deficit than ever, as an Act of Congress called on it to pay a large bonus in cash to war veterans. The entry of this money into circulation helped to stimulate demand. Raw material prices rose, and as the supply did not increase as rapidly, particularly in such cases as rubber, tin and copper, where supply was controlled by international cartel agreements, a commodity boom developed. By the middle of 1937, however, extra supplies were coming on to the market. At the same time the U.S. Government had decided to balance its budget, converting the large deficit of 1936 into a small estimated surplus for 1937. The coincident fall of commodity prices and withdrawal of the government deficit made their impact on an economy where business confidence had never really recovered from the shock of 1929. Between 1937 and 1938 the index of the production of investment goods dropped from 92 to 59, and unemployment increased by two and a half million.

This time the impact on the world economy was not so great. Germany and Japan were now insulated as well as the U.S.S.R., and their production indices continued to move upward. In most other countries there was some decline in 1938, but the extent of the decline was arrested by the commencement of rearmament. Beginning in 1937, the volume of expenditure on defence swells gradually in one country after another until in 1939, with the outbreak of war, it begins to dominate the world economy.

It is with this background of slump, recovery and slump that we must examine the policies pursued by some of the more important countries during the 1930's, which are the interesting as well as the most spectacular feature of the period.

PART II

NATIONAL POLICIES

CHAPTER V

THE UNITED KINGDOM

THE difficulties of Great Britain began in the 1870's. From the beginning of the century until then, industrial production[1] had been increasing at an annual rate of not much less than 4 per cent; thereafter until the war the rate was less than 2 per cent (see Chart II). At the same time, other countries were forging ahead. The cumulative annual increase of manufacturing production[2] from 1873 to 1913 was 4.8 per cent for the United States, 3.9 per cent for Germany, 3.7 per cent for the world as a whole, and only 1.8 per cent for the United Kingdom.

There can be little doubt that the main cause of the relative British stagnation was to be found in the export trade. In the first part of the nineteenth century the growth of British exports was astonishing, the annual rate of growth increasing steadily to the sixties, when it averaged about 8 per cent. The ratio of exports to industrial production increased rapidly. Taking the two indices as 100 in 1913, their ratio rose from 46 in 1826/36 to 97 in 1884/89, in spite of the vigorous increase in industrial production which was occurring at the same time, and then fell below this level for the next twenty years although industrial production was growing much more slowly (see Chart III). At the end of the century the rate of increase of British exports had fallen to less than 1 per cent.

For this there were two main reasons. One was the effect of adverse terms of trade for primary products on the rate of growth of world trade in manufactures, from the 1880's onwards. The quantum of world trade in manufactures was almost stationary between 1880 and 1900, and though some part of this must be attributed to the tariff policies of industrial countries, especially France, Germany and the United States, these three countries in 1881-5 were taking only 19 per cent of world imports of manufactures,[3] and the failure of smaller countries to purchase more manufactures was of greater importance. At the end of the century the terms of trade began to improve for primary products, and world trade in manufactures once more leapt upwards.

The British export of manufactures was adversely affected in the 1880's and 1890's by the decline in the rate of growth of world trade in manufactures. But it was affected even more and permanently by the industrialisation of new countries. In 1876/80 the British share of world exports of manufactures was 38 per cent; in 1911/13, when world trade as a whole was buoyant, the British share was only 27 per cent.

The principal reason for the relative stagnation of British industry was that Britain had ceased to be the workshop of the world.

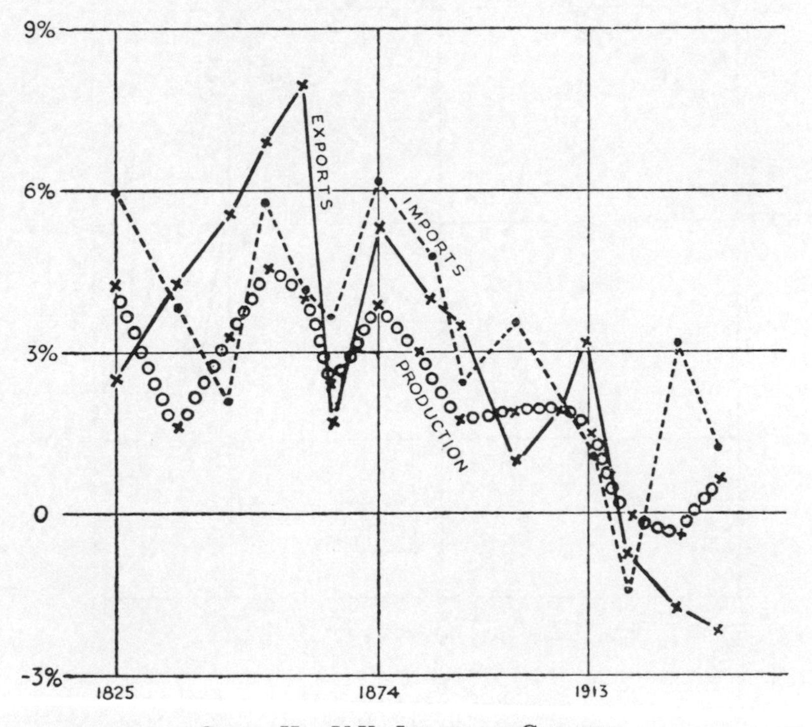

CHART II. U.K. INDICES OF GROWTH.

Annual rates of growth of exports, imports and industrial production, measured in physical quantities. Points of inflexion are averages of cycles ending in 1818, 1825, 1836, 1846, 1853, 1860, 1865, 1874, 1883, 1889, 1899, 1907, 1913, 1920, 1929 and 1937. For figures, see Statistical Appendix, series 15, 16 and 17.

Thanks to an early start she had captured in the first part of the 19th century a much greater share of world trade than she could possibly hope to retain. She had become too dependent on international trade. Production for export could no longer impart to her economy the vigour which had raised industrial production

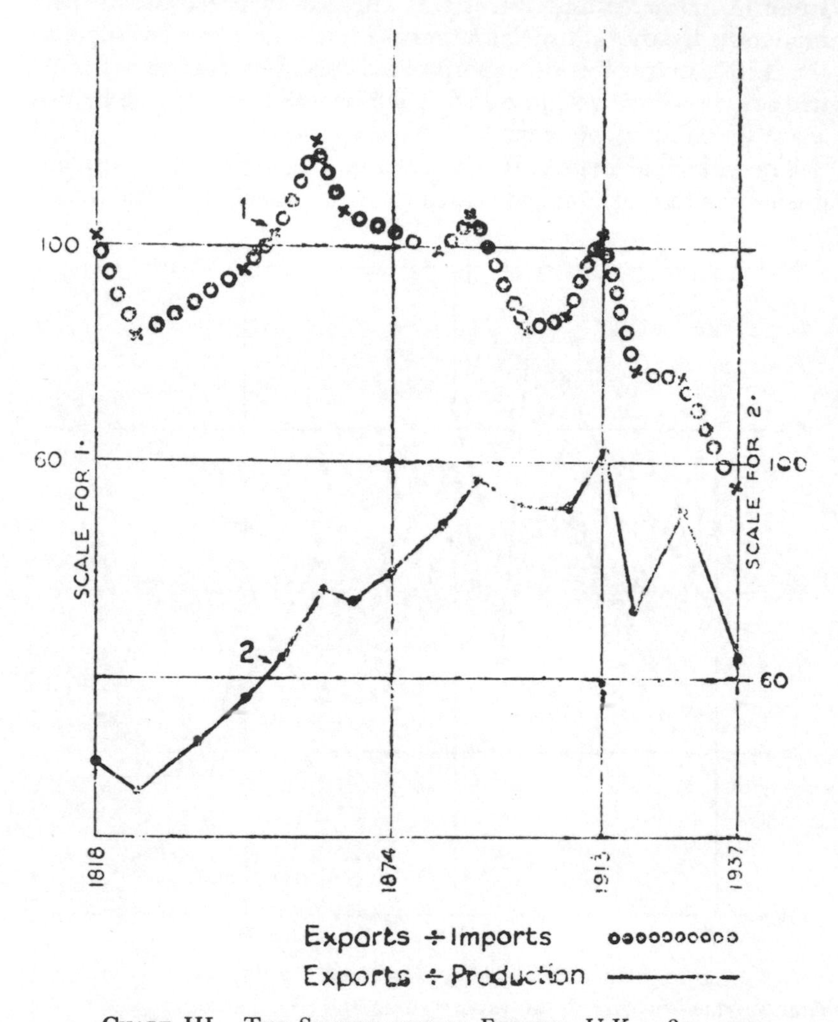

CHART III. THE SIGNIFICANCE OF EXPORTS, U.K., 1811–1937.

Ratio of Exports to Imports and to Industrial Production, in physical terms. Base, 1913 = 100. Points of inflexion are averages for cycles ending in boom years. Based on series 3, 4 and 5 in the Statistical Appendix.

so rapidly; henceforth, if industrial production was to recover its vigorous growth there would have to be much more emphasis on the home market. The readjustment was, however, delayed. Exports could no longer pay for imports, but the country was saved from having to reduce its imports (and, thereby unfortunately diverted from the task of developing production for the home market) by developing new sources of income, in the form of invisible exports. Imports continued their upward rise; measuring in 1913 prices[4], the ratio of retained imports to national income rose from 21 per cent in 1870/76 to 28 per cent in 1911/13. The gap between imports and exports widened constantly. Taking the ratio between the indices of physical volume as 100 in 1913, the export-import ratio rose from 86 in 1819/25 to 121 in 1854/60, then fell back to 86 in 1890/99, rallying again in the years before the war (see Chart III). The gap was filled by the export of services, which developed so considerably that a large surplus was still left to finance a growing export of capital.

In a word, having ceased to be able to command an abnormal share of world trade in manufactures, Britain temporarily maintained her balance of payments by achieving an abnormal share of the world's shipping, insurance, and other commercial services. It is most doubtful whether such a position could have been maintained permanently even if there had been no world war. Sooner or later, surely, other countries would have begun to develop their own shipping and similar services, just as they had developed their own manufactures, and Great Britain would have been forced to adapt her economy to a larger production for home consumption.

The war accelerated the adverse forces at work. It encouraged other countries to supply for themselves both more goods and more services, and forced some realisation of overseas assets, which reduced the income from abroad. In spite of this, Britain was still able to pay her way in the 1920's; she was forced to reduce her export of capital, but her external earnings were still large enough to finance her imports and leave some surplus for foreign investment. Not until after the slump of 1929 was the income from invisible exports so greatly reduced that the country was no longer able to pay its way, and driven to start living on its overseas capital.

It was not inevitable that British exports should have fared as badly as they did; exports would have been larger if the British economy had been more flexible. The industrialisation of new countries brings a shift in the composition of world trade. Consumer good manufactures decline in importance relatively to producer goods. British trade has been making some adjustment to this change for a century, as figures compiled by Dr. Schlote show:[5]

TABLE VII

COMPOSITION OF U.K. EXPORTS OF MANUFACTURES, %

	1827–29	1857–59	1890–92	1911–13	1927–29	1932–33
Textiles	78.2	67.9	58.7	51.2	44.4	39.7
Other consumer goods	9.3	9.1	8.6	10.6	12.0	11.3
Producer goods	8.7	21.8	30.2	33.7	37.5	39.0
Unclassified	3.8	1.2	2.5	4.5	6.1	9.0

There is a steady trend against consumer goods in general and textiles in particular, in favour of producer goods. But the adjustment was not rapid enough. Both the U.S.A. and Germany have advanced rapidly in the producer goods trades, capturing a large share of the market, while the U.K. remained too long wedded to consumer goods, and especially to textiles. This comes out very clearly in an analysis which has been made of world trade. In this German enquiry[6] the growth of world trade between 1913 and 1929 in value terms was measured for a number of manufactured products, amounting to 80 per cent of U.K. exports, 87 per cent of German, and 85 per cent of U.S.A. exports of manufactures. Commodities were then classified according to the growth of world trade in them between 1913 and 1929, three degrees of growth being distinguished, viz. by less than 75 per cent, by more than 150 per cent, and by between 75 per cent and 150 per cent. Next the trade of each country was classified by commodities according to the world growth of trade in those commodities, with the following result:

TABLE VIII

EXPORTS OF MANUFACTURES IN 1929

	Percentage in groups expanding 1913–1929 in world trade by			
	less than 75%	75% to 150%	more than 150%	no data
Great Britain	42.1	33.5	4.3	20.1
Germany	27.3	55.3	4.5	12.9
U.S.A.	17.1	38.8	28.6	15.5

Here we have the clearest proof of the U.K.'s lost leadership in world trade. The largest category of British exports was in those commodities expanding least in world trade. The leader *par excellence* in world trade was the United States; only 17.1 per cent of her manufactures exports were in the lowest category, compared with Britain's 42.1 per cent; and 28.6 per cent were in the highest category, compared with Britain's 4.3 per cent. Germany also was well ahead.

All this could be and was neglected until after 1929. Until then overseas income continued to be large enough to pay for imports, and even to continue some export of capital, and it was possible for the situation to be ignored. It was not completely ignored. The persistence of heavy unemployment did indeed cause much disquiet, but no such drastic measures were taken, or even seriously contemplated in influential circles, as would certainly have been adopted if there had been less unemployment but a passive balance of payments. After 1929 the situation became even more serious; exports and invisible income shrank so much that they were insufficient to pay for imports—throughout the 1930's Britain was living on her capital. Even then some relief was obtained from a very favourable movement of the terms of trade. Taking the ratio of export to import prices in 1913 as 100, the average for 1921/29 was 127 and for 1930/37 it was 138. Having failed to hold her share of the export market, Britain was rescued first by winning an abnormal share of invisible services, and then by a very favourable movement of the terms of trade. It is only in 1946, with invisible income diminished, and the terms of trade moving unfavourably that the British people are beginning to become aware of a problem which had first begun to emerge some sixty years or more ago.

The problem had begun to emerge well before the war, but it was not until after the war that it really became serious. The average level of unemployment was greater after the 1870's than it had been before; but it was still relatively small. Industrial production and exports were growing less rapidly, but they were still growing. Stagnation before 1913 was relative; after 1913, in the export trade, it was absolute. A few indices illustrate the situation.

	1913	1929	1937
World trade quantum	100	133	128
U.K. exports, quantum	100	87	72
U.K. share of world exports, %	14	11	10

	1913	1929	1937
U.K. balance of payments, current account, £m	181	103	−56
U.K. manufacturing production	100	104	128
U.K. percentage unemployed	2	10	11

The index of industrial production which we have to use for all U.K. comparisons—Dr. Hoffman's valuable compilation[7]—is known to underestimate post-war growth by about 20 per cent; but the indices of unemployment and of trade give a fair indication of the stagnation in the export trades.

In the 1920's policy was dominated by two ideas; in the first half of the decade the idea was to restore Britain's position as a great financial centre, and this was pursued up to the restoration of the Gold Standard in 1925 at pre-war parity. Thereafter the main idea of policy was that the wage level was too high for this parity, and ought therefore to be reduced, but after the general strike of 1926 no further great efforts were made to bring this into effect. That the industrial situation was unsatisfactory was common ground, and various enquiries were promoted. They showed that stagnation was due to the loss of export markets, and that unemployment was concentrated in the export trades. Machinery was created to facilitate the transfer of labour from export trade areas into others, but since no special effort was made to stimulate production for home consumption, employment opportunities outside the export trade areas were not expanding rapidly enough to absorb the export unemployment. Total employment increased from year to year, but only enough to absorb the increase in the industrial population.

Much blame lies at the door of the foreign exchange policy pursued after 1920. The determination to return to the Gold Standard at par put Britain's prices well above those of her competitors, and checked production both by hindering competition in old markets and by restricting the development of new ones; much of the lost leadership revealed by Table VIII was due to excessive prices. It would have been possible to find a rate of exchange which would have brought full employment in the second half of the twenties, when all other countries were expanding with full employment, and it would probably have been not more than 20 per cent below par. At this level exports would have been greater, and though imports of food and raw materials would also have been larger, imports of manufactures would have been smaller, and the ratio of total imports to national income would have been smaller than before the war. There would have been less strain on the balance of payments, and the financial crisis of 1931 would have been avoided. There would also have been no "general strike." For the "prestige" of the pound, regained for six years only, an exorbitant price was paid.

THE BALANCE OF PAYMENTS

The slump aggravated the situation by turning an active into a passive balance of payments, and increasing unemployment in the export trades.

In 1929 there was an active balance on current account[8] (excluding gold) of plus £103,000,000; by 1931 this had changed to a passive balance of minus £104,000,000. The main change was not in the merchandise balance, but in the invisible exports, the merchandise balance deteriorated only by £27 million; the invisibles by £180 million. The merchandise balance did not deteriorate despite a big fall in exports, because the terms of trade moved violently in favour of Great Britain, enabling her to buy the same volume of imports[9] for two-thirds of what they cost two years earlier.

	Price of Imports 1927=100	Quantum of Imports 1927=100	Value of Imports £m	Value of Exports £m	Merchandise Balance £m	Quantum of Exports 1927=100	Price of Exports 1927=100
1929	99	101.4	1,229	848	−381	104	97
1931	70	101.0	870	461	−408	69	79

Then came the depreciation of sterling, not so much because of the adverse balance, but because a general loss of confidence in the British economy made foreigners recall their assets, thus causing the Bank of England to lose gold abnormally.

Depreciation had several effects. Imports were cut at once, by depreciation and by the moderate tariff imposed soon afterwards. The volume of imports retained for home consumption had risen slightly between 1929 and 1931 (1927=100) from 102.5 to 103; in 1932 it fell abruptly to 90.5. At the same time, the terms of trade moved against the country; up to 1931 import prices had been falling faster than export prices, but between 1931 and 1932 export prices fell faster than import prices. They did not fall by the full amount of the depreciation, the net effect of which was to check the fall of prices in Britain while prices continued to fall in countries still on gold. The gap that thus developed was not, on the other hand, as great as the degree of depreciation, so in terms of gold British export prices were reduced relatively to the export prices of other countries, and the volume of British exports was maintained while the exports of other countries continued to decline. The volume of exports was so well maintained that, despite the fall of British prices relatively to those of other countries, the share of Britain in world exports, which had declined from 10.75 per cent in 1929 to 9.36 per cent in 1931, advanced to 9.92 per cent in 1932 and 10.37 per cent in 1933. The passive balance was also reduced, from £104 m. in 1931 to £51 m. in 1932 and zero in 1933, mainly by reducing the adverse merchandise balance very substantially, from £408 m. in 1931 to £287 m. in 1932 and £263 m. in 1933.

This good fortune did not, however, last. In 1933 the United States also left the Gold Standard, and soon the pound and the dollar were back to their pre-1931 relation. British and American prices came back into line. Taking 1929 as 100, wholesale prices[10] in 1931 were 76.8 in the U.K. and 76.6 in the U.S.A. Thereafter they diverged, the U.K.'s 74.9 and 75.0 comparing with the U.S.A.'s 68.0 and 69.2 for 1932 and 1933. But in 1934 they were back together, the U.K. at 77.1 and the U.S.A. at 78.6. Similarly French prices came back into line after the French devaluation; in 1936, U.K. prices stood at 82.7 and French at 65.5 in 1937 they were at 95.2 and 92.7 respectively. The effect of all this was that British exports lost the gains secured by devaluation. One by one countries regained their position as they left gold, with the result that Britain's share of world exports, after rising to 10.37 per cent in 1933 declined again to 9.8 per cent in 1937, compared with 10.75 per cent in 1929. Depreciation had been a profitable episode while it lasted, but it could not last long since other countries were bound sooner or later to try to secure the same benefits for themselves. If in 1925 Great Britain had returned to the Gold Standard at a lower parity the repercussions on other countries would have been less noticeable as world trade was expanding, and she might have got away with unilateral action; but in 1931, with a world crisis in progress, the chance was already lost.

The other important line was to try to improve Britain's share of world trade by bilateral agreements. In 1932 the countries of the British commonwealth met at Ottawa, and agreed to extend to each other increased import preferences; the colonies were also instructed to grant preferences to British goods, and very restrictive quotas were applied to Japanese textiles. The same demand was made on some small foreign countries specially dependent on the British market, who were required to increase the proportion of their imports coming from the United Kingdom; the Argentine, Denmark, Sweden, Norway, Estonia, Latvia, Finland, Lithuania and Iceland. In most of these latter agreements special emphasis was laid on extending the market for British coal, these countries being required to ensure that the proportion of their coal imports from Britain should not fall below a figure which varied from 45 per cent for Sweden to 85 per cent for Estonia.[11] A similar result was expected from the loans made to certain countries in 1938 and 1939 through the Export Credits Guarantee Department, for the purchase of British goods.

These arrangements were effective in maintaining Britain's share in the trade of these countries. Nearly every country in the world was buying a smaller percentage of its imports from the United Kingdom in 1929 than in 1913—the U.K. had been losing ground in world trade since at least the 1870's. But after these agreements were made, the share of the U.K. increased in all agreement countries except India (which gave only small preferences to Britain), while continuing to fall in all the others. The figures are set out in Table IX; they are quite striking.[12]

TABLE IX

IMPORTANCE OF THE U.K. AS A SOURCE OF IMPORTS, 1913–1937

	Share in U.K. Exports, 1913 %	Share of U.K. in Imports 1913 %	1929 %	1937 %
Germany	7.74	8.1	6.4	5.7
U.S.A.	5.58	15.2	7.5	6.6
France	5.51	13.2	10.0	8.0
EMPIRE COUNTRIES				
India	13.38	64.2	42.4	31.5
Australia	6.56	51.8	40.0	42.6
Canada	4.53	21.3	15.0	18.2
South Africa	4.22	56.8	43.1	42.6
New Zealand	2.06	59.7	48.7	50.2

AGREEMENT COUNTRIES				
Argentine	4.31	31.0	17.6	20.7
Sweden	1.60	24.4	17.3	19.0
Norway	1.20	26.5	21.2	24.6
Denmark	1.14	15.7	14.7	37.7

The South African figure for 1937 is exceptionally low. The figures for 1936 and 1938 are 46.3 per cent and 43.2 per cent, each being an increase on 1929.

That Britain retained a larger share of the trade of these countries is not open to doubt, but whether the benefit was net remains a subject of dispute. The reason for this is that the effect of the protection for Britain in these markets was to deflect foreign competition into other markets where, on the whole, the British position was in any case already less favourable. It seems likely that Britain would have fared better elsewhere if she had not fared so well in her protected markets. But it is not possible to decide whether on balance the extra loss in unprotected markets exceeded the gain in the protected ones. Supporters of British policy argue that Britain would have lost nearly as much in any case in the unprotected markets, so that nearly all her gain in the protected ones was net; while opponents of the policy disagree. Whichever may be right, Britain's share of world trade continued to decline, being lower in 1937 than it had been in 1929. The gains in protected markets were not enough to compensate for losses in the unprotected.

The British situation could not be improved simply by seeking to have a larger share of world trade. Other nations were sure to resent any such policy, and just as British depreciation in 1931 was followed within a few years by depreciation by all other major countries (except Germany) so also, if British bilateralism had been deemed successful others would surely have followed suit. The British choice lay between maintaining exports by striving for a larger volume of world trade, and alternatively, adapting the economy to a smaller production for export and a larger domestic trade. There is little doubt that British policy in the 1930's helped to diminish world trade. First, depreciation brought only temporary gains, but brought also permanent loss in destroying the international monetary system, by throwing excessive strains on countries remaining on gold, and eventually encouraging other countries to follow the British example; for the collapse of respect for an international monetary standard, and for the network of currency restrictions which followed, the depreciation of sterling must bear a large share of the blame, and as we shall see in a later chapter, this growth of obstacles to trade was one of the prime reasons for the low level of international trade. We shall see also, secondly, that British bilateralism had deflationary consequences for international trade. A high level of international trade could have been attained only if the major countries had collaborated to maintain stability of currencies, and if possible of imports and of prices, and to assist with credits those countries whose balances were most adversely affected by the slump. The decision to pursue unilateral policies ruined the prospects of international trade, and therefore also of British trade. Great Britain was not the only country to take unilateral action. But she started it, and must bear the blame for setting the fashion.

The external problem was never solved. The balance of payments stayed passive throughout the 1930's; Britain was living on her capital.

POUNDS MILLIONS

Balance on current account	1929	1930	1931	1932	1933	1934	1935	1936	1937	1938
	+103	+28	−103	−51	0	−7	+32	−18	−56	−55

INTERNAL POLICY

The process of adapting the British economy to a smaller volume of trade was begun. The number of persons attached to export trades fell substantially, while the numbers attached to domestic industries expanded. The share of exports in national production,[13] estimated at 33 per cent in 1907, and 27 per cent in 1924, fell steadily to 15 per cent in 1938. But progress was inadequate. The average number of unemployed fell from 2.2 millions, its peak in 1932, to 1.3 millions, its lowest level in 1937, but was then still at least twice as large as "normal frictional unemployment" would justify. Imports ceased to grow more rapidly than industrial production; taking 1913 as 100, the 1921/29 average of the quantum of imports was 104 and of industrial production 86, but the 1930/37 averages were 115 and 99 respectively, the ratio of imports to industrial production thus falling from 121 to 114. Thanks to favourable terms of trade, the relative fall in values was even bigger than the relative fall in volume, with the result that the ratio of imports to national income,[14] which was 31 per cent in 1913, fell to 25 per cent in 1929 and 16 per cent in 1938. But even with the terms of trade so favourable to the country, this ratio was still too high. With export trade so low, the country could not afford to be importing so much, and this would have been even more obvious if full employment had been achieved, for the small passive balance would rapidly have changed into a heavy and insupportable drain.

The principal instrument of policy was a reduction of interest rates, achieved by expanding the cash reserves of the banks by open market operations, by converting government securities to a lower rate of interest, and by imposing restrictions on foreign lending. It was hoped that lower interest rates would stimulate private investment. There was, indeed, some revival of private investment, but not to any such great extent as had been expected.

Leading the revival was investment in housing, the increase in which was the dominating factor in British revival during the thirties. It is very doubtful whether the building boom was principally due to either of the factors to which it is usually attributed, the fall in interest rates, and the favourable terms of trade. There is a building boom in Britain about once every 20 to 30 years, and it seems to occur whether prices and interest rates are rising or falling, or whatever is happening to the terms of trade. A boom was due some time in the 1920's, and was delayed, mainly through the affects of rent control in keeping rents below costs. After the fall in prices, this factor ceased to operate, and the boom would probably have come about even if interest rates had not fallen. As for the change in the terms of trade, what was gained on the swings was lost on the roundabouts: the value of exports fell between 1929 and 1931 by slightly more than the value of imports, so that the effect of the trade balance on aggregate purchasing power was not inflationary but slight deflationary. Real wages did rise, for those remaining in employment, and this will have increased their willingness to pay the rent of new houses. But it is difficult to maintain that there would have been no building boom in the 1930's if interest rates had not fallen and the terms of trade had not been favourable.

Whatever the cause, the effects were beneficial. Investment and employment increased not only in building and in related industries, but also in others benefiting from the increased purchasing power generated by investment in building. An estimate[15] attributes one-third of the increased employment in Britain to the direct effects of building, and the indirect effects must have brought this to the neighbourhood of one-half.

The second main line of policy was to try to keep up the rate of profit in some industries by lending support to monopolistic arrangements: coal, cotton, iron and steel, railways, agriculture and shipbuilding. In the case of iron and steel and shipbuilding there was an understanding that new investment should be made and some was made. But generally the nature of the arrangements was such as to discourage the emergence of new and enterprising firms, by protecting by quota the markets of all, irrespective of efficiency. The general effect of this policy was probably to keep declining industries less efficient than they would otherwise have been, and to restrict investment in them.

The third main line of policy was tariff protection, for industry and agriculture. The tariff, however, was low, and while it was of some assistance, it was not enough to prevent employment from continuing to decline in the protected industries as a whole.

CONCLUSION

By 1939 readjustment was proceeding, but it was slow; too slow to absorb the "hard core" of unemployment in the export industries. Nothing could have done this but a vigorous policy designed to increase production for home consumption.

First, there was a great opportunity to modernise the methods and equipment of basic industries, such as coal, cotton, steel and engineering. It was not only since the war that British productivity in these industries had lagged behind. Ever since the 1870's other countries had been equipping themselves with industries more up to date than those of Britain. Estimates show that in the years before 1914 productivity per worker was hardly increasing.[16] Again in the 1920's when France and Germany were reconstructing and the U.S.A. forging ahead, basic British industries were remaining relatively stagnant. A policy of industrial re-equipment would have provided a large volume of employment directly, would have generated additional purchasing power and helped employment indirectly, and would also have eased the export situation by reducing real costs, and by stimulating the export of producer goods (exports thrive best on a good home market base). This was a great opportunity missed. Today the job has to be done, but in most unfavourable circumstances, and the nation pays for twenty years of *laissez faire*.

Secondly, if exports could not be increased, Great Britain was fully entitled to restrict imports to a greater extent than she did, and to meet more of her own needs domestically. Admittedly, imports and exports react on each other, and import control would have had some unfavourable effects on the volume of exports. The first business of the United Kingdom must always be to try to expand the level of international trade, but no conceivable expansion of trade could have sufficed to give the country full employment and to pay for the full employment level of imports. For sixty years the British share of world trade had been falling, and it was necessary for the country to get used to having a smaller ratio of imports to national income. That this fact was not faced adequately before 1931 only makes the problem more difficult in 1946 when the diminution of income from invisible exports, and the prospect of adverse terms of trade to come have added their own urgencies to the need for reducing imports.

Ideas are always behind the events which generate them. British economic doctrine was formed in an era when Britain was securing an ever increasing amount of trade, and in no need to worry about the balance of payments. So long as this continued the role of the government in the economic system was small; the person who counted most was the export trader, and the industrialist whom he fed. After 1920, the export trader was no longer a source of dynamic for the British economy; he was instead, a source of stagnation, and problems were left which only vigorous action by the government could solve. But the philosophy of the twenties and thirties was still the philosophy of the early 19th century; there was no room in it for a vigorous economic policy, and so none was forthcoming. Today these things are seen more clearly, and hardly anyone in Great Britain seriously contemplates any possibility of solving British problems without vigorous governmental planning. Whether the plans will be appropriate to the problems of today rather than to those of the 1920's is not so clear; but that is another matter.

The final lesson of British experience is the importance of international cooperation. The policies pursued by Great Britain in the 1930's were defensible in terms of the strain on her balance of payments, but they were negatived by arbitrary American action, which in effect, deprived Britain of the right to devalue sterling. This is the importance to Britain and to other countries whose international position is weak, of having an international code which restrains unjustified unilateral action. If the rules now proposed in the monetary and tariff spheres had been operating in 1930, the U.K. would have been allowed to adopt the measures needed for readjustment, and the U.S.A. would not have been allowed to take arbitrary action. In the light of this experience the oddest thing about the proposed rules is the fact that those who oppose them most strongly in this country are the very people who think that the time may come again when Britain needs to be able to try out the policies that failed in the thirties; what they do not see is that it is only rules of the kind proposed that may in future substitute success for failure.

CHAPTER VI

GERMANY

THE troubles of Germany were the aftermath of the war. From the 1880's up to the war the country was forging ahead, with its industrial production and exports constantly accelerating. Then came the war; and after it the peace, denuding the country of gold, foreign investments, external investments, ships, and many types of domestic assets, and imposing an annual drain for reparations. Government and people did not rise to the situation. Inflation seized the country in its grip, and not until the middle of the twenties did anything resembling "normal" conditions return. There followed a period of feverish activity, in which all the economic indices moved upwards swiftly. But this was too dependent on foreign credits, and when these began to fail the country plunged once more downward into gloom, adversely affected by the slump more than any other country in the world.

The comparison with Great Britain is specially interesting. The basic problem of both countries in the 1920's was that they had lost their place in world markets.

	1913	1929
Share of world exports	%	%
U.K.	13.9	10.7
Germany	13.1	9.7
Quantum of Exports		
U.K.	100	87
Germany	100	95
Manufacturing index		
U.K.	100	103
Germany	100	117

But the German situation was, in this respect, worse than the British, for while Britain retained her sources of invisible exports, and could still pay her way, Germany had lost hers, and was forced to live on credit, becoming after 1924 the world's largest borrower.

On the other hand, there were also favourable differences. Germany was on the way to solving her problems, which Britain was not. Owing to the inflation and its effects German production had fallen much lower than the British, the manufacturing index (1913 = 100) having dropped to 55 in 1923. But it had also recovered much more swiftly, reaching 122 in 1927, the year before foreign withdrawals began. Exports also were rapidly increasing, their volume doubling between 1924 and 1929, and the adverse trade balance falling steadily. Again, the power of Germany to stand on her own feet was greatly increased by the industrial reconstruction of 1927 and 1928, while the equipment of British industry lagged behind.

Then in 1928 the position started to deteriorate. Foreign funds began to be withdrawn, in 1928 for speculation in Wall Street, in 1929 by the French for political reasons, and thereafter for many reasons—the slump, French political pressure at the time of the proposed Austro-German customs union, Hitler's election success in 1930, and in final culmination the international monetary crisis of 1931. The German authorities reacted at this vital time by restricting credit at home, and in the ensuing deflation, the economy was dragged down.

From 1931 the experiences of Germany and the United Kingdom sharply diverge. The United Kingdom depreciated its currency, while Germany remained on gold; and the United Kingdom balanced its budget, while Germany in 1932 initiated large programmes of public expenditure.

THE BALANCE OF PAYMENTS

By 1931 Germany had achieved a favourable balance of trade by greatly reducing her imports while maintaining her exports, and her only balance of payments problem arose out of the flight of capital. Then came the British depreciation in September 1931, to aggravate all her problems.

It was decided not to devalue. This was a mistake, bringing further problems in its train, but at the time the Government feared that in the public mind devaluation and inflation were inseparably connected, and that fear of a return of inflation would cause a panic. In consequence the balance of payments could be maintained only by one of two means, by exchange control or by deflation, and both were tried.

Foreign exchange control began even before the British depreciation. It was instituted in July 1931 as a result of the international crisis, which was causing too great a flight of capital. At first the control was intended to be temporary, but after the British depreciation it was put, in November, on to a more permanent basis.

Then in December 1931 deflation was attempted. A government decree ordered wages to be reduced to the level of 1927, i.e. by between 10 per cent and 15 per cent, and ordered all prices, rents, salaries, railway fares, etc. to be cut by 10 per cent and interest by 2 per cent (absolute). This had no clear effect. Internally it would have stimulated investment and recovery only if there had been reason to believe that the slump was now over; but it clearly was not over, world prices were still falling, and conditions everywhere were still deteriorating. As to its effects on the external situation, the cut was too small to count. The pound had just lost 30 per cent of its value, and a 10 per cent cut was not much better than no cut, from the point of view of competition.

The result was that while British exports held in 1932, German exports continued to fall until 1934, when they were only half their 1929 volume, compared with a U.K. figure of about 70 per cent. The further result was that the balance of payments was worse than ever. But it was to get still worse, for as recovery proceeded, under the influence of heavy expenditures, the natural tendency was for imports to rise rapidly, and very drastic steps had to be taken in order to maintain equilibrium.

Three principal methods were used to cope with the problem; import licensing, control of foreign payments on loan account, and bilateral trading arrangements.

Import licensing was linked with exchange control. From November 1931 traders were given a quota of foreign exchange based on past performance. Then in 1934 this system was discontinued, and exchange control and import licensing were linked with economic planning. The overall aim of the system was to keep imports within the limits of what could be afforded. The particular aim was to discriminate against imports considered unnecessary, and to develop home production of substitutes wherever possible. Thus great efforts were made to extend German agricultural production,[1] efforts which were unsuccessful because, as soon as labour became scarce in the towns, agricultural workers left the country, and output was very little higher in 1938 than in 1933. It was also desired to foster production of synthetic materials, especially fibres, rubber, and oil, but as it was also desired to build up large reserves of such materials for the event of war, there was not much relief to be found in this direction.

The second method of easing the balance of payments was to eliminate as far as possible interest and dividend payments, so that more exchange could be available for imports. The idea of a moratorium was not invented by Hitler. It was born out of the international monetary crisis in 1931, as a result of which foreign creditors had agreed to standstill arrangements extending into 1932. In 1932 and 1933 foreign withdrawals of capital continued at a high rate, and German reserves of gold and foreign exchange were rapidly depleted, falling in million RM from 2,405 in 1928 to 975 in 1932 and 165 in 1934. Accordingly in June 1933 the Government announced that, while payments on the Dawes and Young Loans would be continued, sinking fund payments on all other loans would be stopped, and only half the interest would be available in foreign exchange, the other half being available only in marks. In June 1934 even these limited payments in foreign exchange were stopped, and a complete moratorium was declared. However, foreign countries did not just accept this declaration. Wherever exports from Germany to a country exceeded imports to Germany there was a balance available which the country could seize for interest payments. Countries favourably placed, like the United Kingdom, accordingly entered into agreements with Germany arranging for their creditors to be paid out of this balance. But other countries simply saw their interest payments accumulating uselessly in German marks.

Thirdly, special arrangements were made with certain countries, especially in South-east Europe and Latin America, exchanging increased imports to Germany for increased exports. The arrangements were varied and complex, because monies arising out of these transactions were available only for bilateral trade, and had therefore to be segregated into special accounts, under what came to be known as clearing agreements. To increase the attractiveness of German goods, the Government in some cases bought goods from clearing countries at prices above world prices or fixed special rates of exchange for the mark below the official rate, or subsidised exports, all these being devices to achieve the benefits of devaluation without actually devaluing. Against these arrangements, as also against the moratoria on interest payments, many foreign commentators protested. They argued that Germany was using her bargaining power to exploit smaller nations. But apart from some tendency to buy more than she sold in exchange, which was due more to shortages of goods in conditions of full employment than to deliberate dishonesty, this charge proved, on further examination, to have little foundation. Bye and large the countries concerned benefited from these arrangements, and the impetus their economies derived may even have spread to the advantage of other countries not party to the arrangements.[2]

The net effects of all this were unimpressive. In spite of a great outcry in foreign countries, and a great fear of a German "trade drive", the quantity of Germany exports in 1937 was only at 69 per cent of the 1929 quantity, whereas the British figure was 83 per cent. On the other hand, German prices not having fallen so low, Germany was getting more for exports, and in terms of gold, the values of German and of British exports had declined just about equally. The U.K. share of world exports had fallen from 10.75 to 9.87, and the German share from 9.73 to 9.11 per cent. British imports were maintained better than German imports, the British at 109 per cent of 1929, and the German at only 80 per cent, but the British in 1937 were partly living on their capital and the Germans in 1929 had been living partly on borrowed money. It is not therefore easy to decide whose policy was the more successful. Germany was more successful in the sense that she got full advantage of the terms of trade, and was therefore able to get more than the U.K. for a smaller volume of exports. But on the other hand, in order to achieve this she had to bind her economy with exchange control and a network of other controls, in order to prevent imports from getting out of hand.

RECOVERY POLICY

The other interesting aspect of German economic policy in the 1930's is the effort to abolish unemployment. The policy of deflation was abandoned in the summer of 1932, and a programme of expenditure on public works took its place. This policy, greatly extended by the Nazis after their assumption of power in January

1933, was the basis on which the country swept on to full employment.

It is true that recovery occurred in other countries where no such large volume of public spending was undertaken, and that there would have been some recovery in Germany even without this policy, but no one can doubt that the degree of recovery was greater in Germany than it would otherwise have been.

In 1933 and 1934 the Government concentrated on schemes for improving the natural resources of the country by afforestation and land work generally, and on improving the public services, such as roads and railways. There were also subsidies to industrialists to stimulate private investment. Something like 4,000 million marks was spent on these purposes in 1933 and 1934, and between January 1933 and December 1934 the number of insured workers unemployed[3] decreased from 6.0 millions to 2.6 millions; the number of insured workers employed rose from 11.5 to 14.5 millions, and the number engaged on relief works rose from 0.3 to 0.6 millions. No other country experienced a comparable recovery in so short a time.

With so many still unemployed there was no reason to fear inflation from this expenditure. Powers of price control existed, but did not have to be used much, except in cases where shortage of imported materials was tending to raise prices unduly. If the trade unions had still been in existence, they might have seized the opportunity of recovery to bargain for higher wages, and this would have raised prices. But one of the Government's first acts had been to dissolve the unions, and wages were thereafter kept stable. The main problem in this period was the balance of payments, since recovery greatly increased the potential demand for imports; but as we have already seen, this was met by strict import licensing.

Unfortunately the German experiment ceased to be helpful just as it was becoming interesting. What interests economists in this sort of situation is whether, after heavy government expenditure has set recovery in motion in this way, private investment will start to grow cumulatively, and so make it possible for government expenditure to be curtailed without the system collapsing once more. The German experience is unhelpful because when private investment began to recover the government did not reduce its own expenditure. It embarked instead, from 1935 onwards, on a policy of rearmament, which compelled it increasingly to restrict and divert private investment, so as to secure for government purposes all the resources that it required. From 1935 onwards the German economy ceases to be an illustration of the methods of "priming the pump." It becomes only an illustration of the workings of a war economy, detailed examination of which, now that we have all had the same sort of experience, is tedious for any but the specialist.

The main features can be sketched rapidly. As government expenditure continued unemployment virtually disappeared in 1938, and the shortage of labour began to be acute. Even before this, particular shortages were tending to drive prices up; to prevent inflation prices were fixed by decree at the level of October 1936, and held pretty effectively. The volume of additional money which it was necessary for the government to create in order to finance its expenditure was kept low by a policy of high taxation, and by public borrowing, voluntary and compulsory, including measures to secure the investment in government bonds of surplus industrial profits. These financial measures prevented the public from having too much money available to spend on consumption. In fact, by means of wage and price stabilisation individual consumption was held down to a level not much above that of 1932, Germany being one of the few countries in the world where real wages did not rise substantially after 1932 (but total national consumption increased proportionately with employment).

By restricting the incomes of private individuals the government was able to get hold of a larger share of the national resources for its own purposes. Nevertheless, there was some competition between the public and the government for resources, especially in certain industries whose output could not be expanded. Financial measures had therefore increasingly to be coupled with direct controls over the economy to ensure that resources be used for the purposes considered most urgent. Starting with control of imported raw materials, economic controls were extended until they comprised most aspects of the economy.

CONCLUSION

By 1936 Germany was one of the best equipped countries in the world. Her private industry had been overhauled in the years 1926 to 1928, and her public services also in those years and again in the public works programmes of 1932–34. Her people could have had a fine standard of living; instead theirs was the only country where the standard of living was stabilised at a low level. Public affairs had passed into the control of a gang of maniacs.

Bad economic policies are largely responsible for this calamity, and for the suffering which in due course it has imposed on all the rest of the world. Too much credit creation at the beginning of the twenties and too little at the end sums up the situation. The inflation ruined the middle classes, and prepared them for desperate leadership. The deflation brought down the economic system, and sowed the final seeds. The most interesting aspects of German inter-war history are sociological—the inter-relation between economic events, social psychology and political movements, but this fertile field is for other ploughs.

CHAPTER VII

FRANCE

FRENCH recovery from the effects of the war was rapid. Agriculture was never restored to its pre-war importance either in area cultivated or in production, but there was a large extension of manufacturing, the index[1] (1913 = 100) rising from 61 in 1921 to 143 in 1929, and these were all years of increasing prosperity, and of relatively full employment. Recovery was helped by immigration, the number of foreigners in the country increasing to about three million, and in this way the grievous wartime losses of manpower were compensated. It was helped also by the "moderate" inflation. The inflation raised prices fourfold, caused the franc to fall, and provoked many dramatic financial and political crises; but it nevertheless kept the economy feverishly active, and was not large enough to bring ruin, as in Germany. The fact that the franc was undervalued in the foreign exchanges throughout this period, and even after stabilisation in 1926, was also helpful to exports, which rose in volume[2] from 71 in 1923 (1927 = 100) to 101 in 1928, while imports in the same period increased only from 100 to 106. At the end of the 1920's France was considered to be financially one of the strongest countries in the world, and much of the safety-seeking capital whose movements so damaged the world economy between 1929 and 1931 took refuge in Paris.

The 1929 slump was felt in France, but the effects were moderate compared with what was happening elsewhere. Exports fell, and imports rose but industrial production was well maintained. What most affected France was the depreciation of sterling in 1931. French prices were now left too high, and strains began to appear. The balance of payments deteriorated, the balance on current account changing[3] in millions of francs, from 5,200 in 1930 to

1,700 in 1931. France was thus faced with the same choice as Germany; she must devalue, or deflate, or take extraordinary measures to control imports.

Devaluation was rejected in France for the same reason as in Germany, namely fear that it was associated in the popular mind with inflation, and that it would therefore cause a panic. Resort had therefore to be taken to deflation and to import controls.

Deflation was continued until 1936. It proved most painful, especially after the U.S.A. depreciated the dollar in 1933, and left France as one of the few countries still on the old parity. The course of wholesale prices shows the effort made in France:[4]

WHOLESALE PRICES

	1929	1932	1935	1937
France	100	68	54	93
U.S.A.	100	68	84	92
U.K.	100	71	74	90

The divergence by the year 1935 is most marked. Indeed French prices fell so low that in July 1935 they were estimated[5] to be only 9 per cent above world prices although the pound and the dollar had depreciated by 40 per cent. Deflation of this magnitude is bound to have adverse effects on employment, because all prices in the system do not move together, and it is difficult to bring costs down as rapidly as prices. Thus, taking 1929 as 100, hourly wage rates[6] fell only from 108 in 1931 to 102 in 1935, in spite of the fall of prices. Unemployment also increased, the numbers receiving benefit[7] rising from 273,000 in 1932 to 432,000 in 1936, and this in spite of the fact that unemployment bore first upon foreign workers, who were repatriated and who did not therefore appear in the statistics. Industrial production (1929=100) fell to 73 in 1935. Government finances were badly affected. As prices fell receipts fell; expenditure was reduced by cutting salaries, and increased by having to pay unemployment benefit, the net result being a budget deficit that not the most frantic efforts could eliminate; from 1931 to 1935 the public debt increased by about 58 million francs. But probably the worst sufferers were the farmers, for farm prices fell much more than industrial prices. As the numbers engaged in primary production in France are rather larger than the numbers in manufactures, their discontent was a factor of the utmos political importance.

The strain on the balance of payments was just as marked; the quantum of exports (1927=100) fell to 54 in 1935, and although the terms of trade were more favourable than for other countries, the share of France in world exports fell from 5.95 per cent in 1929 to 3.66 per cent in 1937. Imports had therefore to be rigidly controlled. This was done not by exchange control, but by tariffs and by imposing quantitative restrictions on imports. As the 1930's proceeded French imports quotas became more numerous and smaller, until after the devaluation, when the system began to be abandoned. Import control, however, could affect only the transactions on current account. On capital account matters deteriorated gravely after the depreciation of the dollar in 1933. It was then generally accepted that the franc would sooner or later have to follow and Frenchmen therefore changed their money from francs, which would depreciate, into pounds and dollars. In consequence there was a heavy drain of gold, amounting to 1,600 million dollars in the three years 1935 to 1937. Sooner or later control of capital exports would have become inevitable.

All these adverse movements reflected themselves in the political situation. During the inflation in the twenties France had had a succession of political crises as government after government failed to balance the budget. The deflation in the thirties brought exactly the same result. But while the crises of the twenties were confined to the circles of politicians and financiers, as the country was generally prosperous, the crises of the 1930's moved the whole nation, the farmers being discontented with the adverse terms of trade, the workers with unemployment, the industrialists with low production, the civil servants with salary cuts, and the financiers with the insecure future of the franc. In France, as in Germany, political violence thrived on deflation, the extreme parties gaining at the expense of the more moderate.

But still the deflation continued. In July 1935 Laval became Prime Minister, and made a last desperate effort to "save the franc". His activities were prodigious, 549 decrees being issued in his six months of office; but they were unsuccessful. His main effort was to balance the budget. Taxation was increased, and expenditure cut; receipts were still, however, less than expenditure, and the main effect of these measures was greatly to increase political discontent. The farmers were already so discontented that further deflation could not be enforced on them. M. Laval was forced, on the contrary, to subsidise agriculture, and to try to raise farm prices; this in turn raised the cost of living, and increased the discontent in the towns. In January 1936 the Laval government fell, and when later, in the year, elections were held, a "Popular Front" coalition of parties, pledged to end deflation, was swept into power.

THE BLUM EXPERIMENT

There were several strands in the policy of M. Blum, and we can follow only some of these here. The first, was a policy of raising wages. On this the government had no option, for the workers celebrated its arrival in power by a wave of "sit down" strikes. The Government brought the strikes to an end by negotiating with the employers' representatives what came to be known as the Matignon agreement, under which wages were increased by about 12 per cent. There was also legislation providing holidays with pay, which came into effect immediately, and for a week of 40 hours with the pay previously given for 48, which began to come into effect at the end of 1936. As a result of these changes, hourly wages increased, it is estimated,[9] by about 60 per cent during the year of the Blum regime.

The farmers also received assistance. A Wheat Board was established to fix a minumum price for wheat, and it fixed a price almost double that of the previous year. All agricultural prices together increased, it is estimated,[10] by between 40 per cent and 50 per cent.

The third strand of policy followed from these two. The increase in costs affected all those manufacturers who could not easily adjust their selling prices, and some had to curtail production; the government was driven to adopt measures to help them to carry on. More important, French prices were now more out of line with world prices than ever before. Exports contracted, and unemployment rose swiftly. At last the effort to "save the franc" was abandoned. In September 1936 France left the gold standard and the value of the franc was allowed to fall.

The situation was now reversed. French prices were below world prices. Exports, employment and production increased rapidly. The effect of devaluation was all the more spectacular as other adverse trends were still at work. The fourth strand of policy in operation at the same time seems to have been neutralised; it was the policy of spending money on public works in order to reduce employment both directly and indirectly. This did not work out as planned. For the increased expenditure made the budget deficit still larger; and the growing deficit, coupled with continued uncertainty about the foreign exchange value of the franc, stimulated a still greater export of capital. It seems that the increased expenditure and the increased export of capital just about neutralised each other.[11] In France, as in the United States, private investment failed to revive. The growth of production after September 1936 is to be attributed almost entirely to devaluation.

By the spring of 1937 recovery had gone as far as was possible. France had achieved full employment. What was remarkable was that it had reached full employment with industrial production at only 82 per cent of the 1929 level. For this there were several reasons. One was that in France unlike most other countries the natural increase of population is small; the increase in production up to 1929 was largely associated with immigration of foreign workers. Net annual immigration[12] dropped from an average of 120,700 in 1928/30 to an average of 1,900 in 1933/36. The second reason is that the population available for manufacturing industry had been reduced by the return to the farms of some of the unemployed, France being so largely a nation of small peasants. Thus, between 1929 and 1937 the numbers engaged in industry[13] diminished by 21 per cent. And, thirdly, production was restricted by the application of the forty hour week, so that total hours worked in industry, allowing both for the fall in numbers and for the decline in hours, fell between 1929 and 1937 by 34 per cent. Thus, on the eve of the second world war, when industrial potential was to prove so decisive, France was less of a manufacturing nation, and more rural, than it had been in the 1920's.

To sum up, then, the original experiment, to increase production by increasing wages, failed. Then came devaluation which increased production but was unable to increase it very much because another part of the experiment, the 40 hour week restricted the available labour supply. And meantime the franc continued to be insecure, capital was exported and investment at home remained low.

There remains one aspect which must be considered. The Blum Government was of the "left", and interested therefore in increasing the share of the workers and of the peasants in the national income. This was the other main purpose of raising wages and agricultural prices. Industrial prices increased in the same ratio as wages; the employing class therefore had its profits increased in the same ratio as the workers' wages, confirming the argument from theory which suggest that the ratio of wages to profits cannot be altered merely by increasing money wages. The cost of living did not rise by as much as industrial prices, so both employer and industrial worker were better off; but the worker took his increased standard of living entirely in having greater leisure. His income would have been about one-fifth higher if he had worked as long hours in 1937 as in 1936; as he cut his hours by slightly less than one-fifth, his weekly purchasing power increased by about 3 per cent. Farmers' incomes and the prices of what they buy seem to have risen in about the same proportion. The losers in the experiment were the people in receipt of fixed incomes, whether salaries, pensions, rent or interest; the gain of the industrialists in profits and of the industrial workers in leisure was mainly at their expense. The big industrialists gained more than any other group.[14]

The Blum experiment was thus a decisive failure. The people who were regarded as "the enemy" were those who gained most from it, and though its principal supporters the industrial workers also gained, to the extent of having the same living standards for shorter hours, their gain was at the expense of many hundreds of thousands of no less deserving people whom the workers had had no intention of despoiling. The most valuable action taken by the Government was the devaluation of the franc, and this it had done not of set policy but because it was forced reluctantly to do it. The other important action which the government might have taken was to reconstruct French public finances, using them to redistribute the national income in favour of the workers, but nothing was actually done on these lines. The experiment proves only that good intentions are no substitute for sound economic analysis.

CHAPTER VIII

UNITED STATES OF AMERICA

THE problems of the United States were domestic. In 1929 the ratio of imports to national income[1] was only 5 per cent and of exports was only 6 per cent, and while changes in American foreign trade most profoundly affected the rest of the world, they were of little importance to the American economy itself. We can therefore concentrate in this chapter on domestic problems.

In previous chapters we have traced in outline the events of the 1920's in the United States, the collapse of 1929, and the long depression of the thirties. The great American problem, still unsolved—and indeed the world problem—is why a country which had been progressing so vigorously for at least sixty years should suddenly regress and stagnate for something like a decade. We have considered the theories, and tried to see what the facts support, in Chapter IV. There remains to study in this chapter the great experiments made by the administration of Mr. Roosevelt in his effort to solve America's problems.

No single chapter can contain the New Deal. Here combined in one administration were innumerable great measures grappling with innumerable problems. No single objective can be selected as the major objective of the New Deal. Consider, to begin with, the three major planes on which the President was operating. On the plane of foreign policy, the major events in inter-American relations, and in American intervention in European affairs would themselves be enough to write the name of any other President securely in American history. On the domestic political plane, the relations of federal and state governments, of North and South, of the Supreme Court and the executive, and of old established departments and of new government agencies each raised issues with which any other President might well have contented himself. And then there was the economic plane. Here there was not one New Deal, but many. A New Deal for the unemployed, for farmers, for debtors—a Relief New Deal. A New Deal for Labour, for trust-busting, for control of Wall Street, for progressive taxation—a "left" New Deal. A Recovery New Deal, designed to "prime the pump" and to send the economy once more vigorously upward. A social security New Deal. Each pursued in detail with vast expenditure through an ever growing network of government agencies; each changing its direction whenever some new idea rejected an old; each liable to contradict or neutralise some other whose objectives were not quite consistent with its own. We cannot hope in this chapter to follow so many different strands. We select for consideration just three major types of policy which, for the grandeur of their conceptions, illustrate the vastness and vigour of this great experiment. We shall take a brief look at the industrial, the agricultural and the Recovery programmes.

INDUSTRIAL POLICY

"Industrial programme" is a wide term. It can include many matters which will not be considered here—labour policy, reorganisation of banking and of marketing securities, the devaluation of the dollar, the trade agreement programme and many other matters whose impact on industrialists was large. In this section, however, we are confining ourselves to the organisation of industry.

The traditional policy of the Democratic Party in the United States is "anti-big business", in favour of competition and the small man. This policy culminated in 1890 in the passing of the Sherman Act, which sought to make monopolisation illegal, and in further measures passed during the war to tighten up the Sherman Act. This anti-trust legislation had had only moderate success. For one thing, it had not been very carefully drafted, and the lawyers and the Supreme Court had frequently let through undertakings which the legislature had intended to prevent. But beyond this, adequate machinery for enforcing the Act was not provided. In Theodore Roosevelt's day the anti-trust division's staff included only five lawyers, and in the 1920's the number never exceeded twenty.[2] With such a small staff, policing the affairs of a country of the size of the United States was just impracticable. When Roosevelt came to power in 1933 the job had hardly begun.

On the other hand the immediate problem was the slump; industrial production at 53 per cent of the 1929 level; 13 to 15 millions unemployed; and a banking crisis. The President's advisers told him that the slump was due to the lack of profits to stimulate investment; that lack of profits was due to prices having fallen below costs; and that this was due to excessive competition. They advised, therefore, measures to force prices up by restricting competition, in direct opposition to the traditional anti-trust policy of the party. Told that he must choose between recovery and anti-trust, the President chose recovery.

In June 1933 there was passed the National Industrial Recovery Act. Part II of this Act authorised the President to spend up to 3,300 million dollars on public works, in order to provide employment. Our concern here is with Part I which empowered him to establish for each industry a code of business practices designed to ensure "fair competition". Each code was also to ensure freedom of the workers to organise in unions of their own choice and to bargain collectively, and the President was also empowered to lay down minimum wages, maximum hours, and other conditions of employment.

That the issue was stated in terms of "fair competition" arose out of the fact that under legislation of 1914 "unfair competition" was declared to be illegal, and a Federal Trade Commission was established having the enforcement of this prohibition as one of its purposes. The Federal Trade Commission found in the course of the twenties that the easiest way to enforce the provision was to get the entrepreneurs in an industry together to define which trade practices were unfair in their industry. The principal effect of the N.R.A. was to generalise these conferences, by drawing up a code for each industry—some 600 codes were approved—and to absolve provisions sanctioned under these codes from fear of violating the Sherman Act.

Such absolution was necessary because in practice attempts to prohibit unfair competition merged very frequently into attempts to prohibit all effective competition, which was otherwise illegal under the Sherman Act. Thus a few of the codes established under the N.R.A. permitted the fixing of minimum prices; a few more prohibited selling "below cost"; very many permitted "open price filing", an arrangement by which firms declare and circulate the prices that they are charging, an apparently harmless policy which in practice operates to discourage price cutting; and a few even fixed production quotas. Many of the provisions of the codes had no monopolistic purpose or effect, e.g. provisions against misrepresentation on labels, or against bribery of a rival's employees; but such provisions were not in violation of the Sherman Act, and were in any case already covered by the Federal Trade Commission Act. What was new and important about the codes was the cover they gave to essentially monopolistic devices.

The trade practice part of the codes was naturally more popular with business men than the part designed to regulate labour conditions. The Act did not specifically state that the representatives of labour must take part in the framing of the code, and frequently they were absent. Government agencies sought to ensure that the provisions relating to labour should be adequate, but they were not always successful. Nevertheless nearly every code restricted hours of manual workers to 40 per week, and fixed minimum wages. But the effect of the N.R.A. in stirring the American Labour Movement into action, and in stimulating collective bargaining was more important than the precise terms laid down in codes.

What, then, was the outcome? The President's hope was that the N.R.A. would promote recovery in two ways; by raising prices, and so dissipating the gloom of business men and encouraging investment; and by raising wages, and so increasing purchasing power. In the summer of 1933 the codes seemed to be making some contribution to recovery, as a small boom was in progress. Their psychological effect was good; business men took heart from the prospect of rising prices, and began to give orders for goods. Unemployment fell a little. But there was no firmer basis than this. Wages were rising, both because of the codes and because of other forces operating at the same time, and rising about as fast as prices, so that business was not really becoming more profitable. If prices had risen faster than costs, the recovery would probably have been sustained; for though the consumption of workers would have been reduced relatively and savings increased, investment at that time was probably most sensitive to low profits, and could probably have increased faster than savings, carrying the economy upward.[3] The fact is that the President was working at the same time with two inconsistent theories. According to one of them higher prices would bring higher profits and stimulate recovery; according to the other recovery was to be brought about by raising wages relatively to prices, and this, if it had been successful, would have lowered profits. Neither theory was put to the test; the increases in prices and in wages neutralised each other. In the autumn business declined again and the N.R.A. boom was over.

This left the N.R.A. contributing more problems than useful results. The codes were giving much trouble. Industries overlapped, with different codes. The interpretation of words like "selling below cost" were numerous and conflicting. Enforcement was proving a gigantic task, with the number of firms covered by codes exceeding two million. Small business men were complaining that the codes in practice operated against them. The public complained that in raising prices they raised the cost of living. Above all, the distrust of their monopolistic intentions and effects gathered force. When in May 1936 the Supreme Court declared the N.R.A. to be unconstitutional there was general relief.

The disappearance of the N.R.A. left the President free to return to the traditional anti-trust policy of his party. In his next term of office, he increased the staff of the anti-trust division to include over 200 lawyers, provided much bigger funds, and appointed a vigorous chief. The results were remarkable. Always before big business had had more money to spend than the anti-trust division, and had been able to strain the division by long drawn legal quibbles taken to the highest court. Now the situation was reversed; it was the anti-trust division that could afford to stand the strain; and to stand it in several major cases simultaneously. Business men suddenly grew nervous of its charges, and became very amenable. They sought to avoid long legal battles by admitting rapidly what was provable, and by undertaking to discontinue doubtful practices. Cases went into court and came out rapidly, the parties having agreed beforehand to a "consent decree". Other business men re-read the Acts, and were more careful to avoid practices that might contravene them. Within a few years the officer responsible for the division was claiming that immense sums had been saved to the nation through the effect on prices of restoring competition.[4] Roosevelt had proved that it is possible to use the law to maintain a competitive economic pattern if adequate vigour is put into its enforcement. However, the gains were not all net; one more item was added to the grievances of big business against the New Deal, along with the regulation of securities, labour policy, tariff reductions, and many others, real and imagined. The antagonism of big business men towards the administration is believed, by some people, to have been an important factor depressing business confidence and holding down investment and recovery. But we shall come to this in a moment.

AGRICULTURAL POLICY

The farmers were the section of the community hit hardest by the depression. As consumption declined, stocks mounted, as farmers do not, like manufacturers, close down in depression—farm output in 1932 was just as large as in 1929[5]—and agricultural prices fell much more rapidly than industrial prices. American farmers were carrying a large load of debt in 1929, owing to their having been investing in equipment for their farms, and the slump left them quite unable to meet their commitments. As some 20 per cent to 25 per cent of the population is engaged in agriculture, the Government was compelled to take special measures to relieve agricultural distress.

President Hoover took the initial steps. In 1929 he created the Federal Farm Relief Board, the object of which was to try to keep up prices by buying stocks and holding them off the markets. The slump was too severe and too world-wide for the Board to achieve this object. It merely found itself acquiring larger and larger stocks.

To the policy of holding stocks President Roosevelt added crop restriction. The Agricultural Adjustment Act of 1933 gave the government the power to give each farmer a quota, and to pay him "benefit payments" for restricting his planted acreage. In January 1936 the Supreme Court declared this also to be unconstitutional; but a loophole was found. Instead of paying farmers not to grow wheat or other staple crops the Government paid them to leave land fallow, or to plant it with leguminous crops. This kind of payment was made under its powers (indeed its duty) to conserve the natural resources of the country; leaving land fallow or planting it with leguminous crops improves the quality of the soil, and could not therefore be attacked through the courts. The effect of this policy can be seen in agricultural employment and in acreages. The number gainfully employed in agriculture diminished by 7 per cent between 1932 and 1939, and the acreages in wheat, maize, cotton and tobacco diminished by nearly one-fifth. On the other hand the soil conservation measures had the (apparently unexpected!) result of increasing productivity; output per worker increased by 22 per cent between 1932 and 1939, so that the net result was an increase of 11 per cent in agricultural output.[6] The cotton and wheat surpluses were as great at the end of the thirties as they had been at the beginning.

Measures to restrict output had therefore to be coupled with still more direct operation on prices. The government began to raise prices by making crop advances on the basis of minimum prices, and being prepared to take the crop in repayment of the advance; this automatically set a floor to market prices. The aim was to raise prices to "parity", which was calculated in the following manner. An index number of the prices of things farmers buy is calculated year by year, using the average prices of 1909 to 1914 as base. This index, multiplied by the average price of any commodity in 1909/14, gives the parity price for that commodity. When this policy was first adopted market prices were so far below parity prices calculated in this way that immediate equalisation was considered impracticable. Prices were, however, raised gradually, towards the objective of 75 per cent of parity. The further result of this was that American agricultural prices rose above world prices. Exports were discouraged, especially of wheat and cotton, and in 1938 the government began to subsidise export to certain countries in order to be able to dispose of surpluses.

These measures raised the income of farmers substantially. Benefit payments were substantial, and agricultural prices also rose much faster than industrial prices. Farmers were also assisted by a third measure, the provision of credit. In 1933 the burden of agricultural mortgages was very heavy, and the government established agencies which were willing to take over the mortgages, reduce the rate of interest and postpone payment until better times came.

The farmers benefited more from the New Deal than did any other class of the community. But the agricultural problem was still unsolved. The major cause of agricultural troubles in the thirties was the slump, which reduced demand, and if the slump had been exorcised, the surpluses would not have been so large. But the farmers' troubles had not started with the slump. The basic problem was that there were too many farmers. The origins of this went all the way back to the war; between 1914 and 1918 European agriculture contracted and American agriculture expanded. After 1918 European agriculture began to be restored, returning to its pre-war output by the middle twenties; American agriculture was contracting in terms of numbers employed, but output per worker was rising even faster, and so total output was still increasing. Farmers' troubles began in the middle twenties, and could have been avoided only if the numbers engaged in agriculture had contracted more rapidly. The restrictions imposed by the New Deal were a step in the right direction. But the most successful agricultural policy of all is to provide full employment in industry, which keeps demand at a maximum and curtails supply by attracting workers from the country to the town. Fixing minimum agricultural prices has the disadvantage that if they are fixed too high they may make agriculture so profitable as to diminish the incentive for people to leave it. But is is quite likely that the numbers engaged in agriculture depend more on the opportunities for employment in industry than on agricultural prices, and at this point the fixing of minimum prices makes a very useful contribution, for it increases stability. As we have seen, the collapse of agricultural prices in 1929/30 was the principal factor that turned the slump into a catastrophe. Such a swift fall of prices will not in future be possible, under the parity price system, and this will benefit the economic system as a whole (and indeed the world as a whole) by increasing stability.

The basic problem remains, however, to diminish the numbers on the land, and to effect their transfer to other occupations. The war has temporarily covered up this problem by providing an abnormal demand for American agricultural products. The signs are that, as soon as the European output is restored, American agriculture may find itself, in many respects, back where it was in 1925.

RECOVERY POLICY

The problem above all others in the United States was unemployment. Something had happened to the American economy that had never happened before, and the problem was how to get things going again.

The N.R.A. was the goverment's first effort. This policy having failed, policy came gradually to concentrate on deficit spending. By spending money not covered by taxation, or money borrowed from idle balances, the government was putting extra money into circulation, which, by increasing consumption would, it was hoped stimulate investment, and so send the economy moving upwards.

The agencies created for government spending were almost innumerable, and can merely be classified here. First there were the agencies for the relief of debtors, such as the Farm Credit Administration, and the Home Owners Loan Corporation. The money spent by these did not directly help employment; creditors were repaid, and for the most part held the money idle waiting for better times to come. The same applied, secondly to much of the money lent through the Reconstruction Finance Corporation to industry, to the banks and to other institutions, which was simply used to pay off debt. But many R.F.C. loans were also used for investment purposes, adding to the money in circulation. Thirdly, there were the relief payments—benefit payments to farmers, the Veterans' bonus, and unemployment relief. And fourthly, there was the public works programme, which absorbed ever increasing sums of money. The federal budget[7] balanced in 1930 with expenditures of about 3.6 milliard dollars, rose to over 9 milliard dollars in 1936, with a deficit of about 5 milliard dollars; the national debt increased from just over 16 to over 32 milliard dollars, and was still growing, passing the 40 milliard level in 1939.

The results were meagre. Employment increased under the pressure of these expenditures, by about 8 millions from 1933 to 1937, but as population continued to grow, unemployment fell only by 5 million, and over 7 million workers were still unemployed on the average in 1937.[8] Government expenditures stimulated consumption, and employment in the consumers' goods industries increased substantially, but private investment failed to revive. In 1937 the index of industrial production[9] (1929=100) stood only at 103; for consumers' goods at 114 and for investment goods at 92.

Most disappointing was the further collapse in 1937 with production at such low levels. The boom of 1937 was a commodity boom. According to Professor Slichter,[10] its origin lay in the coincidence at the end of 1936 of four factors expected to raise prices; first the Spanish war; secondly the payment of the Veterans' bonus; thirdly renewed labour troubles; and fourthly an increased deficit; the last two being associated with the resounding victory of President Roosevelt at the polls. Orders were therefore put in hand. But there was no substantial increase in long-term investment. The orders were delivered, and the boom petered out.

The great question is therefore why private investment so stubbornly failed to recover. Several answers have been attempted. One school lays great stress on antagonism between big business and the government, which depressed business confidence. Another on the increase in the national debt, which did the same. Yet another school argues that the national debt did not grow fast enough; sooner or later, if only the government had spent enough, the volume of money in circulation would have been so large that industrialists would have found it profitable to invest, whether they liked the government and the national debt or not. They also point out that against the growth of federal government expenditure must be set the decline of state and local government expenditures. Thus the net income increasing expenditure[11] of the federal government increased from 249 million dollars in 1930 to 3,366 million dollars in 1936, but the state and local government net income increasing expenditures fell from 845 to 116 million dollars in the same period. However, taking all governments together diminishes the significance of the increase in federal expenditure only from 3,117 to 2,388 millions, or by 23 per cent, and is not as important a point as is sometimes suggested.

Without a doubt industrialists invested so little because profits were so low. Owing partly to the President's labour policy of encouraging trade unions, hourly wages in manufacturing[12] were 10 per cent higher in 1937 than in 1929; but the prices of finished goods were 8 per cent lower. Profits, 7.6 milliard dollars in 1929, had become negative in 1932 to the tune of 2 milliard dollars, and remained negative for three years, rising only to 4.2 milliard in 1937 (all figures in 1929 prices). Recovery was not possible until investment was restored, and investment would not be restored while profits were so low. Investment had to be restored, because it was impracticable in the U.S.A. for government spending fully and permanently to take its place. In terms of 1929 prices, gross capital formation averaged about 18 milliard dollars in 1925/28, being pretty stable at this rate. In 1932 the figure had fallen to less than 4 milliard, and considering that in 1929 total federal expenditures were less than 4 milliard, it would have been difficult to bridge the whole gap of the 14 milliard simply by increasing federal expenditure.

Yet deficit financing had an important part to play, in "priming the pump". What critics of the policy usually ignore is the unprecedented depth of the depression. There was so much idle capital in the United States in 1933 that investment was bound to remain low, notwithstanding technological progress, until some of the idle stock had been reduced—the low level of profits was principally due to the excess of capital overhanging the market. The idle stock could not be reduced without an increase in employment, which in turn depended on a revival of investment. Here was a vicious circle. The quickest way to deal with it was deficit financing which, if pursued far enough, would bring so much capital back into employment that investment would again be profitable. What the New Deal shows is not, as critics allege, the failure of "pump priming," but on the contrary that when a country has fallen so low as the United States fell from 1929 to 1933, only the most drastic measures will suffice to get it up again. Above all, of course, American experience demonstrates the importance of not allowing a country to fall so low. Even the most bitter opponents of the New Deal now agree that the American Government has a duty, on the first sign of a slump, to increase its expenditures in an effort to maintain consumer demand; no government, of whatever political colour, could dare to remain inactive if profits began to fall and unemployment to increase. Enough has been learnt to make it improbable that the United States will ever again experience so large a slump and so prolonged a depression as that of 1929 to 1939.

CHAPTER IX

JAPAN

THE industrial growth of Japan was the most rapid in history until 1929, when the rate of growth of U.S.S.R. industry began to surpass even that of Japan. Manufacturing production[1] increased at a cumulative annual rate of 6.3 per cent between 1905 and 1913, 8.4 per cent from 1913 to 1920, 7.0 per cent from 1920 to 1929, and 6.2 per cent from 1929 to 1937; whereas in the United States of America the cumulative increase from 1905 to 1929 was only 3.7 per cent. The impact of this rate of growth on other industrial countries became considerable in the thirties, when the others were relatively stagnant, and it attracted great attention to the country.

After the Restoration of 1868, when the "westernisation" of the country really started, the impetus to development seems to have been provided in Japan, as in Great Britain in the first three quarters of the 19th century, mainly by the growth of foreign trade, which increased in volume[2] from 1873 to 1913 at a cumulative annual rate of 7.2 per cent, the greatest increase occurring between 1885 and 1905 at a cumulative annual rate of 9.4 per cent. There were, however, two important differences from Great Britain. The first was that the developing export trade was not in manufactures but in primary products, notably silk and tea. Foreign trade did not stimulate manufacturing directly; it merely stimulated the economy as a whole, increasing real income and providing a basis for the growth of manufactures, aimed in the first instance at the home market. The second difference was that the government intervened deliberately to encourage manufacturing in various ways; without their intervention in the early stages Japanese industrialisation would have been much delayed, and slower. Industrial enterpreuneurship is scarce in an undeveloped country;

in taking the lead in developing manufactures the Japanese government showed much greater foresight and understanding of the problems of backward countries than is usual among those responsible for their administration.

The Japanese government did something to help every kind of industry, though its interest was most of all in industries like shipbuilding and iron and steel which are useful in war. But it was the cotton textile industry which grew most rapidly, so rapidly that already in 1913 it was making some contribution to the country's exports.

The war greatly expedited the industrialisation of the country, partly by cutting off imports of manufactures, and partly by enabling Japan to gain a secure footing in Far Eastern markets. Japan's share of world exports[3] increased from 1.73 per cent in 1913 to 2.90 per cent in 1924. All industries continued to expand, but silk and cotton still led the way. This continued throughout the 1920's, with silk exports proving most dynamic of all, in response to a growing American demand for fully-fashioned silk stockings. Between 1913 and 1929 exports increased by 133 per cent. Raw silk increased in proportion from 30 to 37 per cent of total exports, and silk and cotton manufactures from 23 per cent to 28 per cent. Like the United Kingdom before 1914, Japan had become dependent on a relatively small group of export commodities; to an even greater extent she depended on a single country, the United States, principal buyer of silk, who now took 43 per cent of her total exports.[4]

The country was heading for catastrophe, which came when in 1929 the slump started in the U.S.A. The export of silk dropped sharply, and the price came tumbling down. The value of raw silk exports fell from 781 million yen in 1929 to 417 million in 1930, and 355 million 1931. The export of cottons was also affected. The quantum of exports[5] did not fall very heavily, from 116 in 1929 (1928 = 100) to 103 in 1930, the lowest point, but export prices fell by 23 per cent. On the other hand, import prices fell by 21 per cent, and the balance of payments on current account deteriorated only very slightly.[6] It was the domestic economy that was most damaged by the slump, and the drain of gold which began in 1930 was due not to pressure on the exchanges but to lack of confidence in the economic position of the country.

To understand this we must return to the balance of payments position in the twenties. During the war Japan exported much more than she imported, and so accumulated gold and foreign exchange to her credit. As soon as the war was over she started using these accumulations to pay for heavy imports, and they were rapidly dissipated. Prices in Japan fell in 1920 less than in other countries, and in view of the drain on reserves many people urged that the yen was overvalued and should be depreciated. Nevertheless the government kept it at par until the disastrous earthquake of 1923 so greatly increased imports for reconstruction purposes that parity could no longer be maintained. The yen was then allowed to depreciate by 20 per cent. Reconstruction was financed by credit expansion, culminating in a severe financial crisis in 1927. After this, the government was anxious to return to the gold standard at par. Japanese prices were probably still too high to justify this, nevertheless the return was affected in 1930, just as the world slump was gathering force.

The comparison with Great Britain is interesting, for here too it was widely believed in the twenties that the currency was overvalued. And here too, when the slump came, it was not the balance of payments on current account that caused a rapid outflow of gold (though in both cases there was a small passive balance), but lack of confidence in the economic position leading to a big export of capital. Thus Japan lost gold heavily in 1930 although the passive balance on current account was quite small ($14 m. compared with a gold outflow of $142 m.), and lost even more gold in 1931 although the passive balance was not much larger. When finally in September 1931 Great Britain abandoned the Gold Standard, Japan decided to do the same, and the yen fell rapidly below the pound.

REACTIONS TO THE SLUMP

So far there is little that is specially interesting in recent Japanese history, except the abnormal rate of growth of manufacturing (even government assistance to the process has many parallels elsewhere), and that is why we have passed so lightly over the events leading up to the slump. The special interest of this chapter is in Japanese reactions to the slump, to which we now proceed.

The collapse of the price of raw silk, coinciding as it did with a fall in the price of rice, brought great hardship to the farmers. This, as well as the decline in cotton exports, adversely affected manufactures, and employment and production declined. They did not, however, decline as much as in other big industrial countries. In the worst year, 1931, industrial production was only 8 per cent below the level of 1929, while in the U.K. it was 16 per cent below, in Germany 33 per cent below, and in the U.S.A. 32 per cent below the level of 1929. The reason for this was the greater flexibility of the Japanese price structure. Wholesale prices had fallen 30 per cent, compared with 23 per cent, 19 per cent and 23 per cent respectively, and wages by 9 per cent compared with 2 per cent, 3 per cent, and 4 per cent respectively.[7] It is arguable that in a closed economy all-round price adjustments have little effect on employment and production. But Japan, like Germany and the United Kingdom, is not a closed economy; the ratio of exports to national income[8] was 14 per cent in 1930. Falling export prices helped to prevent exports falling as much as they did in other countries; and at the same time falling internal prices enabled the farmers to maintain to some extent their consumption of manufactures.

Deflation was nevertheless unpopular; it always is. Deflation is bound to be more rapid in some sectors of an economy than in others, and it cannot in practice be pursued so rapidly as to prevent production and employment from being curtailed. Japan had also political difficulties of her own. Deflation meant trying to balance the budget, and this meant reducing expenditures, including military expenditures. It was this that sealed the fate of deflation, of liberalism in Japan, and of the Far Eastern situation generally. For the militarist classes, whose political power had been held in check in the twenties, refused to acquiesce in cutting military expenditures, mobilised all the popular resentment of deflation, and brought down the government. The new government was committed to reflationary financing and military expenditure, and the political power of the militarists was established definitively.

Reflation began in 1932. Between the end of 1930 and the end of 1931 the national debt[9] had been reduced by 26 million yen; at the end of 1932 it had increased by 546 million, and it rose steadily from 6,003 million in 1931 to 11,893 million in 1937. The effects were decisive. Industrial production began to increase at once, without waiting for the bottom of the slump to be reached in other countries, moving from 92 in 1931 (1929=100) to 169 in 1937.

This had several effects. First, there was the impact on imports. These tended to rise without any corresponding increase in exports. In Germany, where the problem was similar, this had enforced strict licensing of imports. Japan preferred to let the yen depreciate to whatever level was necessary in order to bring imports and exports into equilibrium. When ultimately stabilised, in 1933, the yen had lost about 65 per cent of its gold value, compared with about 40 per cent for sterling and the dollar. Japanese export prices had become comparatively low, and exports had risen to 38 per cent above the 1928 level (having been only 5 per cent above in 1931). Import prices, on the other hand, had moved against Japan, and the ratio of import to export prices had risen from 100 to 122, and was to rise still further as primary products recovered in world markets, to 165 in 1937. Thus much of the increase in exports was dissipated by adverse prices; in 1933 when exports were up by 38 per cent, imports were up only by 5 per cent, and in 1937 the corresponding figures were 111 per cent and 37 per cent.

It was this enormous effort to sell enough exports to pay for continually increasing imports that so enraged other industrial countries. At first Japan concentrated on pushing her textile exports, especially in the poor tropical countries whose purchasing power had been so reduced by the fall of prices that they welcomed enthusiastically the cheap Japanese goods. Most of these countries, however, were colonies of the big industrial nations, who thereupon took special measures to restrict the import of Japanese textiles in their dependent areas. The international political repercussions were immense. Japan found that to have colonies gives economic advantages, and that not to have them may place a country at a grave economic disadvantage; her militarists were strengthened, and it became inevitable that she should try to carve out her own empire in the Far East where she might do to others as they had done to her.

Our interest, however, is rather in the economic consequences. The American demand for silk having been cut by the slump, and the possibilities of expanding cotton exports being restricted by the actions of other countries, Japan had to develop exports of other types of manufactures. She turned to light engineering products. The ratio of textile to total exports fell from 67 per cent in 1929 to 46 per cent in 1937. The ratio of cotton exports was constant, but silk declined heavily and artificial silk expanded,[10] the Japanese industry becoming the largest in the world.

These changes in exports were reflected in changes in employment, exports as usual setting the pace for the rest of the economy. The ratio of persons employed in textiles to total factory employment[11] fell from 50 per cent in 1929 to 35 per cent in 1937; metals expanded from 6 per cent to 11 per cent, engineering from 14 per cent to 21 per cent, and chemicals from 6 per cent to 11 per cent.

These changes were not all due to the changed structure of the export trade. They were also largely due to increasing military expenditure, especially on iron and steel, engineering, and chemical products. Indeed, the deficit seems largely to have been incurred in financing armament building rather than on relief payments and public works, as in Germany in 1934 and 1935, or in the United States. Taking 1930 as 100, the production of consumers' goods stood in 1937 at 145, and of investment goods at 211, a phenomenon paralleled only by Germany and the U.S.S.R. Reflation was largely war preparation.

What is particularly remarkable about the Japanese reflation is that it was done without control of the foreign exchanges, and without control of prices, but nevertheless without signs of inflationary strain. Wage rates seem to have remained pretty steady from 1931 to 1936, and the increase in wholesale prices from 70 to 90 was not large, in view of the 65 per cent depreciation of the yen and the upward world movement of primary product prices. As retail prices were also increasing, real wages were falling, and were no higher in 1936 than they had been in 1929. The explanation of this lies in the mobility of labour. The decline of silk production, coupled with general agricultural depression, forced hundreds of thousands of young women on to the labour market. Women's wages fell sharply, and industrial expansion occurred without any upward pressure on the wage level. That so large a transfer of labour should occur without wages rising is most unusual; only the weakness of the trade union movement made it possible. The net result was that profits increased enormously as a proportion of the national income, and large voluntary entrepreneurial savings offset the government's expenditure, and prevented inflation.[12]

By the beginning of 1936 the Finance Minister responsible for this policy had come to the conclusion that full employment had been reached, that further deficit expenditure would now start an inflation, and that expenditure should now be curtailed. But the militarists were now too firmly established to be denied. He was murdered. His successor continued the military expenditures, and wages and prices started to move swiftly upwards. Then, in 1937, came the attack on China, and the adoption of a full war economy.

CONCLUSION

It is tempting to argue from Japanese and German experience, as so many do, that reflation has been successful only where coupled with expenditure on armaments. The retort, on the same plane, is that in both countries it was deflation that produced social and political conditions that put the militarists into power. None of the countries which adopted deficit financing in the 1930's is an ideal test of the policy, the United States because the policy was not carried far enough, Sweden because it was adopted when recovery was already well started, and Germany and Japan because it was mixed up with rearmament. But if the Japanese government had spent money on building houses and on public works instead of on armaments, there is no reason to think that reflation would have been less successful.

The peculiar lesson of Japan is in the virtues of flexibility. The problem facing the country in 1930, when its principal market shrank, was of the same order as that which the United Kingdom faced in 1920; but whereas Britain dragged on for twenty years at a low level of activity, Japan set herself to it at once, and in five years had accomplished a remarkable diversification of her production and trade.

At the same time, it was a mistake to devalue the yen by as much as 65 per cent. This turned the terms of trade violently against the country, and made necessary an excessive expansion of exports to pay for imports. It is, indeed, most instructive to compare the experience of different industrial countries in the 1930's in this respect, for it throws considerable light on the effects of price competition in international trade.

Between 1929 and 1938 all industrial countries reduced their export prices in terms of gold, but in different degrees. To the extent that their exports were competitive, those whose prices fell most should have had the greatest expansion of exports, and if the elasticity of demand for exports exceeds unity, their foreign exchange receipts should have contracted least. Table X shows what happened to the leading countries. Belgium and Czechoslovakia should be there, but the League of Nations *Review of World Trade*, on which the figures are based, does not give the relevant figures for these two; Norway, Sweden, Canada and others are excluded because the high proportion of primary commodities in their exports vitiates comparison.

TABLE X

EXPORT INDICES, 1936/38 (1929=100)

	Price in gold	Quantum	Total Value in gold
Germany	64	62	39
Switzerland	59	64	38
France	51	55	28
U.K.	50	78	39
U.S.A.	45	74	33
Italy	39	93	36
Japan	29	168	49

What are we to conclude from this? The most tempting generalisation is that in this period the elasticity of demand for exports was unity or even slightly less than one, but the statistics we are using are subject to too many limitations to permit firm conclusions. It is certainly most remarkable that despite such wide differences in prices the total export values of four countries should lie between 36 and 39. And even the three exceptions are peculiarly interesting. The French figure is not surprising because France is the one country whose industrial production never recovered from the slump. American exports include much primary produce, and indices confined to manufactured exports might well remove this exception. And Japan, the only case that supports an elasticity greater than one, is probably much more the case for a determined and well organised export drive.

1929 to 1936/38 was a period in which world trade contracted violently. It is also interesting to take the figures for a period in which world trade was expanding, 1913 to 1927/29.

TABLE XI

EXPORT INDICES, 1927/29 (1913=100)

	Price in gold	Quantum	Total value in gold
U.K.	162	85	137
Switzerland	149	101	150
U.S.A.	125	163	204
Italy	123	136	167
France	101	147	148

This is quite a different picture. If we discount the high American figure for the favourable assistance of the war in capturing other countries' markets, and write up the French figure to compensate for war destruction and the dislocations of inflation, there is a *prima facie* case for an elasticity of demand greater than one. Might we make, very tentatively, the generalisation that when world trade is expanding elasticity is greater than one, but that when it is contracting over a longish period, and restricted to essentials, elasticity may be one or less?

Whatever the right generalisation may be, it is difficult to escape the conclusion that it was a mistake for Japan to devalue the yen so considerably. A smaller devaluation of the yen would have stimulated exports less, but it would have brought more imports for each unit of exports. Some exchange control or import licensing might have become necessary, as in Germany and France, but real income would have been greater, and, perhaps so violent a change in the structure of production would not have been necessary.

Also, Japan's foreign relations would not have deteriorated so badly. No nation can hope to double its exports in volume within five years, at a time when world trade has been reduced, without arousing the most violent antagonism. Japan was not alone in trying to capture more of a smaller market: the United Kingdom and Germany were doing the same, and France also tried, without success, to use her import quotas for bilateral bargaining. It is a most important lesson that unilateral action of this kind is a breeding ground of war. The first business of all trading nations must be to try to keep international trade continually expanding, for unless it is expanding, the changes in the relative importance of countries which circumstances continually demand cannot be achieved without friction. The world must contrive to make the problems of each the official concern of all, so that they may be solved by discussion and mutal concession. To return to the jungle of the thirties in matters of international currency and trade policy is to return to the inevitability of war.

CHAPTER X

THE U.S.S.R.

BY the year 1926 the U.S.S.R. was well on the way to recovery from the disastrous depths into which the civil war had plunged her. Large-scale industry, the output of which had fallen to less than one-fifth,[1] was in that year restored to its pre-war level. The pre-war agricultural acreage was restored in that year too,[2] though, owing to a decline of productivity, the pre-war output was not to be regained until 1930. The "New Economic Policy" had served its purpose; production was restored, and the country was ready for new progress.

Its rulers had ambitious ideas. The superiority of communism to capitalism was to be proved. Russia must advance faster than any other country had ever done before. She certainly needed rapid advance, as the standard of living of her peoples was among the lowest in the world. And if communism was to be defended from further foreign intervention, the country must become strong industrially. Of its industrial resources there could be no doubt, nor any doubt that industrialisation was the one certain way to increase the standard of living. And so the First Five Year Plan was born.

It is no part of the purpose of this book to describe the machinery of planning in the U.S.S.R.; or the way in which the plans are operated. That is a long story, useless except in detail, and out of keeping with our objective, which is rather to study the processes of growth and decline in the inter-war period, and their lessons. We shall confine ourselves in this chapter to analysing the objectives of Russian policy, and assessing the results.

INDUSTRIALISATION

Rapid industrialisation was the keynote of Russian policy. The annual increase of manufacturing production[3] in the United States was at its greatest at the beginning of the twentieth century, averaging 9 per cent from 1900 to 1906; from 1906 to 1913 Japan, most vigorous industrialiser of all, had averaged 11 per cent. The Russian planners did not think in such terms. The first five year plan demanded an average annual increase[4] of 27 per cent, and what is more, at the cost of considerable deterioration of quality, actually achieved 29 per cent, according to the official figures. Lower tasks were set for the subsequent plans. Nevertheless, industrial production increased from 1929 to 1939 by 382 per cent, a cumulative rate of increase of 17 per cent per annum, according to the official figures. The official figures seem to exaggerate the increase, not wilfully, but through the use of bad statistical techniques. The estimate of a careful enquirer[5] is that gross industrial production increased from 1928 to 1937 at a cumulative rate of 13½ per cent, which is still considerably in excess of what other countries have achieved. Other measures confirm a rapid increase. Thus according to the census[6] the numbers dependent on industry increased by 30 millions from 1926 to 1939, bringing the industrial population up to 45 millions. (Russia has now a larger industrial population than the U.K., and an industrial output larger than the U.K. and about one third of that of the U.S.A.) But even this enormous rate of increase of the industrial population was barely greater than the increase in the total population, which rose by 23 millions, from 147 to 170 millions, the numbers dependent on agriculture declining only by 22 millions, from 114 to 92 millions. In view of the belief in many informed circles that European Russia is rurally overpopulated—estimates put the surplus population in the twenties as high as between 40 and 50 millions[7]—a high rate of industrialisation was certainly needed if Russia was to keep up with the growth of its population, and to provide for absorbing some of its rural surplus.

Nevertheless this great investment could not be achieved without a great increase of saving, as foreign loans were not forthcoming. And the required saving was all the larger as the first plans for industrialisation were to concentrate on building capital equipment rather than on increasing consumers' goods. Taking 1929 as 100, the consumers' goods index stood at 362 in 1939 but the investment goods index stood at 770. Moreover, investment in this period was by no means confined to industry. Every branch of the economy needed capital and was to have it—agriculture, communications, education, public health, housing, were all to have their share. Out of 64.5 milliard roubles to be invested under the First Five Year Plan, only 16.4 were for large-scale industry; the largest item was actually agriculture, with 23.3 milliard roubles.[8] Unfortunately Russian statistics are not in a form which make it possible to calculate easily what portion of the national income was actually saved. An estimate by Prokopovitch shows savings increasing from 22 per cent of the national income in 1928/29 to 31 per cent in 1929/30, according to the plan. Colin Clark[9] rejects these figures on the ground that the prices of capital goods in Russia are artificially inflated, and offers an estimate of 14 per cent for 1934. This estimate is almost certainly too low. The United States was saving rather more than 14 per cent of its income at the end of the 19th century, when it was certainly not making anything like the effort of the U.S.S.R., and many other countries have surpassed 14 per cent at some stage of their growth, including Britain, Germany, Holland, Norway and Japan. Actually, the method of calculation used by Colin Clark is misleading and less appropriate than that used by Prokopovitch.[10] Russia must have been saving at least 20 per cent of her national income during the 1930's, and probably considerably more. Considering that countries with the Russian standard of living are normally considered exceedingly thrifty if they save as much as 10 per cent of their incomes, the immense strain of the Russian effort can be understood.

The strain revealed itself in two important ways, in inflation, and in conflict with the peasants.

INFLATION

In any society that uses money, whether it be capitalist or socialist, there will be inflation if the sums being spent on producing investment goods exceed the sums that people are willing to save, unless the difference is either lent by foreigners or absorbed by a budget surplus. This is because there will be inflation if the sums spent by the public on buying consumer goods exceed the sums spent on producing consumer goods. It is in this framework that we must see and compare the policies of such countries as the U.S.A., Germany, Japan and the U.S.S.R. in the 1930's.

Money can be created freely and spent by the government on

producing goods other than consumer goods (investment or military expenditure, for example) when there is unemployment, without creating inflation. This is because the recipients of income save a part of that income. Suppose that they save 25 per cent of it. Then the 75 per cent that they spend will bring more unemployed resources into production. This second lot will save 25 per cent, and will therefore spend 75 per cent of 75 per cent. The money will circulate, and assuming that one-quarter is saved, for every one person directly employed by the government three others (making a total of four) will receive work. This sets the limit of development by creating money without inflation. If x per cent of income is saved, then (very roughly and subject to modifications into which we need not enter here) the government can create enough money to employ directly x per cent of the unemployed labour, and it will know that this will also indirectly absorb the other (100 – x) per cent of the unemployed, thus bringing full employment without inflation (assuming that private investment does not also increase at the same time). Beyond this it cannot go without inflation. For beyond this, when money is spent on investment, the portion that is not saved will enter into the stream of demand for consumer goods, and, as there is full employment and no extra production of consumer goods, it must cause inflation.

In the U.S.A. in the 1930's this limit was never reached. Much more money could have been created without inflationary effects. But in Germany, in Japan, and in the U.S.S.R. it was reached and passed with serious results.

In Germany the limit was reached in 1936. Up till then the creation of money reduced unemployment without adverse effects on prices. But as unemployment became very small, additional government expenditure threatened to raise prices. The government was thus forced to impose strict price controls. But price controls are no remedy for inflation; their effect is to distort production. All prices cannot be controlled with equal effectiveness. Usually the prices of essentials are best controlled, while the prices of inessentials rise. It then becomes more profitable to produce inessential commodities, and a whole host of regulations has to be made to try to prevent resources from being diverted from essential to less essential purposes. There is also a great growth of black markets. There is, in fact, no adequate remedy for inflation, save withdrawal of the surplus purchasing power, either through a reduction of investment, or through an increase in voluntary saving and in taxation. In Germany the government continued investment at a high level after 1936. But it also imposed very high taxation, and imposed measures designed to keep saving high, with the net effect that the sums withdrawn by saving and taxation were not much less than the sums that were being spent on purposes other than producing consumer goods, and the inflationary pressure, even after 1936, never became very great.

In Japan too, the limit was reached in 1936. Till then the creation of new money by the government merely brought workers into employment without inflationary consequences. But once full employment was reached, every yen invested needed to be balanced by a yen saved. As this was not achieved, some inflation began in 1936; then in 1937 Japan attacked China, and drastic controls of imports, prices, etc., had to be taken in an effort to suppress the inflation. Wage and price statistics show the movement clearly. Wages were stable until 1936. Wholesale prices were rising, not because of inflation, but because world prices were rising, and the simplest way to eliminate this element is to divide the Japanese index of wholesale prices by an index for the United Kingdom (1929 = 100).

	1934	1935	1936	1937	1938	1939
Wages	88	88	88	93	102	111
Corrected prices	113	114	114	120	145	150

The stability of prices up to 1936 is very clear, and so is the inflationary rise that followed as soon as full employment was reached.

In the U.S.S.R. full employment was reached in 1930, within two years of the adoption of the First Five Year Plan, and from then onwards the problems of inflation were very serious. The plans were financed by an enormous increase in the quantity of money. There are no statistics of bank deposits, but notes and coin in circulation increased from 2.8 milliard roubles at the end of 1929 to 11.3 milliard roubles at the end of 1936. Prices increased rapidly, and so did wages. There are no price statistics, but the wage statistics show the inflation clearly.

Monthly	1929	1930	1931	1932	1933	1934	1935	1936	1937	1938
wages	100	107	125	150	164	191	242	293	315	353

What was happening is easily explained. The government's budget was balanced all the time, but the banking system was being used to finance industrial investment, not covered either by voluntary private saving or by budget surplus, and in consequence there was constant pressure on prices. This had the usual consequences of inflation. Price control had to be adopted, with very strict rationing. In place of the usual black markets the government organised its own "commercial" markets where commodities could be had at exorbitant prices, the profits going to the state instead of to private racketeers. There was an acute shortage of labour, and a fantastic turnover of labour. Direction of labour became necessary to secure labour for essential works. The flow of production was most uncertain; factories were held up by shortages of raw materials and of components ordered from other factories, because the surplus of money distorted demand and supply unpredictably. In short, the government produced for itself a nightmare of problems due simply to its failure to balance investment with savings. Gradually the situation was brought under control. The financing of investment came to depend more on the budget and less on the banks, and by imposing an enormous burden of taxation—probably exceeding 40 per cent of the national income—the excess of money was largely mopped up. By 1935 it was considered safe to abandon rationing, and to merge the ordinary markets and the government's "black markets", but even then the gap was not completely closed. It can be shown that most of the problems of organisation which the Soviet Government found so difficult and so tiresome in the 1930's were due simply to its failure to frame financial policy in such a way that the budget would catch the full excess of investment over what the public was willing to save. The economy would have functioned much more smoothly and with fewer controls, including fewer labour controls and fewer police controls, if the government had recognised the simple rule that investment and savings must be kept in equilibrium.

But of course the fundamental problem was that it is not easy to impose saving of 20 per cent or more of the national income upon a backward nation. The administrative machine for collecting taxation was rudimentary, and had the greatest difficulty in coping with the peasants. In these circumstances forced saving through inflation, though crude and troublesome, seemed the easiest way out. And the problem was also specially difficult because, whereas the bulk of the saving would have to be done by the peasants, who in 1926 were 78 per cent of the population, the first benefits of industrialisation would, on the other hand, go to the industrial workers. Their standard of living is always higher than that of the rural population, and had naturally to be kept higher in Russia in order to attract labour from the country into industry. The farmer was being required to save, but would be the last to reap the benefits. No government could hope to pursue such a policy in a predominantly rural country without violent opposition.

AGRICULTURAL POLICY

The farmer opposed from the start. Even before the First Five Year Plan came into operation in 1927/28, the government had been having difficulty with the farmers. In fact it had had difficulty from the days of the revolution itself. From 1917 one of the main preoccupations had been how to obtain grain from the farmers without yielding anything, or at any rate very much in return. Requisitioning had been tried during the period of War Communism, and eventually abandoned, as the peasants simply reduced their sowings. Its place was taken by the "scissors"—increasing industrial prices relatively to farm prices; but this too had been so resented that in 1927 special efforts had to be made to prevent the gap from increasing. Next the government tried heavy taxation, but this, too, the peasants resisted, hiding their grain, or reducing their sowings. In the summer of 1927 forcible requisitioning had once more to be adopted.

By the summer of 1928 it was fairly clear that the peasants were unwilling to cooperate in the high level of savings that had been laid down for them, and since a growing urban population could not be fed without their grain, it was resolved that desperate measures must be taken. In 1929 rationing had to be reintroduced. The hatred of the government concentrated on the upper stratum of peasants, called "kulaks." A kulak was not a big estate owner in the old sense; all such had been liquidated during the revolution. He was simply a peasant whose lands were sufficiently large for him to have to hire some labour. This included about 1 million out of the 20 million farmers. They were not rich or well-to-do in any sense of those words which has meaning; by the standards of any European country they were poor. In any other country their presence would have been welcomed, and they would have been most valued citizens. But in the special circumstances of the U.S.S.R. in 1928 it was inevitable that the government should come to hate them, for of all the peasants it was they who had a marketable surplus. Millions of the poorest peasants were net purchasers of food, and the "middle" peasants had only very little to spare. Everything depended on imposing on the kulaks, and on them principally, the very heavy burden of saving which the economy was called to bear; and naturally they were unwilling to be singled out for this historic privilege. Between the government and its most valuable citizens there could in the circumstances be nothing but bloody war.

In 1929 it was decided to liquidate the kulaks by extending collectivisation and taking their lands into the collective farms. Collectives had existed since the revolution, but were appreciated only by the very poorest farmers. On the 1st of June 1929 only 4 per cent of the farmers were in collectives; by the 20th of January 1930 the figure was up to 22 per cent and by the first of March to 55 per cent. Thereafter the pace was pushed less rapidly, but by 1933 two-thirds of the peasants were in collectives, and by 1936, as many as 90 per cent. The peasants were not given much choice.

Resistance was not confined to the kulaks, and the immediate results were catastrophic. Peasants slaughtered their cattle rather than have them collectivised; the number of horses fell from 33.5 million in 1928 to 16.6 million in 1935; and the number of cattle from 70.5 to 38.4 million[12] and the output of grain also was somewhat reduced, except in 1930 when the weather was exceptionally favourable. As the available margins were in any case very small, shortages were acute; there was famine in parts of Russia in the seasons of 1931–2 and 1932–3. From a careful analysis of Russian population figures made for the League of Nations, Dr. Lorimer concludes that there were some five million abnormal deaths in the 1930's. More than half of these persons perished in the process of collectivisation. (The rest disappeared in the excessive mortality associated with an unprecedented rate of industrialisation and in political purges.)

On the other hand, collectivisation eventually solved the government's agricultural problems. It solved the immediate problem of securing the whole marketable surplus for very little return, partly because loyal communists were put in charge of the collectives, who neither hid the grain, nor tolerated reduction of output, and partly because it was much easier to assess the production of large collective units, and to enforce delivery. It solved ultimately the problem of integrating agriculture into the general planning system. So long as agriculture was conducted by 20 million small farmers its activities could not be controlled from the centre; but in the late thirties it became increasingly practicable to lay down programmes for the collectives of what they should produce, and they came increasingly under this control. But most of all, collectivisation solved the problem of increasing agricultural productivity. The destruction of the large landed estates had reduced the productivity of agriculture, and as the government wanted a larger and larger industrial labour force it was essential that a smaller agricultural population should produce a larger output. Collectivisation achieved this, by facilitating mechanisation and the application of scientific methods. The number of tractors in Russia, increased from 72 thousand in 1929 to 523 thousand in 1940, and soon the universities were pouring out scientists to work in the fields. The results showed themselves in the fact that by 1939 a smaller population was tilling a larger area than in 1929 and getting a harvest 20 per cent larger. The agricultural problem had been solved by collectivisation; solved by brute force, and at a great cost in human misery; but solved. Further increases in productivity could now be expected steadily.

PRODUCTIVITY

In industry also productivity soon emerged as the central problem, and great efforts were made to solve it.

First the trade unions were reformed. The old leaders were dismissed in 1929. The unions were no longer to consider themselves as distinct from the state machinery, representing the workers against the employers. They were to be rather active participators in the national task, which meant in practice that they became fully subordinate to the aims and methods of the plan. From interfering in the management of concerns their attention was diverted to organising campaigns for higher productivity.

Secondly, all the methods of propaganda were turned on. Wireless and newspapers were full of productivity. Competitions between groups of workers and between factories were organised. Great publicity was given to Stakanhov, a miner, who had discovered the principle of the division of labour, and all workers were urged to consider how output could be increased in their jobs by improved methods. Very high titles were conferred upon workers whose output was outstanding. Generally the effort was made to interest the workers in the objects of the plan, and to enlist their socialist pride and their support.

Thirdly, the economic motive was fully restored. In the period of war communism differences of income virtually disappeared, and at the beginning of the Five Year Plan they were still small. This policy was decisively reversed in 1931. Piece rates were substituted for time rates wherever possible, and the margins between skilled and unskilled wages were increased. Quite rapidly the spread of earnings became as wide in the U.S.S.R. as it is in the U.K. or in the U.S.A.[13]

Fourthly, factory discipline became strict. In the early days of the regime factories were run as "democratically" as possible and managerial officials had little control. The result was very bad administration and low productivity. Gradually the personal authority of managers was increased until by 1939 it was in practice more authoritarian than the authority of similar persons in the United Kingdom, where works councils, shop stewards, and trade union officials are a real restriction on managerial power. Great emphasis is placed in Russia on the importance of the managerial class, which is now relatively well paid, given special privileges, and treated with great respect.

And finally, the number of technicians was greatly increased. Foreign technicians were brought in to train Russian students. The number of students in universities and higher technical schools[14] increased from 177,000 in 1929 to 603,000 in 1938/9, which is about ten times as large as the corresponding figure for the United Kingdom.

The results of all this were unexpectedly satisfactory. Productivity was planned[15] to increase during the Second Five Year Plan (1932–37) by 63 per cent; and according to the official figures actually increased by 82 per cent. The estimate for the period 1928 to 1947 is an increase in productivity of 169 per cent, but this is certainly an exaggeration due to faults in the statistical technique. Careful estimation[16] suggests an increase from 1928 to 1937 of 80 per cent in output per man hour, but even this is an astonishing performance compared for example with the United States, where productivity in the twenty-five years from 1899 to 1924 is estimated[17] to have increased only by 63 per cent. There is naturally greater scope for increasing productivity in an underdeveloped country than in a country that is relatively mature. Nevertheless the U.S.S.R. can certainly claim a most remarkable achievement.

REAL INCOME

Finally we must examine the effect of this great effort on the standard of living of the people. To communists, one of the greatest points to be made in favour of the system is the abolition of the private ownership of the means of production. All kinds of advantages are claimed for this, ranging from improving the moral tone of society to preventing wars. On the strictly economic plane, with which alone we are here concerned, two claims are made, first that the distribution of income is altered in favour of the workers, and secondly that the rate of growth of production is accelerated.

The abolition of private property in the means of production has abolished income from property (but not interest on loans to the government). At the same time, many persons who were considered to be living on income from property in Tsarist Russia were in fact performing social functions, e.g. industrialists and landowners. The same functions are performed today and remunerated by salary, and what it would really be interesting to know is how the distribution of income as between workers and the managerial and professional classes compares in present day Russia with pre-war Russia or with other countries. Unfortunately, there are no figures; only impressions. In the 1920's, the impressions were naturally highly favourable to the regime. But since the recognition, in the early thirties, of the importance of productivity and of the managerial classes, the impressions are almost all the other way. There is no reason to believe that the Russian worker gets a larger share of the product of his labour than does the worker in any other country. Probably he gets a smaller share. But the only scientific answer is agnostic.

There is more information on the growth of real income. Colin Clark's estimates of real income per head, in pounds sterling of 1934 purchasing power are as follows.[18]

1870	1913	1921	1928	1934	1937
50.5	58.5	22.4	55.5	51.0	72.3

Real income per head declined heavily during the civil war, and had not regained the pre-war level in 1928. This conclusion is not open to question. Russian figures of agricultural output amply support it. What is more doubtful is the figure for 1934.

That real income per head declined again after 1928 is certain; that was the effect of collectivisation, which again reduced agricultural output. But by 1934 the crop output had been restored and increased, although livestock had not, and industrial production also had increased to an extent which makes the figure unacceptable. On the other hand, the figure for 1937 seems entirely reasonable.

The situation may be summed up as follows. Real income declined in Russia during the war and did not regain the 1913 level in the 1920's. Just as it seemed about to regain it, at the end of the twenties, it sank again because of the unfavourable effects of collectivisation. But by 1934 Russia's major problems were solved. Agriculture had been reorganised on a sound footing, and could be expected to show steadily increasing productivity. The basic industrial framework had been laid down; productivity was rising rapidly and saving could be reduced in favour of consumption. Russia was ready to give her people a steadily rising standard of living. Then came the war, misery and destruction, plunging them once more into the depths of hunger and poverty from which they had only just succeeded in raising themselves. Not many peoples have had so many misfortunes in so short a time.

PART III

TRENDS

CHAPTER XI

THE INTER-WAR PERSPECTIVE

IN Part I we followed the economic history of our period chronologically; in Part II we studied national policies. Now we can take the period as a whole for the world economy as a whole, and attempt to see it in perspective. How did it differ from what had gone before? Why did it differ? Were the differences temporary or have world economic patterns altered permanently? These are the enormous questions to which we must now attempt to find answers.

It is simplest to begin with the contemporary view. Bye and large, those who had lived both pre-war and post-war felt that economic security had deteriorated after 1914, and tended to look back nostalgically to the "good old days before the war". This was not a universal feeling. In the United States of America a sharp distinction was drawn between the twenties and the thirties; the twenties were seen by many people as a "new era", thought to be better than anything that had gone before, while the thirties brought the gravest depression in history. Other countries closely dependent on American trade broadly made the same distinction, though many primary producers were less happy in the twenties than was the United States. Europe also was more prosperous in the twenties than in the thirties; but the twenties were never felt to be a new era. Problems of post-war reconstruction and of reintegration into the world economy set the climate of the twenties; the depression of the thirties was taken, in many cases, simply as proof that the tasks of the twenties had not been achieved, and it is easier to speak for Europe than for the United States of the whole inter-war period as a single unfavourable episode in economic history.

This view is easily exaggerated. The inter-war years were worse than the pre-war years in some respects, but in others they were better, and it is important to remember this. Pros and cons can be catalogued.

To begin with the pros, the world's standard of living was higher in 1938 than in 1929 or in 1913. In the United Kingdom, for example real wages were about 10 per cent higher in 1929 than in 1913, and, despite the great depression, they rose another 10 per cent to 1938. Some other countries did not fare so well between 1929 and 1938, especially primary producers whose loss through an adverse change in the terms of trade was part of the U.K.'s gain. Moreover, because of higher unemployment rates, national income per head did not rise as much as national income per person employed. What is certain and universal is that technical progress continued throughout the inter-war period, in boom and slump; the degree to which standards of living benefited in each country as a result of this varied with such matters as its dependence on changes in the terms of trade, its level of unemployment, and the proportion of its resources devoted to war preparation.[1]

World production continued to increase. The index of world manufacturing industry[2] (1913 = 100) rose (annual averages) from 25 in 1876–80 to 94 in 1911–13, 139 in 1926–9 and 185 in 1936–38; and world trade in primary products also showed continued increase, the quantum rising from 31 in 1876–80 to 97 in 1911–13, 118 in 1926–29, and 119 in 1936–38. In addition, the world economy was still expanding, in the sense that new countries were still developing rapidly; thus between 1913 and 1936/38 the percentage share in world manufacturing of Russia, Japan, India, Sweden and Finland increased, while the share of Italy was unchanged, and the share of the United States, Germany, the United Kingdom, France, Canada and Belgium declined.

As far as production and the standard of living were concerned the inter-war period can certainly claim to have continued the progress of pre-war years. Why then, was it felt to be an unattractive period? The reason is that it seemed less secure. Unemployment was high in some countries throughout the period, and those which had the greatest prosperity in the twenties had also the greatest depression in the thirties. The general level of prices moved downwards from 1920; and even the small boom of the later twenties occurred on a falling price level. Above all, world trade in manufactured products collapsed after 1929 and never regained the 1929 level. In the twenties, though the volume of trade was large and growing there was an uneasiness about its direction. International investment was moving to Europe from America instead of following the reverse movement of pre-war days, and to uneasiness about this was added a sense of insecurity in important countries, notably Great Britain and Germany, which had obviously not fully found their place in the post-war world economy. The collapse of international trade in the thirties, with all the attendant phenomena in the fields of investment, migration, the terms of trade, international currency arrangements, and so on, was not taken simply as a failure of the thirties; despite their differences the collapse of the thirties was obviously related to maladjustments in the twenties; twenties and thirties must stand together in any review of international trade, and the verdict on them together must be unfavourable.

Production and the standard of living rose, but unemployment, prices and international trade caused uneasiness throughout the period. In consequence as the thirties proceeded men began to wonder whether the economic system had not lost its vigour, and more particularly to search the records of its past performance. The records revealed at once that the "Great Depression" of the 1930's was not by any means the first great depression in history. The label "Great Depression" had indeed already been reserved by the historians for a period stretching from about 1873 to 1896; and before that an earlier period of insecurity had long carried the label "The Hungry Forties." It was clear that the unfavourable experiences of the inter-war period were by no means a unique historical phenomenon; indeed there seemed even to be evidence for the theory that "great depressions" go in cycles; that the economy proceeds by means of long periods of rapid progress sandwiched between periods of relative stagnation, of which the inter-war period just happened to be one.

LONG WAVES

The study of long waves in economic progress is relatively new, and much of it still in the realm of brilliant speculation rather than of unchallengeable fact. We cannot even be sure that it will ever finally emerge from this uncertainty because the relevant statistical material is so sparse. Nevertheless, we must gather together some of the material in order to enable us to see our period in perspective. There is no pretence, in what follows of exhaustive treatment of a subject which is so clearly only incidental to the main purpose of this book.

In order to establish long term trends it is necessary when using statistics first to eliminate from them the effects of the trade cycle. There are many ways of doing this. The simplest, adopted in these pages, is to take each cycle as a unit, average the annual figures for the cycle and compare only these averages.

Even to establish the periods of the cycle raises problems; for example most historians consider one cycle to have reached its crisis in 1873, this perhaps the most famous of all cycles, but Lord Beveridge, after much detailed work, chooses rather the year 1874 as marking the crest in the United Kingdom; 1873 is the year of downward price change, but 1874 the year of downward change in business activity, which is the more significant. The dates taken for this chapter are those given by Lord Beveridge.[3] Again the cycle has different dates in each country, especially in the 19th century, before the international economy was fully developed, nevertheless we have used the British dates throughout to facilitate comparison. Finally the cycle is counted from the year after the crest of one cycle to the crest year of the next, thus including the whole of the depression and subsequent boom. Other points might be chosen; it merely seems convenient to consider for our purpose movements ending in a boom. For convenience the results of this analysis have been put into tables in an Appendix.

The first fact which emerges is that there have been definitely wave like movements in wholesale prices, and also in interest rates. Prices fell from the cycle ending in 1818 to the cycle ending in 1846, then rose to the cycle ending in 1865, fell again to the cycle ending in 1899, rose to the cycle ending in 1920, and then fell steadily through the two inter-war cycles. The movement is illustrated clearly in Chart IV. The long term rate of interest (the yield on consols) shows an exactly similar movement.

Three main explanations have been given for this "long wave" in prices and interest rates. The first is that it is due to wars and their inflationary effects on prices. Prices were rising at the end of the 18th century owing to the inflationary effects of the Napoleonic wars. After the wars they fell as war expenditures were curtailed. The big fall is from the cycle of 1818 to the cycle of 1825; the downward movement thereafter is one of the order of only about 1 per cent per annum, which might be explained by the effects of technical progress on costs. The next two cycles show upward movements again explained by war, the first by the Crimean War, and the second by the American Civil War. The Austrian and Franco-German wars prevented prices from falling much in the cycle of 1874 below the heights of 1865, but in the succeeding years of peace prices fell again to the cycle of 1899. The rise in the two pre-1914 cycles is not so easily explained by war. There was the Boer War and increased expenditure on preparation for war, but these are hardly enough to justify so big an increase in prices. Neither can the continued fall in the cycle of the 1930's be explained either by cessation of war expenditure, which had exhausted itself ten years earlier, or by technical progress. The war explanation of the long wave works well for the 19th century but is less convincing for the twentieth.

The second explanation attributes the long wave to changes in gold supplies, attributing the increase of prices in the fifties and sixties to new gold from California and Australia, and the rise in the years before 1914 to new gold from South Africa. The periods of falling prices have coincided with a reduced output of gold, and on each occasion contemporaries have sought to attribute the fall of prices to this cause. But while increased gold doubtless contributed to rising prices, a fall in gold production should not itself cause prices to fall; also the fall of prices is largely explainable in terms of technical progress, save in the cycles immediately after major wars, when the curtailment of war expenditure doubtless contributes to the heavy fall in prices; and certainly the heavy fall in the cycle of the 1930's cannot be explained in terms of changes in gold production.

The third and most modern explanation, and that which is most interesting, attributes the long waves in prices to parallel waves in the rate of industrial growth. The theory was first developed by the Russian economist Kondratieff, and has been given its fullest expression in a remarkable work by the American economist Schumpeter[4] who attempts to provide a theoretical mechanism for explaining why long waves of prosperity and depression, of about 50 or 60 years duration, should be generated by the economic system irrespective of war and of changes in gold supplies. On this thesis, the long waves in prices should be matched by similar waves in the indices of industrial growth.

The original conclusions of Kondratieff were based on statistical

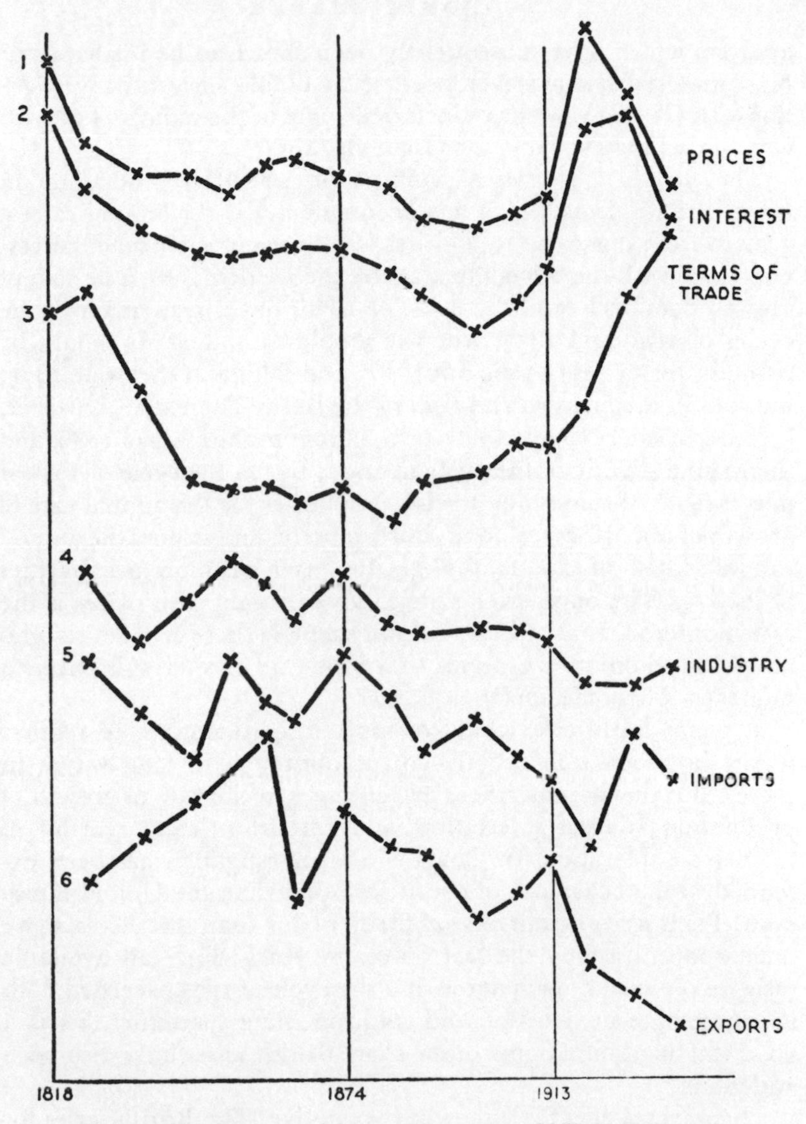

CHART IV. SECULAR MOVEMENTS IN THE U.K., 1811–1937.

1.	Wholesale Prices.	4.	Annual Rate of Growth of Industry.
2.	Rate of Interest.	5.	Annual Rate of Growth of Imports.
3.	Terms of Trade.	6.	Annual Rate of Growth of Exports.

Points of inflexion are averages of cycles ending in 1818, 1825, 1836, 1846, 1853, 1860, 1865, 1874, 1883, 1889, 1899, 1907, 1913, 1920, 1929 and 1937. For figures see Statistical Appendix, series 1, 2, 6, 15, 16 and 17.

analyses which have subsequently been shown to be inadequate.[5] New material has however become available since his investigations. In Chart IV we have included some of the indices of growth which are now available for Great Britain.

The first is the physical volume of industrial production in Great Britain, from which has been calculated the annual rate of growth from one cycle to another. It shows no such exact correspondence with the price index as the theory demands. The rate of growth does decline in the cycle of 1836, but it rises again in the cycles of 1846 and 1853, when it should be falling. It should be rising in the cycles of 1860 and 1865 and falling in the cycle 1874, but falls in the first two and rises in the third. Thereafter, however, it conforms more closely to pattern, falling to the cycle of 1889, and then rising slightly to the cycle of 1907; but in the cycle of 1913 it falls instead of continuing to rise. The series for the annual rate of growth of imports corresponds fairly closely, and so does the annual rate of growth of exports, though the latter has more peculiarities of its own. The only series which moves closely with prices is the rate of interest, a fact which will not surprise those economists who have argued on other grounds that "the rate of interest is purely a monetary phenomenon."

It seems fairly clear that we must discard notions of regular waves in production exactly corresponding with long waves in prices. But the fact that there are changes in the rate of growth of production is itself interesting and important, and worthy of further consideration. In Chart V the investigation has been extended to the behaviour of countries other than the United Kingdom. Their series do not extend further back than the 1860's, so we must concentrate on the last 60 or 70 years. Since all available series of physical growth agree that the cycle of 1874 exceeded both its immediate predecessor and its immediate successor, this is a good starting point. Some other short British series have also been added.

The general effect is somewhat wave like. The British series for the growth of industrial production, for the ratio of home investment to industrial production and for the level of unemployment all tell the same tale. From a peak in the cycle of 1874 conditions deteriorated for the next two cycles till 1889; then for two cycles they improved, to 1907, and then decline set in again to 1913. The series relating to external trade have irreconcilable problems of

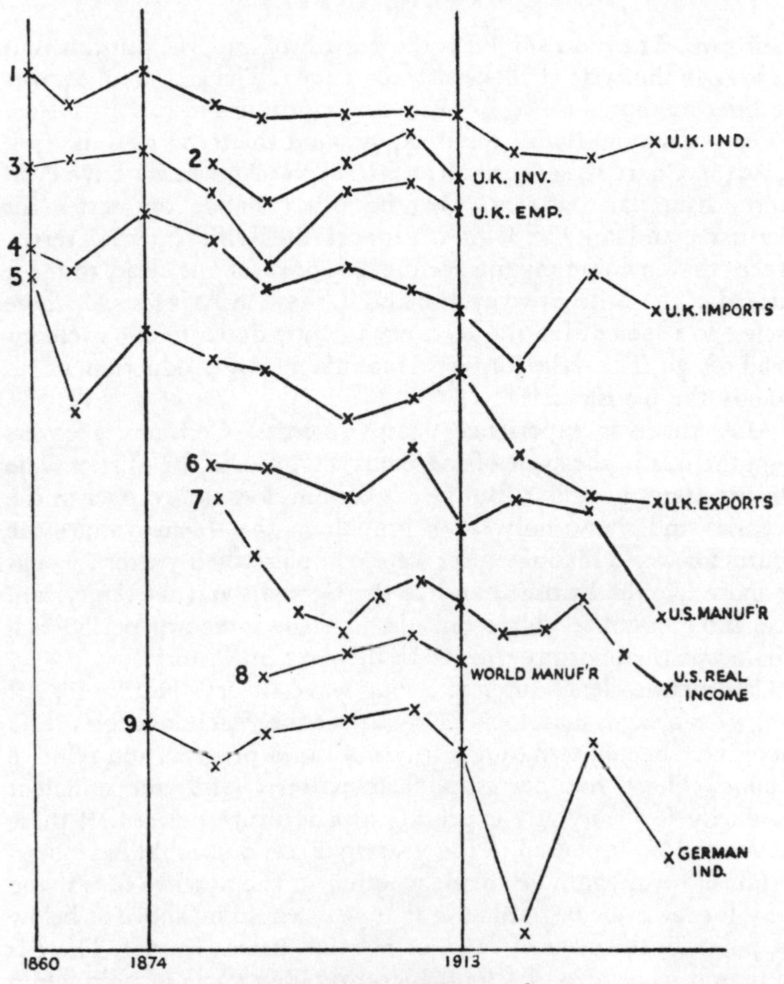

CHART V. SECULAR TRENDS, 1854–1937.

1. Annual rate of growth of Industry, U.K.
2. Ratio of Investment index to index of Industrial Production, U.K.
3. Employment percentage, U.K.
4. Annual rate of growth of Imports, U.K.
5. Annual rate of growth of Exports, U.K.
6. Annual rate of growth of Manufacturing, U.S.A.
7. Annual rate of growth of Real Income, U.S.A.
8. Annual rate of growth of World Manufacturing.
9. Annual rate of growth of Industrial Production, Germany.

Series 7 (U.S. real income) plots quinquennial averages. In the other series, points of inflexion are averages of cycles ending in boom years. For figures see Statistical Appendix, series 7, 9, 15, 16, 17. 18, 19, 20 and 23.

their own. The most similar is the growth of imports, but this is at its peak in the cycle of 1899, instead of 1907. The growth of exports declines to 1899, instead of 1889, and continues to rise after 1907 instead of falling. Both capital exports and the terms of trade (not shown in Chart V; see series 6 and 10 in the Appendix) have even more dissimilar patterns. On the other hand, the series for Germany and for the U.S.A. support the U.K. internal series, except that in Germany the decline lasts only for one cycle, to 1883, instead of the British two cycles; and in the U.S.A. it lasts for three cycles, to 1899 cutting the recovery to 1907 down to one cycle instead of two. The series for world manufacturing production moves exactly the British series.

After the war experience again diverges. Germany recovers from the war in the cycle of 1929, but stagnates in the thirties. The United States is similar. But Great Britain does not recover in the twenties and shows only small growth in the thirties, and if the figures for world manufactures were complete their pattern would be more like the British than like the German and the American. The three countries agree only in that the inter-war period as a whole was the least progressive in their recent history.

Can such evidence support a long wave theory? Hardly so. All that we can say is that, looking back over the years since the 1860's there have been alternating periods of rapid progress and relative decline. There has been no clear pattern, and not sufficient regularity to justify any expectation of a future pattern. If these curves had been plotted in the year 1938, no one could have been certain how to continue them; whether in the absence of war the point for the cycle beginning in that year would be above or below the point for the cycle of 1937, or how far distant from it. There is no reason to believe in a self-generating long cycle in production on the Kondratieff-Schumpeter model. There are changes in the rate of progress, but each change must be explained *ad hoc* by reference to its own facts.

OTHER THEORIES

This is the central object of Part III, to discover why the experience of the inter-war years was so unfavourable. That it was especially unfavourable is confirmed by the pre-war comparisons which we have just made. They showed that our great depression was not the first in history, bearing as it does comparison with the long decline of the 1870's and 80's, and with an earlier decline in the 1820's and 30's; and even though we saw no reason to accept the 50-year intervals as more than a coincidence, especially as each was punctuated by a second short depression, we are left to find an explanation for this unfavourable change in the world's fortunes. The comparison also shows that the inter-war period was not just unfavourable; it was more unfavourable than anything that had happened in the 19th century. The rate of growth of industrial production had declined from one cycle to another before, but never before had it actually been negative, average annual production being less in one cycle than its predecessor; with relative stagnation we were familiar, but here, for some countries in the inter-war period, was absolute decline.

There have been many theories to explain this phenomenon: the effects of the war; the decline of population growth among European peoples; the reaching of the agricultural frontier in new regions of overseas settlement; the exhaustion of investment opportunities in mature countries and so on. In long wave theories, the decline of the inter-war period was a mere phase; to be followed in due course by another burst of vigour and prosperity, say from the middle 1940's to the 1970's, when a new period of decline would set in. But in many other theories the decline was not temporary but permanent; the sources of 19th century expansion had dried up; the economic system was played out, and its collapse in the near future inevitable. To thread one's way through all the possible theories would be entertaining, but it would be out of keeping with the character of this book, whose general purpose is to collect the necessary facts together, with theory in the background rather than on the centre of the stage. What we need is rather a suitable framework for displaying the relevant material.

Such a framework is provided by studying the behaviour of international trade. The disintegration of the international economic system is even more characteristic a feature of our period than the declining growth of production. Throughout the 19th century the volume of international trade was growing and more and more countries were being drawn in to participate in a world economy. In the 1930's production and trade declined together, but whereas world production recovered, to surpass the level of the 1920's, world trade did not, and the international network seemed irreparably damaged. To many observers the stagnation of international trade was not only the most obvious but also the central feature of the inter-war period, in that all other features were directly related to it, either as cause or as effect. Doubtless this could be said of almost any other feature of the economy, since all parts are inter-related. Nevertheless, the study of international trade is a very convenient vehicle for discussing the major trends in the world economy, and we shall use it for this purpose.

Chapter XII sets out the main facts on the behaviour of international trade, revealing its relative stagnation. That stagnation was due to two main groups of factors, to obstacles to international trade, and to changes in the long-run trends of demand and supply. ChapterXII treats also of the first group, and the following chapter of the second group.

CHAPTER XII

INTERNATIONAL TRADE: OBSTACLES

THAT international trade declined after 1929 is well known, and generally attributed to the slump and its aftermath—international currency restrictions, tariffs, the decline of production, and so on. What is not generally realised is that even in the twenties international trade was already failing to retain its pre-war place. Taking 1913 as 100, and averaging the years 1926–29, world manufacturing production stood at 139, and world production of primary products at 125; but world trade in manufactures stood only at 112, and world trade in primary products at 118.

It is not difficult to account for the low level of trade in manufactures. Manufactures are imported principally by countries producing primary products; a League of Nations calculation[1] shows that in 1935 the twelve most industrialised countries in the world took only 35 per cent of world imports of manufactures; such countries are more important in the market for primary products, where they took 74 per cent of world imports. Now the demand of primary producers for manufactured products depends principally on the terms of trade, and can be almost exactly calculated if we know both the export volume of primary products and the terms of trade. This fact can be illustrated in various ways. The League of Nations has published a diagram showing how the ratio of world trade in primary to world trade in manufactured products has varied with the terms of trade since 1876, and it shows the inverse relation we should expect.[2] Another illustration is to compare the indices of the value of world trade in primary and world trade in manufactured products; these would move absolutely in step if the demand for manufactures were determined only by the sales of primary products in volume, and the terms of trade. The correspondence is not in fact exact, but it is very close.[3]

TABLE XII

VALUE OF WORLD TRADE, AVERAGES, 1913=100

Year	Primary Products	Manufactures
1876/80 .	32.8	31.4
1881/85 .	35.7	35.7
1886/90 .	36.5	36.9
1891/95 .	40.1	37.0
1896/00 .	47.0	43.5
1901/05 .	58.0	53.7
1906/10 .	74.8	72.6
1911/13 .	95.0	93.4
1913 .	100	100

It is not exact because there is a considerable exchange of primary commodities against primary commodities—the value of world trade in primary products is twice as great as the value of world trade in manufactures—but it is close because the price and quantum behaviour of the primary commodities exchanged against other primary commodities is very similar to that of the primary commodities exchanged against manufactures.

In 1926/29 the quantum of trade in primary products (taking 1913 as base) stood at 117.7; the price index was at 135.9, and the price of manufactures at 149.4, the terms of trade being therefore at 110. Applying the terms of trade to the trade in primary products would give the quantum of trade in manufactures as 107. The actual figure was 111.7. We can say, therefore, that given the volume of trade in primary products and the terms of trade, the trade in manufactures was at a reasonable level, such as might be expected.

What has to be explained is why the trade in primary products was so low. The trade in primary products is a function first and foremost of the demand of industrial countries of which the first twelve, as we have seen, import 74 per cent. In the years before 1913 the trade in primary products increased *pari passu* with the index of world manufacturing. The ratio of the increase in the quantum of trade to the increase in manufacturing from 1876/80 to 1911/13 was 74 per cent, the quinquennial average figures varying between 64 per cent and 100 per cent. If this relation had continued after the war, i.e. if trade in primary products had increased say three-quarters as much as manufacturing, with the manufacturing index at 139 in 1926/29, the trade in primary products would have been at around 129; it was, in fact, only at 118.

This failure of the trade in primary products to attain its "proper" level was not due to any increase in tariffs. The only indices we have of agricultural tariffs are those which Dr. Liepmann has published for Europe.[4] Striking an average for Europe, excluding the U.K. and the U.S.S.R., they show that the agrarian tariff level (ratio of duties to price) was the same in 1927 as in 1913.

1913	1927	1931
26	26	65

Some countries had increased their tariffs, but others had reduced theirs; the big all-round increase in agrarian tariffs did not occur until after the slump in 1929. In the twenties the big increase was in manufacturing tariffs.

1913	1927	1931
18	25	30

The principal reason why the trade in primary products was not higher was the decline of population growth. If we exclude the populations of Asia and of Africa, whose contribution to world trade is small, the population of the rest of the world[5] grew from 551 million in 1900 to 666 million in 1913, and to 757 million in 1929. The cumulative annual rate of increase thus dropped from 1.5 per cent to 0.9 per cent. This was due not so much to a decline of the birthrate as to the war. As a result of the war, it is estimated,[6] the population of Europe was 22 million smaller in 1920 than it would have been if there had been no war (6.6 million military deaths, 5.0 million excess of civilian deaths over normal, plus 10.8 million net deficit of births). In addition the population of Russia was 26 million smaller than it would have been in the absence of war and civil war.

Now this deficit of population meant that the demand for foodstuffs was correspondingly smaller than it would have been because that demand depends most of all on the number of stomachs to be fed. The world's capacity to consume manufactured products is, in the long run, unlimited, but its capacity for foodstuffs is limited strictly by the size of the human stomach. In consequence a decline in the rate of growth of population must slow down the rate of increase of demand for primary products, while it need not have the same effect on the rate of increase of demand for manufactures.

The decline of population growth explains not only why the trade in primary products grew at a smaller rate relatively to world manufacturing production than was the case before the war. It also explains why the trade in primary products grew less than production of primary products. For, of the increase in population (excluding Asia and Africa) between 1913 and 1929, only 33 per cent occurred in Europe although Europe's population was in 1913 as much as 70 per cent of the whole. Production of primary products increased very much outside Europe, but only a part of the increase was sent to Europe, the large part being needed at home for consumption by the increased populations of the producing countries. This situation was already established by the middle twenties. Thus, while world trade did not regain its 1913 level until the year 1924 (corresponding perhaps to a 4 per cent increase in trade in primary products and an 8 per cent decrease in trade in manufactures), world manufacturing in 1924 was already 11 per cent above pre-war, and world primary production 10 per cent above. The war had made countries more "self-sufficient", and had diminished international specialisation. Nevertheless this was a "once for all" change, rather than a continuing trend. From 1925 to 1929 world manufacturing increased by 27 per cent, and world trade by 19 per cent, or by 70 per cent as much. The "proper" relation had been resumed, even though there was no tendency for the specialisation lost by the war to be made up.

Then came the slump, and with the slump repercussions in the form of greatly increased obstacles to trade which further widened the gap between world production and world trade. Taking 1913 as base, manufacturing production in 1936/38 stood at 185; the trade in primary products, assuming 75 per cent as great an increase, should have been around 164, but was only at 119. Taking 1926/29 as base, manufacturing production stood at 133 and the trade in primaries, which should have been at 125, was only at 101. The gap had increased still more in the thirties. The trade in manufactures, on the other hand, was still at a reasonable level despite tariff increases. The terms of trade had deteriorated to 130; this applied to the trade in primary products would give the trade in manufactures as 92; the actual figure was 97.

From this follows an important conclusion. There was much groaning in the inter-war years at the low level of the trade in manufactures, especially by those industrial countries whose export industries were so badly affected. But in fact the trade in manufactures was throughout the period at a reasonable level.

This conclusion that the trade in manufactures was at a reasonable level does not of course follow directly from the figures presented here. These figures prove no more than that, for the sixty years for which we have figures, the volume of trade in manufactures and the volume of trade in primary products have been directly connected by the terms of trade. Given the trade in primary products, we have shown, the trade in manufactures was at a reasonable level; but it might equally well be said that, given the trade in manufactures the trade in primary products was at a reasonable level. Which is the more important?

In deciding to treat the trade in manufactures as the dependent factor we are in effect arguing that in these sixty years it has been the growing demand of industrial countries for primary produce that has dispensed purchasing power to primary producers for buying manufactures, and not the growing demand of primary producers for manufactures that has dispensed purchasing power to the industrial countries with which to buy primary products. This seems reasonable enough, from what we know of nineteenth century history. The dynamic factor in that century was the growth of the industrial countries; what happened in primary producing countries, by way of increased production of primary products, and increased trade, was merely by way of reaction to disturbances originating in the industrial countries; no one can argue seriously that the original disturbances making for growth were occurring in the primary producing countries, and that the industrial countries were merely adjusting themselves to what was happening to primary producers. Statistics, again, prove nothing, but it is interesting to observe that whereas the volume of trade in primary products grew fairly steadily in the nineteenth century, it was the volume of trade in manufactures that reacted sharply to changes in the terms of trade:

TABLE XIII

ANNUAL RATE OF GROWTH OF WORLD TRADE

Year	Primary Products	Manufactures
1876/80 to 1881/85	4.4	4.9
1881/85 to 1886/90	3.4	2.5

Year	Primary Products	Manufactures
1886/90 to 1891/95	3.1	0.4
1891/95 to 1896/00	3.4	0.9
1896/00 to 1901/05	3.5	6.3
1901/05 to 1906/10	3.5	4.7
1906/10 to 1911/13	3.3	4.5

The steady growth of the volume of trade in primary products, which links with the steady growth of population, suggests that this was the independent factor; if it were dependent, and the trade in manufactures independent, the steadiness of the dependent and the wide fluctuations of the independent factor would make a strange coincidence.

But even if one agrees that in the nineteenth century the demand of the industrial countries was the cause, and the demand of the primary producers the result, in international trade, it is still possible to believe that this position was reversed after the war. But such a conclusion would not be consistent with all the facts. If the independent factor had been the unwillingness of primary producers to buy manufactured imports because they had industrialised, the terms of trade would more probably have moved against manufactures; the fact that they had moved in favour of manufactures even in the 1920's when the world was still relatively prosperous suggests that it was diminished demand for primary products rather than for manufactures that was causal. This argument, however, is not decisive, since, even if the diminished demand for manufactures was the causal factor, the diminished demand for primary products which resulted might have made the terms of trade move against primary products, whose prices are more flexible than the prices of manufactures. More suggestive is the fact that in the 1920's the industrial countries (excluding Germany) continued to lend money freely to the primary producing countries, as they had done before the war. This is hardly consistent with the view that they were forced to curtail their purchases of primary products because primary producers were not putting enough purchasing power at their disposal; if they had been as " hard up" as this, they would have diminished their capital export rather than their purchases of foodstuffs and raw materials. Once we accept, as the statistics compel us to, that the trade in primary products and the trade in manufactures are linked in a way suggesting that the demand for one is limited to the purchasing power generated by the demand for the other, we are forced to take the demand for primary products as the independent and dominant factor, since it seems much more the case that the small countries are limited by what happens in the big industrial countries, than that the latter have had their demands limited in international trade by what they could sell to primary producers.

It is for these reasons that we conclude that the low level of trade in the inter-war period was due not to a reduced rate of growth in the demand for manufactures by primary producers, but to a reduced rate of growth of demand for primary products by manufacturing countries. *The decline of trade in manufactures was due neither to tariffs nor to the industrialisation of new countries.* The trade in manufactures was low only because the industrial countries were buying too little of primary products and paying so low a price for what they bought. If therefore we wish to understand the decline of international trade it is on the demand of industrial countries for primary products and on the prices they pay that we must concentrate attention.

Now the demand for primary products and the terms of trade were affected in the 1930's by two different sets of influences. First, as a result of the slump many countries had created obstacles to international trade greater than at any period in the previous 70 years. And secondly, demand and supply were affected by long run forces other than obstacles the effects of which had gradually accumulated. These require separate diagnosis. The long run trends are examined in the next chapter; first, in this chapter we must examine the obstacles.

The big increase of obstacles to international trade came after the slump of 1929. It was then that the international currency system seemed finally to break down; that currency controls multiplied; that tariffs reached enormous proportions and licences became diminutive; and that the free multilateral flow of trade was constrained into bilateral channels. All these obstacles existed in 1920, as an aftermath of the war. But while in 1920 men regarded them as temporary, looked forward to their speedy removal, and did in fact proceed to remove them as the twenties progressed, in the 1930's the obstacles came to be regarded by a much larger circle as desirable in themselves, and not just as temporary weapons for coping with a slump, but as a necessary part of national economic systems. In our analysis, therefore, of these obstacles, we cannot confine ourselves to examining their immediate causes and effects; they merge into the long-run problem in that we are compelled to enquire whether their growth is not itself part of a long-run trend, and destined to as much permanence as other long-run trends in demand and supply.

Indeed there is nothing specially important to say about the causes and effects of the obstacles to international trade. Their great growth was due to the slump; their main effect was to curtail international trade more than production. What is interesting about these obstacles is to enquire what lessons were learnt from their operation which help us to assess whether they should be or will be permanent. Men are not governed in such matters only by reason, and it does not follow that controls will be retained if they are valuable, or rejected if they are only a hindrance; but if we can discover how far controls have served a useful purpose in the 1930's, we shall be better able to assess their likely future.

The two principal controls were in the fields of foreign exchange and of tariff policy.

INTERNATIONAL CURRENCY EXPERIENCE

The aim of policy for most governments in the 1920's was to get their countries into the position where their currencies could maintain a stable international value, and be freely convertible into other currencies without control. This state was attained by nearly every country in the world by the year 1929. From that year onward, however, the number of countries repudiating stability and free convertibility increased rapidly. Some countries retained free convertibility, but made no effort to secure stability; others maintained stability, but controlled convertibility, and yet others rejected both stability and free convertibility. For a while, in the first half of the 1930's, there seemed to be emerging a feeling that neither stability nor convertibility was specially desirable, and that no efforts need be made to attain to these conditions. The principal advantage of stability and of free convertibility is that if these twin conditions are present international trade is facilitated, and if either is absent, international trade is hindered. It was therefore only natural that when, as a result of the slump, international trade started to contract and to become or seem to become less important to countries, even perhaps to be a hindrance to their recovery programmes, less importance should be attached to stability and convertibility; they ceased to be major objects of policy because the maintenance of a large foreign trade ceased to be a primary object, and became secondary to internal domestic policies. This phase of opinion, however, passed. As the thirties proceeded and international trade once more revived, its slow revival was seen as a hindrance to internal recovery. Value was once more attached to its promotion, and to currency arrangements likely to facilitate it. The gay unilateral abandonment of the Gold Standard gave place to new efforts to promote stability by agreement, starting with the tripartite agreement of 1936; and the mood turned against restrictive currency controls, which with the revival of trade began to be relaxed in many countries. That stability and free convertibility are desirable is a proposition which no longer needs to be defended; the question now asked is rather what conditions are necessary in order that stability and convertibility can be maintained.

The answer to this question divides into short-term conditions, and long-run conditions, the latter concerned with adjusting to long-run adverse movements in the balance of payments, the former concerned with day to day movements in a position which is fundamentally sound.

We take first the short run conditions, assuming that the long-run position of the balance of payments is fundamentally sound.

It is of the nature of trade that there should be day to day fluctuations in the balance of payments, sometimes to the credit, and sometimes to the debit. To meet such fluctuations every country needs a buffer stock of internationally acceptable currency, otherwise there will be day to day fluctuations in the price of the national currency, and these fluctuations are undesirable. They would not occur even if there were no buffer stock if foreigners had complete confidence in the balance of payments position of the country; day to day fluctuations would then be met by foreign credits, through the market for forward exchange. Such complete confidence does not however exist at any time in the currency of more than one or two major countries; all others need a buffer stock, and usually even those in which there is confidence receive this confidence mainly because it is known that they possess such stocks.

In the 19th century gold served as the buffer stock of each country, gold being the only commodity acceptable to nearly all countries. After 1918, however, the stocks of gold were too unevenly distributed for gold to continue to exercise this function by itself, and the heavy drain on the reserves of European importers in the early twenties aggravated the maldistribution. Thus the U.S. holding of central bank reserves which in 1913 was 24 per cent of the world total, had risen to 44 per cent at the end of 1923, and the U.K. share from 3 per cent to 9 per cent, while several countries, such as Germany, Italy, Russia, India, and Brazil had lost gold not only relatively but absolutely.[7] The countries whose balances of payments were the most insecure, and whose need for a buffer stock was most acute, were the very ones which possessed an inadequate stock of gold. The buffer could therefore no longer be gold exclusively; gold had to be supplemented by some other acceptable means of payment.

This was the significance of the Gold Exchange Standard, which replaced the pre-war gold specie standard. In this system gold holdings were supplemented by holdings of foreign exchange. Countries with small gold reserves supplemented their buffer stocks by holding stocks of claims on foreign currencies.

There were three snags in the operation of the system. The first was that certain countries possessed little gold and were not in a position to amass claims on foreign currencies. They therefore acquired their stock by borrowing. Had they borrowed on long term, there would have been no embarrassment. But they borrowed on short term. Their stocks were therefore peculiarly vulnerable to changes in confidence. Just when the buffer was most needed, it was also most likely to disappear. The weakness of Austria and of Germany in this respect eventually destroyed the Gold Standard. When in 1931 confidence in the stability of those countries was lost, the rapid withdrawal of short term loans so reduced their buffer stock of international currency that they were forced to abandon free convertibility. The first lesson from inter-war experience is therefore that if countries do not possess reserves, and are driven to borrow in order to build up reserves, the loan must be of such a nature that it cannot suddenly be withdrawn. It wil be observed that this lesson has been incorporated into post-war monetary arrangements, the effect of which is to give each country an initial limited credit of international money on which it can draw.

The second snag arose out of the decision by some countries to keep as a buffer claims on foreign currencies, especially sterling and the dollar. This decision imposed on London and New York the necessity of having at their disposal larger stocks of gold than they would have needed if they had not been chosen as insurance for the needs of other countries as well. New York had adequate gold reserves for the purpose, but London had not. In the decades before 1914 London had managed on extraordinarily small gold reserves, much smaller than those of New York or Paris or Berlin or even of Rome or Moscow. Her balance of payments position was known to be so impregnable that she really needed no gold at all, and could have operated the Gold Standard equally well by dealing in foreign currencies. After the war, the position demanded greater reserves; and the additional obligation of insuring the reserves of Gold Exchange standard countries imposed on her the need for still larger stocks. But adequate stocks were never acquired. As we have seen in Chapter III, London was having difficulties in the twenties in preventing an outflow of gold, largely because she was lending more than her balance of payments permitted, and was possibly on balance borrowing short and lending long. When confidence finally departed in 1931, her buffer stock of gold was not adequate to meet all claims, and she was driven off the Gold Standard. New York was immediately subjected to the strain, but her gold reserves were so large that she was able to meet all claims promptly, and the panic soon subsided. The real lesson was that London was no longer fit to serve as a financial centre after 1913. To have fulfilled the function she would have needed to begin the twenties by importing and holding much larger stocks of gold, and this she could have done only by imposing a ban temporarily on the export of capital; but since a centre is expected also to be an exporter of capital, she could not properly have fulfilled the functions of a financial centre in either case. Already in 1918 New York was the only suitable centre for an international monetary system.

The third snag was the abnormal strain on the foreign exchange mechanism imposed by large short-term international movements of capital. These arose out of the general insecurity of the twenties, and more particularly out of violent inflationary movements, especially in France and in Germany. When international confidence is high, only the smallest buffer stocks are necessary; but the lower the state of confidence, the greater is the need for a reserve. Now there are not many countries that can afford to keep such large buffer stocks of gold and foreign reserves that they can meet any demand however large for capital export in a political and financial crisis. Most countries are bound to exhaust their reserves at an early stage of such a crisis, and then to be unable to maintain stability and free convertibility. The only real remedy for this is for each country to pursue only such domestic policies as win the confidence of persons who might otherwise export their capital in mass panic. Since it is unlikely, if not also undesirable, that all countries will behave in this way, no type of international monetary mechanism can guarantee that there shall always be stability and convertibility and no international system can demand of its members that they maintain stability and convertibility in all circumstances. The Bretton Woods agreement, for example, specifically reserves to member countries the right to maintain exchange control over capital movements.

These three snags have been provided for in the new monetary system which comes into operation in 1947. Each country is provided the means of acquiring international currency to meet short term needs if its balance of payments situation is fundamentally sound; no one country is subjected to special strain; and capital movements are exempted for control. The sums provided are small, and hedged with restrictions; possibly too small and too restricted for normal working. (They are certainly too small for postwar reconstruction needs, but this is not their purpose). We shall have to wait until fundament l maladjustments are eliminated to see whether they are adequate or not. Meanwhile we turn to examine the problems that remain of adjustment to fundamental movements.

First there is the cyclical problem. The balance of payments of many countries is peculiarly susceptible to cyclical influences. Primary producers, especially, are in a position to accumulate balances in the upswing, and are usually subjected to heavy adverse movements in the downswing. If they did accumulate balances in the upswing, they could use them in the downswing to finance fixed interest commitments and the excess of imports over exports, but they do not. The more strongly subject to cyclical influences a country may be, the greater is its need for a large average reserve, but it is precisely such countries which tend to keep small reserves of foreign exchange, spending to the hilt whatever they acquire. It may be that some of them will have learnt lessons from the thirties, and particularly where the powers of central banks have been strengthened, they may in future pursue policies more appropriate to cyclical movements. But so long as they do not, they will be unable to maintain stability and free convertibility of their currencies whenever the international cycle recurs. The special difficulties of such countries are now recognised and provision is made in international agreements for them to take special measures.

The new situation is not however, as simple as it is made out to be. For the past hundred years or so prices in all major countries have moved very closely together, partly because of and partly facilitating the maintenance of stable rates of exchange. The new situation is that some countries have decided to try to stabilise their internal prices. The dominant country in the world economy is now the United States, whose prices are not subject to close control, and will doubtless continue to fluctuate cyclically. The result for countries which wish to combine free convertibility with internal stability must be a fluctuating rate of exchange, rising with rising world prices, and falling with falling world prices. If a country is committed not to keep its own price level in step with world prices, it will find itself committed not to keep the exchange value of its currency stable. Most of the lessons of the inter-war period seem to have been learnt, save this.

Secular movements are not as difficult as cyclical movements. If owing to permanent changes the balance of payments becomes passive, stability and free convertibility cannot be maintained for long unless steps are taken to correct the disequilibrium. The required steps may be very varied; the development of new types of production, the search for new markets, the discouragement of certain types of consumption, and so on. Whatever they may be, they are likely to involve some lowering of the relation between the domestic price level and the world price level; the adjustment can be described simply, but not exactly, by saying that the country's price level must be brought into line with world prices. Thus, after Great Britain returned to the Gold Standard in 1925, it was widely believed that her troubles were due to a price level too high in relation to world prices, and it is now even more widely believed that it was this that forced her off the Gold Standard in 1931. The oversimplicity of stating the problem solely in terms of prices is well illustrated by this case. Great Britain had lost old markets and needed to develop new industries and new markets. A general lowering of the British price level would have helped somewhat, but much more direct and vigorous methods were needed than this. Neither is it the case that Britain was forced off the Gold Standard because of an adverse balance on current account. There was an adverse balance in 1931 but it was short term capital movements which drained British reserves, and they were due to an international panic in which adverse movements on current account were of negligible importance.

It nevertheless remains true and fundamental that a country cannot long maintain stability and convertibility unless its prices are in line with world prices. If therefore they are out of line, it must sooner or later deflate, devalue, or restrict convertibility. Deflation is a difficult process, productive of violent industrial disputes, and most countries have now renounced it. Restricting convertibility is cumbersome, and its special value is to countries wishing to discriminate in their trade relations, a problem which we reserve for later consideration. Devaluation is relatively simple, and the right of any country to devalue if there is no prospect of balancing its accounts at the current rate with full employment is recognised and safeguarded in the new international monetary agreements. (If the account can be balanced only by having unemployment, the current rate is not an equilibrium rate; e.g., sterling in the 1920's). Still more important, the new arrangements may help such countries by prohibiting unjustified and retaliatory devaluations which render useless the efforts of countries to whom devaluation is essential. United States devaluation in 1933 was an arbitrary act, and it is essential to the world economy to have a code which in future permits only the justifiable devaluations.

The opposite case is that of the country with a permanent tendency to have an export surplus. Neither an import nor an export surplus creates any difficulties if the surplus is fully covered by long term borrowing or lending. Problems arise only if the surplus is not desired, and not associated with deliberate capital movements.

A persistent export surplus on the part of one country can have deflationary consequences that destroy international trade. Suppose, to take a hypothetical example, that we have *x* countries to start off, all trading with each other, doing the same amount of trade, and in balance. Then suppose that in all but one the sources of food production are blasted, and that all those affected have in consequence to buy more from the unaffected one, increasing their imports by 10 per cent. And suppose that the fortunate country will not, or cannot, import more, so that it has a large export surplus. Then each of the affected will have a deficit on current account. In order to eliminate this it will cut its less essential imports, reducing imports by 10 per cent. But since each country cuts imports by 10 per cent each country will find its exports diminished, and the gap will still remain. This calls for another import cut, which since it is universal brings another fall in exports and still leaves the gap. The gap will be closed if the unfortunate countries cut imports all round, but the fortunate country maintains its imports; but the final result will be to diminish international trade by a multiple of the gap. In this rather abstract example if there were five countries, each exporting 100 units at the start, world exports would rise from 500 to 540, and then fall to 380, the trade of the four affected countries contracting not by 10% but by 30%.

The remedy is an appreciation of the currency of the country with the persistent surplus, and if international trade is to be preserved against deflation, it is imperative that a country with a persistent surplus should be compelled to appreciate the value of its currency to whatever degree is needed to wipe out the surplus. The alternative is to permit all other countries to discriminate against the exports of that country, so that they can balance their payments without having to cut their trade by a multiple of the gap. This is the purpose of the "scarce currency" clause in the Bretton Woods agreement. The same effect is also produced if countries enter into customs unions excluding the country with a surplus, and thus discriminate against its goods, but such unions are difficult to arrange.

In practice disequilibrium cannot long continue. A country cannot persistently have an export surplus unless its citizens are willing to acquire foreign assets. For if they are not, sooner or later they will sell heavily the currencies accumulating to their credit, and their own currency will rise sharply in terms of the others. Alternatively, sooner or later the inflationary pressure of the export surplus will raise internal prices and eliminate the surplus. The trouble lies in the "sooner or later"; in that interval there may be great damage to international trade. It is therefore as important to have a code requiring surplus countries to appreciate their currencies as it is to have a code that permits deficit countries effectively to devalue. The new international arrangements do not impose sufficient obligations upon surplus countries, and throw too much of the burden of adjustment upon those that are in deficit.

Secular movements, once they are recognised, can be dealt with appropriately, usually once and for all. Nearly all the really difficult problems in maintaining stable exchange rates and free convertibility arise out of the international trade cycle. If the cycle could be eliminated nations would have no hesitation in committing themselves with little reservation to stability and convertibility. If, however, the world economy remains subject to major cycles, currency disorder will become endemic, and will slowly strangle international trade. To this subject we shall return.

TARIFF POLICY

The growth of tariffs is not so clearly a product of the international cycle. Industrial tariffs were higher in 1927 than in 1913, largely because of the determination of undeveloped regions to industrialise. It is beyond dispute that many countries have been persuaded by vested interests or by fallacious reasoning to promote industrialisation by tariffs in circumstances where this policy is harmful as much to themselves as to the rest of the world. But it is equally beyond dispute that there are many countries and circumstances where further industrialisation is essential, and beneficial both to the countries concerned and to the world, and where tariff or quota protection may justifiably be a part of the development process. It may therefore confidently be expected, come what may, that there will be tariffs for industrialisation, and even that the importance of such tariffs may increase in the future. Such a development need not harm international trade; if it increases the real incomes of developing countries, it is pretty certain to increase international trade, rather than to diminish it. To this we shall return in the next chapter.

Agricultural tariffs, also, are not a product of the cycle. Their future depends on the political influence of farmers. In the inter-war period that influence was strengthened by the arguments that agriculture is a necessary war industry, and that a nation of farmers is specially healthy and strong. World War II has, however, emphasised that the strong nation, militarily, is the nation with the greatest industrial resources, and realisation of this fact may help to weaken the political strength of farmers.

While it is true that the tariff is not a product of the trade cycle, it is nevertheless true that it was the slump that caused the great burgeoning of tariffs, quotas and trade restrictions in the 1930's, which in turn by strangling international trade, subsequently reduced the rate of recovery.

The use of tariffs to deal with problems created by the slump was strongly criticised in the thirties. It was pointed out that the tariff is not as effective as was thought in that when a large country cuts its imports the countries from whom it ceases to buy must in turn contract their purchases, and so the large country's exports fall; against any employment created by cutting imports must be set the resultant increase in unemployment in export trades. It was further pointed out that while there may be a net gain if the country is the only one increasing its tariffs, these gains disappear as other countries adopt the same policy, to the detriment of its exports. We have already considered these arguments in Chapter IV, when analysing the progress of the cycle. A tariff raised exclusively against the country generating a slump might isolate the slump, or at least greatly reduce its effects on other countries. General tariffs all round are not so good, but even these have the advantage, in the downswing, of cutting the link between international trade and national production. A fall in exports reduces imports not directly but indirectly by reducing production severalfold; if, instead, imports are cut directly by tariffs, the ultimate fall in international trade will still be great, but the fall in production will be smaller. The same argument, however, also applies in the upswing. The case for raising tariffs when the slump starts is also a case for lowering them once the bottom is reached.

Even apart from this general case, which has not been widely recognised, there are also special cases for the tariff as an anti-slump weapon which have gained recognition. First, the slump causes some countries to have acutely passive balances of payments, especially primary producing countries with large fixed interest payments. In the absence of direct import controls such countries would have to face either a violent fall in the foreign exchange value of their currency or a violent fall in income, several times as large as the fall in their exports, through the multiplier linking income and foreign trade. Such countries have no alternative save directly to restrict imports, whether by currency control, by tariff, by quota or by licence. Even if general prohibition of tariffs were desirable and agreeable, this special case would have to be recognised. Secondly, if the slump brings a violent fall in agricultural prices, the consequences may be highly deflationary, as in the United States in 1930–31, and a country may well take steps to prevent its own agricultural prices from falling and spreading depression. This is not necessarily a balance of payments matter at all, nor need it in any way affect other countries; the case is not for reducing agricultural imports, or increasing the domestic output, but for maintaining domestic prices, to prevent spiral effects, and if confined to this, it may be universally beneficial. And thirdly tariffs harm no one if combined with a reflationary monetary policy, and if designed not to reduce imports but simply to prevent them from increasing with reflation. A country may hesitate to take vigorous reflationary action for fear that a consequent increase in imports would denude it of foreign reserves. To seek to restore domestic employment is an act of good behaviour, and no nation is entitled to complain if its neighbour has to control imports because fellow countries are not following its good example. If reflation were pursued internationally tariffs would be unnecessary in this case.

From this has followed the argument that since it seems impossible to get international reflationary action, groups of like-minded countries should be free to act together, setting off additional imports from each other by special arrangements. This brings us to the subject of bilateralism, of which anti-cyclical policy is only a part.

BILATERALISM

In the 19th century the principle of non-discrimination in trade was gradually established, each country being bound to afford all countries any privileges that it afforded to any one of them. The chief protagonist of this principle was Great Britain, which in every trade treaty that it made sought to have a clause, which came to be known as the Most Favoured Nation clause, agreeing that each signatory should have as good treatment in the markets of the other as might be afforded to any other country. Many countries, notably France and the United States, resisted acceptance of the

M.F.N. clause, but its use was gradually extended, and after 1920 non-discrimination was generally accepted to be the most desirable policy.

After 1930 there was a retreat from non-discrimination in favour of bilateral arrangements, whether by way of special currency provisions, or by tariff treatment, by import licensing, or by bulk purchase agreements. The principle of non-discrimination, however, continued to secure wide respect, and not all attempts to defy it were successful. Thus the request of Eastern European grain producers for discriminatory treatment in the cereals markets of Western Europe was rejected, the United States in particular pointing out that such treatment would violate the M.F.N. clause. Again, proposals for customs unions, between Germany and Austria, between the Scandinavian countries, and between Holland and Belgium and Luxembourg were rejected, this time with Great Britain as the principal protester (but the first of these was rejected also on political grounds). On the other hand, both Germany and the United Kingdom made bilateral arrangements with other countries, which were greatly resented elsewhere.

The British protest against customs unions was all the more resented because Britain herself was simultaneously making bilateral arrangements of her own. It has always been felt that customs unions between adjacent countries are a legitimate exception to non-discrimination, and this feeling was strengthened after 1918 by the disruption of the Austro-Hungarian empire. The break-up of that Empire brought into existence a new set of trade barriers, currency and tariff, in a region where previously trade had flowed without restriction, and it was generally felt that it would be best if the new countries could see their way to creating a customs union, maintaining as large as possible a free trade area. No one would argue that the formation of a customs union must increase the welfare either of the world or of the participating nations. Such a union implies discrimination in favour of some against others, and this discrimination may distort the flow of trade out of its natural channels, and may even reduce welfare all round. There is, however, some presumption in favour of countries trading with their neighbours rather than with more distant countries, and a presumption that the increased flow of local trade resulting from removing barriers will do more good than the harmful effects of the discrimination against the more distant ones.

The case is also strong where countries are anxious to industrialise. Successful industrialisation depends on large markets, and if three or four adjacent countries are determined to industralise it is better that they should do so according to an agreement such that their industries are complementary rather than competitive, and that each secures the largest possible local market. Finally apart from the economic considerations, customs unions are welcomed because they are a form of political cooperation, and raise hopes of more. For all these reasons opinion has hardened in favour of recognising customs unions as a legitimate exception to M.F.N. treatment, and even the British Government is unlikely in future to protest against such proposals.

The British urge to bilateralism was different; it was simply a case of exploiting bargaining power. As Great Britain had an unfavourable balance of trade with most countries, the Government felt itself able to insist that countries should buy rather more from Great Britain, so that the share of the latter in a diminished world trade might be increased, and so a number of small countries were made, as we saw earlier, to purchase more British goods. At the same time, the Empire countries were agreeing to increase their preferential margins, and the dependent colonies also were required to give greater preferences to British imports.

We have considered earlier the effects of British bilateralism in diverting trade. The share of empire countries in each other's trade increased, and so did the share of Great Britain in the trade of other countries which gave her discriminatory treatment. There has also recently been some tendency to argue that the net effects on world trade were in general beneficial, and it is this that we must now consider.

In the closing decades of the 19th century and the first three decades of the 20th, a complicated network of multilateral trade had been built up. It can best be described in terms of trade balances. The United Kingdom was entitled to payments for "invisible exports" in the form of shipping and other services, and of interest and dividend payments. The newly developed countries —the tropics and the new regions in the temperate zones settled by European migration—were heavy debtors on "invisible" account, but they met their obligations not so much by having favourable balances with the United Kingdom as by having an export surplus to Europe and the United States, which in turn had an export surplus to the United Kingdom. Thus the U.K. received its payments not directly but indirectly through the multilateral circulation of trade balances. We are greatly indebted to a League of Nations study, *The Network of World Trade*, for a masterly analysis laying bare the framework of the system. In that study the world is divided into six regions, Non-continental Europe (mostly the United Kingdom), Europe, the United States, New Areas (mostly Canada, Australasia and temperate South America), the Tropics, and the Rest (mostly North Africa, Asia and the U.S.S.R.) The merchandise balances of each of these areas is calculated and shown separately.[8]

Two interesting results emerge. The first is clear evidence of the deterioration of multilateral trade between 1928 and 1938. In 1928 world trade amounted to $68,090 millions, and the balances of these six regions with each other to $12,510 millions or 18.4 per cent of world trade. In 1938 world trade amounted to $46,500 millions, and the balances to $7,340 or 15.8 per cent. Bilateral settlements had relatively increased.

The other result is of even clearer significance. The trade balances of Non-Continental Europe with the other regions in these two years were as shown in Table XIV.

TABLE XIV

TRADE BALANCES OF NON-CONTINENTAL EUROPE, 1928 AND 1938

$ million

	1928	1938	Difference
With Tropics	+190	−270	−460
New Areas	−290	−490	−200
Rest	− 80	−140	− 60
Non-Con. Europe	− 10	− 10	0
U.S.A.	−680	−470	+210
Europe	−900	−580	+320
	−1770	−1960	−190

The difference column reveals the dramatic change in the flow of British payments. In 1928 Great Britain received her dues mainly by way of heavy import surpluses from Europe and the United States, to the extent of 89 per cent. But in 1938 payments via these routes were greatly reduced, to 54 per cent, and payments directly from the Tropics, the New Areas and the Rest correspondingly increased. Now this change in flow would not have affected the volume of world trade if it meant only that Britain was buying less from certain regions and correspondingly more from others. But what happened was that Britain bought much less from the U.S.A. and Europe and sold much less to the Tropics, the New Areas and the Rest. These two were inter-related, had Britain continued to buy from the former, they would have bought more from the latter, who in turn would have bought more from Great Britain. The flow of world trade cannot be violently disrupted without deflationary consequences.

Now German bilateralism was different, both in cause and in effect. As we have seen in an earlier chapter, German bilateralism was associated with a reflationary monetary policy. Reflation increases the demand for imports without helping to expand exports. It cannot therefore be pursued for long without control of imports. When the Germans made bilateral arrangements increasing both their imports and their exports, the consequence was not a deflationary diversion of trade, as in the British case, but a reflationary increase in trade which would not have been possible but for the existence of these arrangements. And the Germans could argue that in arranging to buy more they were giving a stimulus to the economies of satellite countries which would promote revival in those countries and so benefit not only Germany but also all other countries which might consequently sell more to the satellites. It is this argument for bilateralism which has most attracted some of its supporters—only in their extravagant claims they usually fail to distinguish between the British experience, which is unfavourable to bilateralism, and the German, arguing as if all bilateralism were of the same nature.

Even the supporters of bilateralism would admit that what is important to their case is reflation. If there could be universal reflation in all countries simultaneously, they would admit that multilateral trade is better for the world than bilateralism, because it makes possible a greater amount of trade and fuller enjoyment of the fruits of international specialisation. They fall back on bilateralism only because they fear that agreement to simultaneous reflationary action cannot be secured, and they are anxious that such individual countries as wish to reflate should be free to pursue unrestricted trade with each other, without the danger that their balances with other countries will deteriorate. To some extent this argument has been accepted internationally, its clearest embodiment being the "scarce currency" clause in the Bretton Woods agreement, which, if generously interpreted, will permit countries to discriminate in their trade against other countries whose policies are having deflationary effects.

But bilateralism designed merely to increase one country's share of world trade at the expense of the rest is of a different order. What is most dangerous in this is the possibility that it may be generally adopted. British supporters of this kind of bilateralism usually argue as if Britain would be permitted to do this without retaliation; or alternatively as if they were confident that in the event of retaliation Great Britain would necessarily be victorious. But this is by no means clear. The United States is a powerful nation which, if it insisted on bilateralism, could do great harm to British prospects in many markets. Indeed it is not clear that Great Britain can find many countries willing to make bilateral agreements with her. Most countries today look to the United States for loans, and for markets, and will not allow themselves to be browbeaten into arrangements of which the United States would disapprove. The argument whether Britain would gain more by bilateralism or by multilateralism is therefore simply academic: the number of countries with which she could pursue a bilateral policy is very limited. Her interest is clearly more in seeking a large total volume of world trade than in adopting methods of trading which are likely to have small appeal. Trade discrimination is acceptable as an anti-slump weapon, as an element in a customs union between adjacent countries, and possibly as an alternative to currency devaluation against a large country with a persistent tendency to have a deflationary export surplus. But it is not likely to be accepted simply as a means of assuring to Great Britain a larger share of the markets of foreign countries than she could win solely on the basis of competition.

STABILISATION

The analysis of bilateralism leads to the same conclusion as the analysis of currency experience and of tariff policy, namely, that the importance of obstacles to the free flow of trade will depend on the degree of stability in the economic system. If international trade is stable it will be freed of obstacles, and will correspondingly be increased. But if it remains subject to fluctuation, countries will take precautions to control it, and its general level will be correspondingly small. We pass therefore to consider measures for increasing international economic stability.

The instability of international trade has followed from the instability of national economies, and would disappear if each country took successful measures to maintain its own stability. This was the point of the proposal sponsored by the International Labour Office in 1931, urging that governments should cooperate in initiating schemes of large-scale public works simultaneously in their own countries, such cooperation being required partly because poor countries would need to be permitted to borrow from wealthier ones, and partly because unilateral action might cause balance of payments positions to deteriorate. The I.L.O. continued to press this proposal throughout the 1930's, and did considerable research into its problems, but the proposal was never even seriously considered by governments.

The other important proposal designed to maintain international trade was that the prices of primary products should be raised. It was clear that the violent fall of these prices after 1929 had had deflationary effects. It did not, however, follow that to raise these prices would be reflationary since, while the violence of the fall had caused the volume of monetary circulation to contract, it was not so obvious that a rise in prices would increase monetary circulation rather than merely divert purchasing power from urban consumers to rural producers. This proposal also failed to win general acceptance.

Nevertheless, in their own interest, producers of primary products began to consider schemes by which their prices could be raised. The most obvious was to restrict output, so that the heavy accumulation of stocks hanging over the market could be reduced, and output brought down to a level nearer to that of consumption. There was nothing new in the principle of output control; in many countries there had long been cartel arrangements with precisely the same object. What was new in the 1930's, was the international cooperation of governments in such schemes. Previous cartel arrangements had been made by the producers themselves, without government participation. But voluntary arrangements between producers are practicable only where the number of producers is small enough for their representatives all to be able to gather together and remove the obstacles. This is the case with many lines of manufacturing industry, and of mining, but it is not the case in agriculture, where the number of farmers of any commodity runs into thousands; in such cases negotiations must be made by governments, and the agreement must be enforced on all farmers by law, if the cartel is to be practicable. The principle of governments participating in such arrangements was violently attacked in some quarters, but with little justification. In industrial countries producers were keeping up their prices by monopolistic arrangements of various kinds, to the detriment of producers of primary commodities; when the latter began to act likewise in defence of themselves, they could not help feeling that the attacks made on their much less successful efforts at cartelisation, on the ground that the participation of governments which was involved put primary cartels into a different and more immoral category, were quite unjustified.

Accordingly international restriction schemes were organised for the following commodities, by agreement between governments: rubber, tin, sugar, wheat (an abortive scheme) and tea (during the war of 1939–45 schemes were added for coffee and sisal). Such schemes were difficult to arrange. It was important that all producing countries should agree to participate, otherwise while some were restricting output others would be expanding and the scheme would fail; e.g. the first sugar restriction scheme failed for this reason. In consequence, some countries were able to hold out against participation unless offered specially favourable terms; quotas came to be allocated not on economic principles but largely on the basis of bargaining power. As a method of regulating the production of commodities the international restriction schemes of the 1930's are certainly not models of economic wisdom.

On the other hand, much criticism was misplaced. For example, these restriction schemes did not reduce world consumption. Output was restricted, but it was merely brought into line with demand, and there is no reason to believe that world consumption would have been significantly (if any) larger in the absence of such schemes. Primary producers would have been somewhat poorer, and industrial producers somewhat wealthier; but since industrial producers are already on the average much better off than primary producers, this is an argument in favour of the schemes. Even so, there is not much in it. The schemes had only very small success in raising prices, and the terms of trade remained throughout the 1930's very heavily adverse to primary producers.

As the decade proceeded a different technique began to be debated, and was actually operated in the case of tin. This was to stabilise prices by creating buffer stocks to be increased in time of slump, and reduced during the boom. This is an immensely superior technique. From the point of view of primary producers, it assures them stability while doing away with the cumbersome and unsatisfactory process of quota bargaining and enforcement. And from the point of view of industrial producers it introduces a new element which restriction schemes do not possess, and which is an important answer to the need of industrial countries for stability. If when a slump begins in an industrial country, that country buys less primary products, primary producers in turn are forced to reduce their purchases of industrial products, and so the slump spreads cumulatively. But if instead, when the demand of the industrial country falls off, buffer stock authorities enter the market for primary products and maintain the demand, then the primary producers can continue to buy as much industrial products as before, and the spread of the slump is arrested. The buffer stock technique is an international mechanism which automatically maintains purchasing power. In a boom it sells stocks, and receives and hoards money, thus checking the inflationary tendency. In a slump it buys stocks, thus putting money into circulation and checking the deflationary tendency. From this point of view it does not matter what stocks are held, i.e. whether they are stocks of primary commodities or of manufactures or of both. What matters is a mechanism for stabilising demand.

The creation of international buffer stocks would be the greatest single contribution that could be made to international stability. If the machinery for operating such stocks had existed in 1929 there would have been no major slump, much higher standards of living all round, and no second world war.

Ideas percolate slowly into men's minds, and only against fierce resistance. The international buffer stock technique has already been considered by an international committee since the war, and rejected, the difficulties in operating it being exaggerated.[9] Its value to mankind is, nevertheless so obvious that its ultimate adoption, say within the next twenty or thirty years is most probable. All over the world men demand that violent fluctuations in activity should be abolished, and the buffer stock technique is so far the only automatic mechanism which anyone has suggested that goes a long way towards maintaining international stability. Unless some new and better device appears, its adoption is therefore only a matter of time.

CONCLUSION

We are left, therefore, with the conclusion that the level of obstacles to international trade will depend on whether or not measures are adopted to promote stability. If such measures are not taken, countries will insist on the right to control their currencies and their tariff policies, and to make bilateral arrangements; international trade will be viewed with suspicion, as one of the ways in which depression is transmitted from country to country, and its level will be low. But if stability is assured—and it can be, and sooner or later must be—the principal incentive to the creation of obstacles to international trade will be removed, and, men being bye and large and in the long run reasonable, international trade will once more be valued and cultivated, and the experience of the 1930's will prove to have been only a passing phase in economic history. The prospects are not too bad. The U.S.A. whose fluctuations dominate the world economy, has learnt much since 1929. Agricultural prices can no longer topple catastrophically, because the parity formula puts a floor to them, and nearly all responsible Americans now seem to agree that it is the duty of their government to pursue a budgetary policy which will minimise industrial fluctuations. The world will yet see many slumps; but it is unlikely to repeat the horrors of the 1930's.

If reasonable stability is assured, the barriers to international trade will be relaxed. Movements in the volume of trade will then depend on the working out of long term trends in world economic development, to the consideration of which we now turn.

CHAPTER XIII

INTERNATIONAL TRADE: TRENDS

THE growth of international trade in the nineteenth century was associated with a great increase in international specialisation. This is not to say that trade grew faster than production. British trade grew faster than British production throughout the nineteenth century, as the figures in the Appendix show. But world trade, at least in the forty years before 1913, was growing more slowly than world production. From 1850 to 1913, world production of primary products increased steadily at about 3.2 per cent per annum;[1] and from 1876/80 to 1913 the cumulative annual increase[2] in manufacturing production was 4.1 per cent, in trade in manufactures 3.3 per cent and in trade in primary products 3.4 per cent. World production and trade in primary products increased in almost exact proportions, but world trade in manufactures lagged behind world production of manufactures. Nevertheless, international specialisation was occurring rapidly, some countries curtailing primary and expanding industrial production, and becoming net importers of primary and net exporters of manufactured products, while other specialised in exporting primary and importing manufactured commodities.

In the inter-war period, and more particularly in the thirties, this process was halted. International specialisation was diminished and an increased production was not associated with increased trade. To some extent this was obviously due to the growth of barriers to trade, discussed in the previous chapter. But it was also widely believed that other long term factors were at work dissociating increased production from trade, and diminishing permanently the relative importance of international trade. It is this belief that we must now examine.

Looking at the problem conceptually, there are two main ways in which the growth of international specialisation might be checked. The first is on the side of the demand for primary products. A declining rate of growth of the demand for primary products from the industrial countries might so change the terms of trade against such products that primary producers were driven to industrialise. Alternatively, if the supply of primary products ceased to grow rapidly, the terms of trade might move in favour of primary products, and industrial countries be driven to preserve and increase their primary production. We can thus analyse the problem in terms of the demand and supply of primary products, and will find that all the trends fit into this framework.

But first we must consider the theoretical possibility that there may be more or less specialisation not only as between primary and manufactured products, but also as between some primary and other primary, and between some manufactures and other manufactures. Of the interchange of primary products for primary products there does not seem to be much to say. It is large. On one estimate[3] it amounts to 36 per cent of world trade, an estimate which we can compare with an alternative calculation[4] that the non-industrial countries import 26 per cent of the primary products entering into world trade. It is large, but there seems no reason to expect it either to grow or to diminish. For the exchange of primary products is determined largely by geographical factors. This does not mean that this exchange cannot be altered. For example, the discovery of coal may cause a coal importing country to diminish its exports of agricultural products and its imports of minerals, both of which are primary products, and so to diminish international specialisation. But since such changes depend largely on unpredictable scientific advances, there is not much that can usefully be said about them.

The exchange of some manufactures against others is less important, but there is more to be said about it. The estimate that it accounts for 18 per cent of international trade[5] is to be compared with the alternative calculation that manufacturing countries import 35 per cent of the manufactures entering into world trade.

Now the principle of comparative costs operates in manufacturing industry no less than it does in comparing industry with agriculture. Industries differ in their requirements of fuel, raw materials, capital, skill, and so forth, and the advantages of some countries are therefore greater in some lines of production than in others. But when this has been said it must nevertheless be added that the proportion of manufactures in international trade does not seem to have altered much since the 1870's; the indices of values, as we have seen, have kept in step, and the quantum relations have varied mainly with changes in the terms of trade. It is true that if the principle of comparative costs were operated, the exchange of manufactures for manufactures could greatly increase. But there is not much reason to expect any notable change of policy here in the near future.

What therefore is most likely to affect the degree of international specialisation and the level of world trade is the relation between primary products and manufactures. If we study the changing trends in the demand and supply of primary products we shall get as near as is feasible to an understanding of trends in world trade.

Let us then begin with the demand for primary products in international trade. We have already seen that the trade in primary products is dominated by the demands of industrial countries. The principal problem is therefore the rate of growth of the demand of such countries. We have seen also that the trade in primary products was increasing before 1913 at a rate equal on the average to rather more than three-quarters of the increase in world manufacturing production. We may thus analyse the possibilities in three stages. The trade in primary products depends (a) on the continued growth of already industrialised countries (b) on whether the ratio of the increase of demand for primary products to the increase of manufacturing production continues to be maintained for such countries, and (c) on the effects of the industrialisation of new countries.

THE GROWTH OF OLD COUNTRIES

The stagnation of the United States in the 1930's gave birth to the idea that old, developed countries must slow down in their growth. It had long been argued that, with increasing wealth, savings must increase, and the rate of interest show a permanent tendency to decline, and the apparent exhaustion of investment opportunities in the United States gave wide currency to these opinions. In fact U.S. stagnation in the 1930's has no relevance to the argument. The sudden collapse cannot be explained in terms of long trends which must have been maturing over several decades, and in any case, the United Kingdom, a much older country, was progressing quite rapidly at the very time when the theory was becoming most popular. For evidence of declining trends we must take much longer periods, and not confine ourselves to the experience of a single cycle.[6]

The expectation that a mature economy should grow slowly is based on several arguments. First it is argued that it is natural that a newly developing country should have great opportunities for investment in improving its basic public facilities. Roads must be built, railways, harbours, hospitals, schools, and all the other needs of a modern community. When once these are built, the need for further investment in these lines diminishes, capital accumulation falls, and wealth grows more slowly. This argument has been countered vigorously. In the first place, one has never reached the stage that the basic services have been built once and for all, and that further building is confined to replacement. The basic services themselves change continually through technological improvement—much capital is invested in canals; then these are scrapped and replaced by heavy investment in railways; and these in turn give way to some extent to road and air transport, with their correspondingly heavy investment. The degree of technological change is such that if it is true that a mature country needs to invest less in basic services than a new country, the difference need not be great. Only if technological progress were to halt would mature and new countries diverge greatly in this respect. And secondly, even if it may be true that mature countries need to invest less in basic services, this should cause no decline if it merely results in their spending more in other ways, including the provision of consumer goods and services.

What does the relevant evidence show? Has the rate of interest been falling, with capital saturation? The rate of interest does not, in fact, throw much light on the situation. The rate of interest depends on the demand for and the supply of funds, and if it were lower it would not necessarily be evidence of a lower demand for funds, but might equally be due to a larger supply. In fact, the rate of interest in Great Britain has not shown a secular tendency to decline; we have already observed that it has moved with prices, rising and falling alternatively over long periods. Its average level in the inter-war period was higher than it had been for a hundred years.

What then, has happened to savings? Has the rate of saving shown a secular tendency to decline? Evidence on this subject is scanty. The most complete figures are Kuznets's figures of net capital formation in the United States, which are included in the Appendix. They show net saving (as a percentage of income) at its highest in the decade of 1889 to 1898, and declining fairly steadily since then. Figures for other countries are not continuous. Colin Clark estimates that in Great Britain[7] the percentage of income saved in the years 1860–69 was 16.6, the figure falling to 12.2 in 1907 and 7.2 in 1929. Plotting such data as he can find for different countries at different dates,[8] he draws a curve relating savings per head to real income per head, which show savings increasing as a percentage of income up to an income of about 1,200 "international units" per occupied person (an I.U. represents the average purchasing of the U.S. dollar over the years 1925–34) and thereafter declining. The conclusion seems plausible, and supports the argument that as countries grow they invest after a while a smaller part of their income.

But is net saving the relevant phenomenon? As capital equipment grows depreciation allowances become an ever greater part of the national income, and if net capital formation declines it seems to be only because depreciation increases in importance while gross capital formation remains constant. Thus Kuznets's figures for gross capital formation in the United States, in current prices, bear the following ratio to gross national income:

	%		%		%
1869–78	18.9	1894–03	21.1	1919–28	20.8
1874–83	19.0	1899–08	20.1	1924–33	17.3
1879–88	19.2	1904–13	19.7	1929–38	14.2
1884–93	20.8	1909–18	20.7		
1889–98	21.3	1914–23	21.7		

There is a fall after 1929; but no evidence of secular decline before that.

Even this, however, is not what we are seeking. Savings may be a constant proportion of income, and yet income may be declining because saving is declining, not in proportion to national income, but in terms of its own rate of growth. The following figures show that the annual rate of growth of gross capital formation, measured in 1929 prices, has declined secularly:

	%		%
1869/78 to 74/83	8.0	1884/93 to 89/98	3.7
74/83 „ 79/88	6.3	89/98 „ 94/03	3.3
79/88 „ 84/93	6.2	94/03 „ 99/08	3.6

	%		%
1899/08 to 04/13	4.0	1914/23 to 19/28	2.8
1904/13 „ 09/18	3.4	19/28 „ 24/33	—2.3
09/18 „ 14/23	2.0	24/33 „ 29/38	—4.6

The rate declined from the seventies to the nineties, was then stable until the first world war, and then declined again, and the rate of growth of gross national income, in 1929 prices, was very similar to this. Gross savings have not declined as a percentage of national income, but nevertheless the rates of growth of capital accumulation and of national income have been declining secularly.

How has this been associated with the declining growth of population, which is the second argument usually advanced to support the expectation of secular decline? In its more complex form this argument postulates that income per head should rise most rapidly in countries when their population is growing most, because population growth stimulates great investment, and this keeps the economy buoyant. Terborgh[9] produces diagrams to dispute this argument, and though there is a slight correlation between the rate of growth of population and the rate of growth of real income per head, as calculated by Kuznets, it is too small to bear much weight. In the U.S.A. the rate of growth of real income per head seems to have been steady, when cyclical and longer fluctuations are eliminated; it was the same in the 80's, at the beginning of the century, and in the 20's. The long-term decline in the rate of growth of total production is due mainly to the decline in the rate of growth of population and not to declining growth per head.[10] Now the rate of population increase has been declining for some time among most European peoples; in Great Britain since 1881, and in the United States since about the same time (Chart VI). It should not be concluded that this decline is permanent. In Great Britain the rate increased up to 1821, then declined to 1861, rose again to 1881 and then started to fall again; and no one can be certain that the rate of increase will never again turn upwards. All that we can say is that at present there seems to be a tendency for the increase of populations in the older industrial countries to decline, and that we should expect a corresponding decline in the rate of growth of their production.

Thirdly, in countries not yet industrialised there is necessarily greater scope for increasing industrial production because workers can be transferred from primary to industrial production, whereas

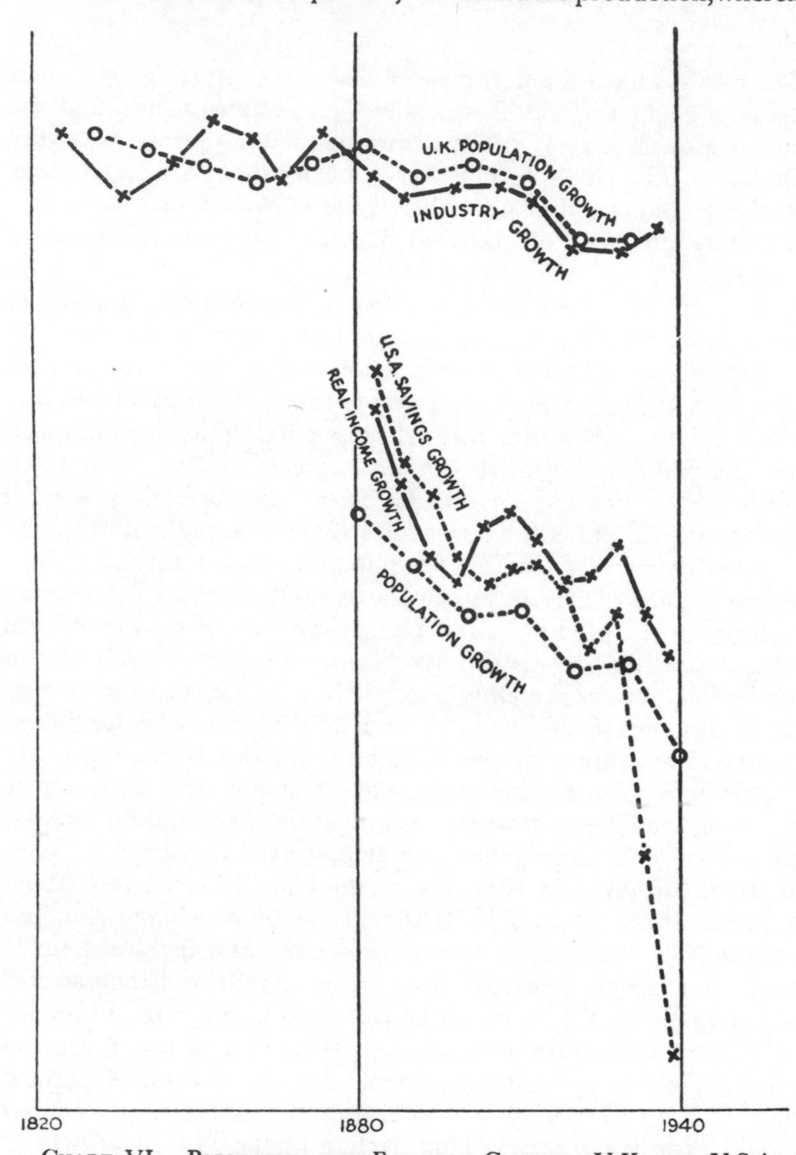

CHART VI. POPULATION AND ECONOMIC GROWTH, U.K. AND U.S.A.

Scales for population are four times other scales. Origins are different. For figures see Statistical Appendix, series 15, 22, 23, 24 and25.

in highly industrialised countries no further transfer is possible, and the growth of industrial production depends solely on population increase and technical progress. Thus we should expect the demand of young countries for primary products through international trade to grow more rapidly than the demand after the transfer from primary to industrial production has been completed.

Fourthly, as real income increases, the demand for services grows more rapidly than the demand for primary and industrial products. Colin Clark has shown that at the highest levels of real income the percentage of the population engaged in industrial production tends to decline,[11] and this would support the expectation that the rate of growth of industrial production should decline as countries mature.

What, then, is the evidence from industrial production itself? It is marshalled in the Appendix. The most complete figures are those of Great Britain. They show the peak growth of industrial production from the cycle ending in 1846 to the cycle of 1853; thereafter the rate of growth is smaller, and after 1874 does not greatly exceed the rate of growth of population. The growth of imports bears this out; the peak here is 1874, but thereafter the rate of growth is remarkably smaller than in the earlier part of the nineteenth century. The series for the U.S.A. are neither so long nor so conclusive, but if we omit the remarkable growth from the cycle of 1899 to the cycle of 1907, we can say that the rate of growth seems to have been declining from 1874 to 1913, and this conclusion for industry as a whole can be made more confidently in the light of what is known of the behaviour of individual industries.[12] The German picture is quite different. After a short setback in the seventies, the rate of growth increased steadily until 1907: here are the phenomena of the still "young" country, rather than the ageing country.

It is important to be sceptical about all these figures. All measures of physical volume tend to be distorted by weighting. Indices of industrial production, in particular, tend to underestimate industrial production in later years, relatively to early years, because they give too much weight to old "staple" industries, whose growth is small, and too little weight to new industries, whose growth is vigorous. Yet even when this is remembered, there does seem to be enough evidence for the view that as industrialisation proceeds it reaches a point beyond which the rate of growth shows a secular decline. In so far, therefore, as the demand for primary products depends on the growth of industrial production in older countries, that demand should increase at a declining rate, owing chiefly to failing population growth.

THE TREND OF PRIMARY DEMAND

In fact, there is reason to believe that the demand for primary products should decline in these countries even if their production maintained its growth, and therefore to an extent greater than is required by the declining growth of their industrial production. There are two reasons for this, one relating to foodstuffs, and the other to raw materials.

The demand for food does not grow proportionately with income. The decline is most marked in the demand for cereals where it is not just relative but absolute, bread consumption per head falling steadily as income grows. The decline in bread consumption is associated with increased consumption of other foods, especially livestock products, and farmers are able to maintain their incomes and the value of their lands if they can switch over to livestock production. Nevertheless, it seems to have been generally considered in the inter-war period that the decline in the proportion of income spent on food was one of the causes of farmers' troubles.

The future here is uncertain. Nutritional investigations and propaganda have tended to stress the value of consuming foods which make heavy demands on cereal production, to feed livestock, and many countries have decided to subsidise the food consumption of special groups, such as expectant mothers and babies. There has been in consequence since 1939 a per capita increase in the indirect demand for cereals, and if such policies are maintained farmers may find the cereal demand maintained much longer than they had hoped. The fears of the world for 1947 and 1948 are food shortage, not a glut, and this is partly due to increased per capita consumption. However, this phase can only be transitory; sooner or later even the lowest income groups, in old industrial countries, must be receiving the "optimum diet", at the present rate of progress, and then farmers will be faced once more with only a slow per capita increase in demand for food, if not indeed stagnation.

Similar forces are at work with raw materials. Technical progress finds constantly new ways of economising on raw materials, finding new methods of getting the same product from a smaller amount of material. The situation, it is true, is complex. These economies, whether they simply reduce materials per unit of output, or utilise waste products or substitute synthetic for natural materials, may expand elastic demands for finished products so much in some cases as to increase the demand for raw materials. With foodstuffs there is a limit to human consumption which would make such economies fatal to farmers, but with raw materials there is no limit to the possible expansion of demand as costs fall. Nevertheless, the point remains that with the passage of time a unit of output requires a smaller volume of raw materials, and therefore the ratio between the increase in manufacturing production and the increase in demand for raw materials must increase.

When we add together a tendency for the rate of industrial growth to decline, and a tendency for the ratio of growth of primary demand to industrial growth also to decline, we must expect the demand of old industrial countries to show a long term deceleration. This is amply borne out by the figures for Great Britain. Imports increased rapidly in the first half of the nineteenth century and up to the cycle of 1874. Thereafter the rate of growth declines steadily, except for a small spurt in the cycle ending in 1899. As this was a free trade country, its statistics are particularly useful; it is also most interesting to observe that the rate of growth of imports was much greater under protection than after free trade was adopted: tariffs are less important determinants of international trade than are the long term factors such as we are discussing in this chapter.

This is not to say that tariffs are not important. On the contrary, it is important to world trade that industrial countries should not place obstacles in the way of importing primary produce. And their tariffs on primary produce are more important than their manufacturing tariffs. For example, most economists attack the U.S. manufacturing tariff as if a reduction of that tariff would make a big difference to U.S. imports of manufactures. This is not likely. The U.K., even at the height of its free trade career, had only a small import of manufactures, and it is unlikely that the U.S.A., whose range of manufacturing industry is much wider, and whose competitive power is much greater, would be a great importer of manufactures under any circumstances. With lower tariffs she might import a few more luxury articles, like tweeds, china, and other commodities to which foreign make adds prestige, but very little of the staples of manufacturing industry. The American tariffs that matter are the tariffs on such commodities as wool, sugar, and copper. Almost equally important are American subsidies to agricultural exports, which reduce America's net import of primary products, and retard agricultural expansion in smaller countries where such expansion would increase the demand for manufactures in international trade.

INDUSTRIALISATION OF NEW COUNTRIES

Changes in tariffs could, however, have only a temporary effect. The trend is for old countries to decline in their rate of growth, and for their demand for primary products to decline still more in rate of growth. Against these forces in old countries making for declining rates of growth, we must set the results of the industrialisation of new countries, which are of the opposite order.

There has been much speculation as to the effects on international trade of the industrialisation of new countries. Some have argued that if capital is invested in old countries like India and China the effect will be to increase both primary and industrial production, and that in consequence the export of primary products will increase and the import of manufactures decline. This argument is particularly plausible when applied to relatively stagnant and overpopulated countries. Their overpopulation means that they can increase manufacturing output without reducing primary output; and as development proceeds the increased productivity of primary industry may be so great that primary and secondary production grow *pari passu*. Others have shown[13] that as countries industrialise they increase their imports of manufactures, and that modern industrial countries tend to have larger per capita imports of manufactures than have undeveloped primary producers.

It is true that countries increase their primary production in their first stages of development. It is also true that as they industrialise they import more manufactures. But it is nevertheless true that as industrialisation proceeds and the numbers engaged in industry grow proportionately, a country becomes a *net* importer of primary products and a *net* exporter of manufactures, and it is with these net effects that we are concerned.

The statistics show this clearly.[14] For example, counting in millions of dollars, the United States in 1881/85 exported net 250 primary products and imported net 142 manufactures; this situation altered gradually, and by 1936/38 she imported net 246 primary, and exported net 519 manufactures. Japan is another example; comparing 1891/95 and 1936/38 a net export of 8 primary changes to a net import of 309, and a net import of 5 manufactures changes to a net export of 272. The only clear exception to this is the U.S.S.R. There industrialisation occurred under a regime which kept foreign trade under strict control, and at levels wel below those of 1913. However, there is no reason to doubt that, in the absence of control, the trend would have been the same, for whereas between 1913 and 1937 the increase in agricultural production barely exceeded the growth of population, manufacturing production was multiplied four fold. There can be no doubt that in the absence of such rigid controls the net effect of the industrialisation of new countries must be to increase the demand for primary products in international trade, and the supply of manufactures.

Now the process of world development did not cease in the inter-war period. Taking 1913 as 100 the manufacturing indices[15] in 1937 for the old countries stood well below those of the new: the United States stood at 186, Germany 138, U.K. 128, France 124; but the world index exceeded all these, standing at 196; and this was because new countries had increased at an enormous pace: U.S.S.R. 772 (the official figure), Japan 551, India 235, Sweden 229, Finland 300, and so on. The declining growth of old countries had been largely offset by the rapid progress of new countries.

The future level of international trade obviously depends greatly on the continuation of this process. If more and more countries industrialise, the demand for primary products in international trade must grow. But if new countries do not industrialise the rate of growth of international trade must decline.

The future of industrialisation itself depends to a great extent on the future of international investment. Russia has industrialised without borrowing, but only at great cost in human suffering, and not many countries will wish to repeat her experience. We must therefore pause here to consider the prospects of international investment.

INTERNATIONAL INVESTMENT

In the 1930's international investment ceased, and capital repayment to the creditor countries exceeded new loans. This was due largely to the effects of the slump. In the first place, Germany and primary producing countries had been the chief borrowers in the 1920's; with the collapse of Germany and of primary prices from 1929, these countries went out of the market for new capital. Secondly relations between debtors and creditors became very strained. Debtors, unable to pay, defaulted, and made foolish and rude remarks in doing so which forgot how convenient it had been to be able to borrow; creditors were correspondingly disgusted, and unwilling to make new loans. Thirdly the slump badly affected the position of the United Kingdom by diminishing her invisible exports. She ceased to have a disposable surplus to lend, and so ended her long career as a capital exporter. This role passed to the United States, who, fourthly, had no well organised capital export market, or tradition of lending, and was still smarting under her first unfavourable experiences.

During the 1930's it was sometimes argued that this collection of circumstances would finally end international investment. There is, however, no reason to expect this. Creditors have often burnt their fingers before, and nevertheless returned to lending as soon as prices have risen and profitability returned. Memories are short. If economic conditions warrant, the United States and some of the smaller creditor countries will once more lend. In the United States the capital market is not so well adapted for foreign lending. It seems that most American foreign lending will be done via government agencies, such as the Import-Export Bank, or direct government loans, or the U.S. contribution to the World Bank. The methods may be different from those of Great Britain in the past, but the amount will not necessarily be smaller.

It has further been argued that while industrial countries can lend easily for developing primary production elsewhere, lending to develop industry creates peculiar complications, for three reasons; that direct investment in industry is not so easy as direct investment in agriculture, that industry does not so easily create an exportable surplus as agriculture, and that the creditors cannot so easily receive dividend and sinking fund payments in the form of manufactures as they can in the form of primary products.

It is true that direct investment in industry is not as simple as direct investment in agriculture. Plantation companies could be floated in London directly in the capital market, and so could mining companies, but the London market has never been so directly interested in promoting factory industry abroad. The importance of this must not, however, be exaggerated. Direct investment in productive enterprise has never been a large part of foreign investment. Most of the foreign money has gone to develop public utility services, either by loan to government or by direct investment in railway and electricity enterprises. These are just as necessary to a country whether it is developing primary or secondary industry, and so the main flow of foreign investment need not be affected by the change from primary to industrial development. Capital for productive enterprise has usually been financed from local savings, and it is these which will continue to bear the main burden. Industry has also an additional source of capital, namely the establishment of branch factories in new countries by companies already operating in old industrial centres. This has been one of the principal sources of new factory enterprise in Latin America and in many other new countries. Industrial development is unlikely to be held up because of technical difficulties in raising capital.

As for the creation of an exportable surplus it simply is not true that it is easier to create an exportable surplus of agricultural than of industrial products. All industrial countries have achieved this in the past, witness the figures just quoted for the U.S.A. and for Japan. It is not merely possible but usually necessary to create an export surplus in industry because the scale on which industrial operations must be conducted if they are to be economic frequently exceeds the local market for any one commodity.

More relevant is the argument that, as the creditor countries are themselves manufacturers, they will be reluctant to receive an exportable surplus in the form of manufactures. Here there are several things to be said. The first is that the creditor countries were just as reluctant to receive payment in agricultural products. Their farmers protested, and in many countries secured for themselves heavy protection. The problems created by industrialisation overseas are in this respect no different from those created by the development of primary production overseas. It is true that in the latter case the problem was eased by growing populations at home; but it could equally be eased by an expansion of demand for industrial products, which operates within no such limits as restrict the demand for foodstuffs. What eased the acceptance of payment was the recognition of the principle of comparative costs. Creditor countries found that they benefited by reducing their production of some commodities and by concentrating on others, in accordance with the principle of comparative costs, which, as we have already argued, is as potent in comparing different industries as in comparing industry and agriculture. Adjustments are always painful, especially if they are resisted rather than facilitated, but they are possible, and old industrial countries can adjust to the development of new ones if they try. Moreover it is not necessary that the creditor should receive its payment directly from the debtor in the form of goods produced by the debtor. We saw earlier that the U.K. received her dues not directly but indirectly. The debtors sold to whichever countries wished their wares; and the U.K. bought from whichever countries were producing her requirements. Payment was settled by the system of multilateral trade, which minimises adjustments of this kind. And finally, once a country has become a creditor, and is entitled to receive payments, it is no longer open to that country to decide whether or not it shall have an import surplus. Fears that the U.S. policy of heavy protection will prove inconsistent with her creditor status are unfounded. If a creditor country will not import more, it will have to export less; an import surplus is bound to emerge if debtors have to make payments, and all that the creditor can decide is whether it should come through larger imports or through smaller exports. The experience of the United Kingdom is ample evidence of this. The U.K. began to develop a large income from invisible items just about the same time as the rate of growth of her imports began to decline. All that then happened was that the growth of her exports declined even faster. The U.S.A. has become a creditor country, and will develop an import surplus. Her people can choose whether adjustment must fall principally on industries producing for export or on those that would compete with imports. But they cannot avoid the adjustment.

It follows from this digression that failure of international investment is not likely to hold up the industrialisation of new countries. The rate of growth in old countries may decline, but some, if not all, of this decline will be offset by the emergence of new countries in the future as it has been in the past. The rate of growth of world manufacturing shows no such downward tendency as the rate of growth of manufactures in the U.K. or the U.S.A.

In so far, therefore, as new countries do not take any special steps to curtail their international trade, but develop on the pattern of say Japan rather than the U.S.S.R., then the demand for primary products in international trade should be maintained. The level of trade must then depend on the supply of primary products, on the terms of trade, and on the effects on demand and supply of changes in the terms of trade.

SUPPLY OF PRIMARY PRODUCTS

According to Snyder's calculation, the production of primary products increased from 1850 to 1913 at a cumulative rate of over 3 per cent per annum. Two forces were mainly responsible; increasing productivity, and the opening up of new areas by migration.

Material on the productivity of primary industry is not very satisfactory. Figures collected by Colin Clark[16] stress the importance of increased productivity, at least in advanced countries. Thus productivity per worker in the U.S.A. is estimated to have increased between 1870 and 1930 at a cumulative annual rate of 1.5 per cent in agriculture and slightly less than 1.5 per cent in manufacturing. Other figures do not show so great an increase as this whether for the United States or elsewhere. Nevertheless it is clear that technological progress is no less important in primary production than in industry.

A greater part of the increase since 1850, however, has been due to the increase in numbers engaged rather than in their productivity. This increase was dominated by migration from Europe to overseas countries, which came to its peak in the decade before the war when about a million emigrated every year from Europe. After the war, emigration was restricted. In the United States, where the agricultural frontier had been closed for fifty years, restrictions were applied in 1921, giving Europe a quota of about 360,000, and again tightened in 1924 reducing the European quota to about 150,000. In fact in the 1930's imigration to the United States averaged much less than 100,000 per annum.

There does not seem to be much prospect of European emigration being resumed on the pre-1914 scale. The spaces that were then empty are now either filled, or else considered to be unsuitable for settlement. There may still be room for some expansion of the agricultural acreage (we are considering here only immigration for developing primary production) in Australasia and in temperate South America, but there seems no reason at all to expect that the area will prove to be large or that it will give rise to large scale migration. Emigration of non-Europeans is a more doubtful matter. There is much room in the islands of South East Asia; the three islands of Borneo, Sumatra and New Guinea have an area nearly one-third that of the United States, and are still largely unoccupied. There are also very large areas in Africa which cannot be occupied until means of eliminating the tsetse fly are perfected. Emigration of non-Europeans is today held up by political restrictions rather than by lack of empty spaces, and the future of such restrictions is unpredictable.

In these matters there can be no certainty. Scientific changes may make it possible to cultivate areas which are now beyond the margin. Still more, agriculture is as yet only on the verge of its scientific revolution. Even if only what is already known were applied generally throughout world agriculture, eliminating the primitive techniques of Asia and Africa and of much of Europe and America, the increase in agricultural output per man would be phenomenal. We are fairly safe in saying that there will be some increase in productivity, and that even if there is no increase in area and no scientific revolution the annual increase in world production of primary commodities can easily attain a rate of 2 per cent. If science is widely applied, the increase may be much greater.

TERMS OF TRADE

We are thus left with two imponderables. The future depends on the one hand on the rate of industrialisation of new countries, and on the other hand, on the growth of productivity in primary production. Some observers believe that the further industrialisation of Eastern Europe, of Russia, of China and of India will be immense and rapid; and that, with the cessation of migration, the growth of primary production will be relatively small. They therefore expect the terms of trade to move rather substantially in favour of primary commodities. Other observers are more doubtful of the prospects of rapid industrial development in Asia, and expect a rapid increase of agricultural productivity, with the terms of trade moving substantially against primary commodities. The reader may take his choice.

The pattern of international trade will depend on the outcome, which will affect the volume of trade in primary products, the volume of trade in manufactures, the nature of trade in manufactures, and the relative prosperity of different countries. The stability of the world economy may also be dependent on the outcome.

The volume of trade in primary products will be large if the terms of trade move against them, and smaller if it moves in their favour. If primary products are cheap, industrial countries will have less concern for their agriculture, but if they are dear, agriculture will be maintained, and international specialisation diminished. It is possible that industrial production may grow so much more rapidly than primary production, and primary commodities become so dear, that world trade in them is absolutely reduced because the new countries keep more and more of their own supplies, while the old countries revert more and more to feeding themselves. This is akin to the old Malthusian fear. It may happen, but with so much scientific knowledge still not yet applied to agriculture, it seems even less likely today than it was at the beginning of the nineteenth century.

The volume of trade in manufactures will depend on what happens to the volume of trade in primary commodities, and to the terms of trade. Given the terms of trade, it is likely to grow because the demand for primary commodities in world trade is likely to grow. But it will be so much the larger if primary commodities are dear, and so much the smaller if primary commodities are cheap. In any case, the trade in manufactures will change in nature; trade will shift away from the simpler consumer goods, which the new countries will be making for themselves, to heavy industrial products, to goods that can only be made cheaply on a large scale, and to products of expert craftsmanship.

This shift will affect the relative prosperity of different countries. Industrial countries that are well suited to the production of the kind of goods for which demand will grow may benefit even if the terms of trade are moving, in a general sense, against manufactures. For while other industrial countries will be severely hit, in having to give up much more for their imports, the terms of trade may nevertheless be improving for specialised manufactures, and for those industrial countries that keep well in the lead.

Prosperity depends as much on flexibility as it does on prices, not only in this respect, but in others too. Thus, if the terms of trade move against primary products, industrial countries may gain quite considerably, because they will need to give less exports for their imports. But they will not get the fullest benefit in real income if this results simply in unemployment in their export trades, as it did in the inter-war years. And, indeed, they will even be poorer if the weakness of agricultural prices turns slumps into great depressions, and causes long spells of unemployment. For these two reasons industrial countries might have been much better off in the inter-war years if the terms of trade had been less favourable to industrial products.

If industrial countries become more flexible and learn to control their slumps, an adverse movement of the terms of trade must be unprofitable. But if this is itself due to the expansion of industry elsewhere (and not just to a smaller supply of primary products), there is to be set on the other side the gain from the widening of the market for manufactures. As the world industrialises the opportunities for specialisation grow. World industrialisation must benefit everybody, provided that it does not cause primary products to become relatively dearer. The industrialisation of the world up to 1914 clearly did not hurt anybody, though some gained more than others. International specialisation grew, and, at any rate after 1880, the supply of primary products did not lag behind.

The course of the terms of trade in the last century or so is most interesting. Figures have been collected in the Appendix showing the terms of trade between British imports and exports since 1811. This is not the same as the terms of trade between primary and manufactured products, because the U.K. imports and exports some of each, but it is a useful first approximation. Chart VII shows the result.

In the first half of the 19th century the rate of growth of industry was high. Primary production, however, did not keep pace, and the terms of trade moved steadily against manufactures—this is the age when Malthusian fears were born, and the Law of Diminishing Returns considered to be the most important of all economic principles. The relative fall of manufacturing prices continued for nearly the whole of the century, the terms of trade falling from 128 in the cycle ending in 1825 to their lowest point of 84 in the cycle of 1883. Thereafter they began to rise, fairly steadily, and the high levels of the inter-war period appear, in a chart, to be no more than the natural continuation of a process begun thirty years before the war.

What caused the terms of trade to move against primary products after 1883? There is no doubt of the answer: the opening up of new countries as the result of migration, capital investment, and improvements in transport. Men rushed overseas to these new opportunities in increasing numbers right up to 1914, and as their produce came on to the market its price fell.

Was this migration excessive, and was this the reason why the terms of trade continued to move adversely during the 1920's? The rate of growth of primary production was not excessive from 1913 to 1929—it rose to 134—either when compared with the pre-war rate of growth of over 3 per cent per annum, or when compared with the growth of manufacturing, which rose to 153. Nevertheless it does seem to have been excessive when compared

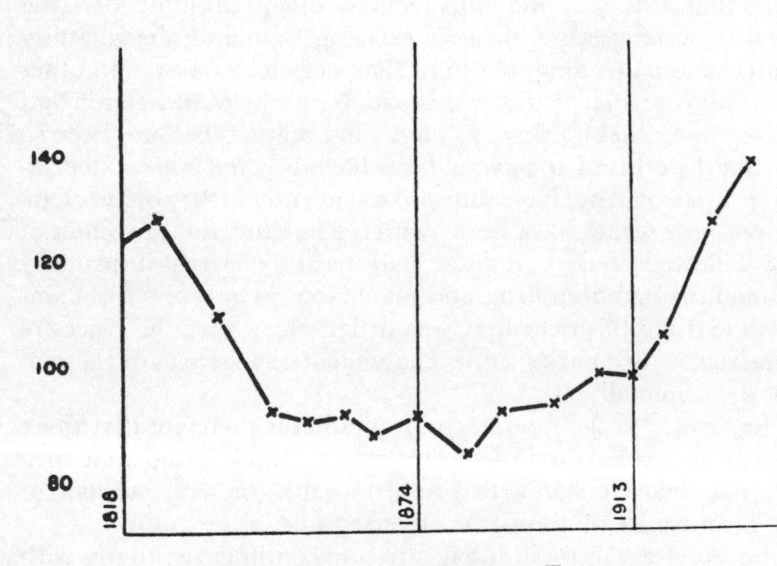

CHART VII. U.K. TERMS OF TRADE.

Export prices divided by import prices. 1913 = 100.

with the growth of population. The production of food in overseas countries, stimulated by the war, continued to grow after the war at too high a rate, in view of the return to normal of European production, and in consequence wheat prices were weakening already in the second half of the twenties. This was also the case with sugar. And to this was added the over-expansion of some other commodities not connected with population growth, such as rubber and tin. We have already seen that it was this insecurity in the markets for primary commodities that was so decisive in converting the crisis of 1929 into a major depression.

CONCLUSION

This is the answer to the fundamental question which any survey of this period raises. Its misfortunes were due principally to the fact that the production of primary commodities after the war was somewhat in excess of demand. It was this which, by keeping the terms of trade unfavourable to primary producers, kept the trade in manufactures so low, to the detriment of such countries as the U.K., even in the twenties, and it was this which pulled the world economy down in the early thirties. To say this is not of course to argue that this was the only source disequilibrium; banking structures were insecure, the gold exchange standard, the volatility of international lending, the high level of indebtedness, and other factors all contributed to the debacle. Nevertheless the significant point remains that if primary commodity markets had not been so insecure the crisis of 1929 would not have become a great depression. Prices would not have slumped as violently as they did in 1930, and recovery would have been swifter. The same result would not have followed if the situation had been reversed—if primary commodities had been firm, and manufactures insecure; for it was the violent fall of prices that was deflationary, and the prices of manufactures are not as subject to violent change as are those of primary commodities.

The answer to the fundamental question is therefore that there is an *ad hoc* explanation of the inter-war troubles; and that they were not linked either with pre-war trends, or with permanent long term trends that must be adverse to us in the future.

The secret of success in the future is to continue vigorously with world development, both in industry and in agriculture, but taking care that the rates of growth do not diverge disastrously. In the second half of the nineteenth century equilibrium was maintained with manufactures growing at a cumulative annual rate of 4 per cent per annum, and primary commodities at a cumulative annual rate of 3 per cent. After the war, economic expansion slackened because equilibrium ceased to be maintained between the rates of growth of primary and of industrial production. It is frequently asserted that the trouble was that industrial production grew too rapidly in comparison with primary production but the truth is the exact opposite of this. In the inter-war period it was primary production that was relatively excessive. The decline of world trade in manufactures was due, not as is alleged to the industrialisation of new countries, but on the contrary to the decelerated demand for primary commodities, and to the resultant movement of the terms of trade. World trade in manufactures would have been larger in the inter-war period than it was, unemployment lower, and the world's standard of living much higher, if there had been more industrialisation and a less rapid growth of primary production.

It may be that the problem will be different in the future, and that the future menace to prosperity may prove to be the failure of primary production to keep up with growing demand. This was what Malthus was expecting at the beginning of the nineteenth century. He was wrong then, but this does not prove that his successors today must also be wrong. In the past hundred years primary production has not failed to respond to the growth of manufactures; and if the economies of Asia are fructified by an inflow of knowledge and of capital, which will stimulate both their manufactures and their primary production, there is no *a priori* reason to expect these two to grow at incompatible rates. History has shown Malthus to be wrong in thinking that population must grow faster than food supply; our problem, in the inter-war period was rather how easy it is for primary production to outstrip the growth of population.

The lesson of the inter-war period is fairly clear. The prosperity of the world has depended in the past on rapid industrialisation, achieved by a steady transfer of resources out of primary production; and when we fail to maintain a sufficiently rapid transfer, the whole world economy is upset. But the inter-war period is not the whole of human history, and it is quite conceivable that in the future, near or far, the need may be rather to concentrate on expanding primary production, at the expense of too rapid industrialisation. The true lesson, and the real secret of success, is to steer our way between the opposite dangers; to retain the nineteenth century goal of expanding both industry and agriculture, but to increase, if we can, the flexibility of the world economy so that resources may move more easily and swiftly between industry and agriculture, in whichever direction the future may demand.

CHAPTER XIV

CONCLUSION

IT is not possible to summarise in one chapter all the lessons of the inter-war period. They were too varied, testing the whole subject matter of economics at one point or another. Neither is it necessary; the lessons have already emerged from each episode as we analysed it, and just to string them together in a series of disconnected generalisations would mislead rather than help. We confine ourselves in this chapter to one or two general reflections.

When one begins to study the inter-war period through its literature one is struck at once by the contrasting approaches of writers in the twenties and in the later thirties. In the twenties economists write of current events as meteorologists write of sun and rain. Whether conditions will improve or deteriorate is taken as a matter beyond human control; business forecasting develops side by side with weather forecasting; the rules governing upward and downward movements are sought, and symptoms isolated. In the thirties, on the other hand, this attitude disappears altogether; it comes to be regarded as the duty of governments to alter and control the course of economic events, and to eliminate adverse movements; and governments do indeed apply themselves with vigour to types of policy which would have commanded universal disrespect in the twenties. The war has still further heightened the contrast; the belief that governments can entirely determine the course of economic events has been exaggerated to the point of naïvety. In twenty years the climate of economic opinion has changed completely.

To judge governments by what they did does not inspire much confidence in them, for they did many foolish things in these twenty years. And yet, it remains true that the climate of the twenties is not one to which we should be wise to return. For it is one of the outstanding lessons of the inter-war period that the economic system cannot just be left to look after itself. The price mechanism has wonderful virtues, not usually adequately appreciated. But there are limits to what should be asked of it. All along the line it requires to be supplemented by positive and intelligent government action.

The great problem for our generation is to learn to make government action positive and intelligent. It is no longer necessary to argue the case for action, except in rarefied circles; governments in these days are not allowed to stand aside from economic events, even if they would. It would not be unfair to say that, on the record, governments failed hopelessly in the inter-war period, both in doing the wrong things, and in refraining from doing the right things, and it will be no easy task to improve their quality. For there is no magic formula. It simply is not true that, given the will to plan, any child can see what should be done; and those political parties, both right and left, which have traded on such phrases as "planning" and "State control" have merely deceived themselves with catchwords if they believe that the will to plan itself solves any problems. They have still to learn to distinguish between good plans and bad, and to suit the objectives of state control to the particular problems and circumstances of the moment. To learn to control our economy will be a long and patient process.

The other great lesson of the inter-war period is that without international cooperation we are lost. The difficulties of Central Europe in the early post-war years; the long period it took for European output to regain its pre-war level; the deflationary curtailment of international trade after 1929; the debtor-creditor muddles; competitive exchange depreciation; all these serve only to remind us that nations cannot prosper in isolation. National sovereignty in economic relations spells chaos. In all matters where the actions of one country impinge upon others—in tariff policy, currency valuation, migration, international investment, control of the trade cycle—change of national policy must be internationally discussed, and if possible, internationally controlled; and also, international action to promote stability is a vital necessity if international cooperation in other fields is to be sustained.

The signs are that we are beginning to learn some of the lessons, if only in part. Last time there were five runaway inflations in Europe; this time there have only been two. The transition from war to peace time economies seems to be proceeding more wisely on the whole, and international assistance to the most needy countries has already proved more generous and more prompt. Governments are beginning to make official surveys of their country's problems, and—for surveys are not new—seem more likely to act on the results in future than they have been in the past. New proposals for an international monetary system and for international trade policy recognise the difficulties which proved so troublesome in these spheres between the wars, and make some provision towards removing them. International capital investment receives unexpected provision. No one can consider for one moment that the battle is won, but it is good to find that agreement can be secured even as far as we have gone. Each generation looks contemptuously on the failures of its predecessors; it is for ours to show that it can learn also from their mistakes.

APPENDICES

TABLE XV

BRITISH SERIES, 1811–1937. ANNUAL AVERAGES. (For choice of dates see Chapter XI, p. 141)

	Prices	Interest	Production	Imports	Exports	Terms of Trade	Employment	Investment	Investment ÷ Industrial Production	Capital Export	Cap. Export Ratio
	1	2	3	4	5	6	7	8	9	10	11
1811–18	176	4-63	9	4	4	123	—	—	—	—	—
1819–25	129	3-87	11	5	5	128	—	—	—	—	—
1826–36	111	3-50	13	7	6	110	—	—	—	—	—
1837–46	109	3-23	17	10	10	92	—	—	—	—	—
1847–53	96	3-21	24	15	15	90	—	—	—	—	—
1854–60	116	3-23	31	20	24	91	*96.14*	—	—	—	—
1861–65	119	3-29	34	24	26	88	96.36	—	—	—	—
1866–74	108	3-27	44	33	36	91	96.58	*44*	*99*	*61*	*56*
1875–83	103	3-08	53	47	47	84	95.47	60	115	11	10
1884–89	83	2-86	60	55	59	92	93.56	57	94	58	53
1890–99	77	2-46	69	70	63	93	95.56	79	114	36	22
1900–07	85	2-75	80	84	74	99	95.71	104	130	52	21
1908–13	93	3-14	89	92	91	97	94.87	92	104	165	82
1914–20	193	4-36	88	83	65	106	98.42	—	—	—	—
1921–29	154	4-57	86	104	79	127	88.2	—	—	*92*	—
1930–37	102	3-52	99	115	64	138	83.2	—	—	−29	—

1913 = 100 except in columns 2, 7, 10, and 11.

1. Sauerbeck index of wholesale prices. (*a*)
2. Yield on consols. (*b*)
3. Index of industrial production. (*c*)
4. Quantum of imports, at 1694 prices. (*d*)
5. Quantum of exports, at 1694 prices. (*e*)
6. Terms of trade (export prices divided by import prices). (*f*)
7. Employment rate (unemployment percentage inverted); (*g*) the first figure is for 1856–1860.
8. Quantum of domestic capital investment; the first figure is for 1870–74. (*h*)
9. Index of capital (8) divided by index of industrial production (3); the first figure is for 1870–74.
10. Export of capital, in £ million; the first figure is for 1870–74 and the penultimate figure is for 1922–9. (*i*)
11. Ratio of capital export to home investment (values); the first figure is for 1870–74. (*j*)

TABLE XVI

MISCELLANEOUS PRODUCTION SERIES. ANNUAL AVERAGES. 1913=100

	U.S.A. Manufactures 12	Germany Industry 13	World Manufactures 14
1861–65 .	—	15	—
1866–74 .	12	20	—
1875–83 .	19	25	26
1884–89 .	29	34	34
1890–99 .	40	49	46
1900–07 .	68	74	69
1908–13 .	84	91	87
1914–20 .	112	61	—
1921–29 .	145	80	108
1930–37 .	137	72	144

12. U.S.A. index of manufacturing production. (*k*)
13. Germany: index of industrial production. (*l*)
14. World: index of manufacturing production. (*m*)

TABLE XVII

Inter Cyclical Percentage Average Annual Rates of Growth

	U.K. Industrial Production	U.K. Imports	U.K. Exports	U.S.A. Manufacturing Production	Germany Industrial Production	World Manufacturing Production
	15	16	17	18	19	20
1811/18 to 1819/25 . .	4.1	5.9	2.4	—	—	—
1819/25 to 1826/36 . .	1.6	3.9	4.1	—	—	—
1826/36 to 1837/46 . .	3.0	2.0	5.4	—	—	—
1837/46 to 1847/53 . .	4.6	5.9	6.8	—	—	—
1847/53 to 1854/60 . .	4.0	4.3	8.0	—	—	—
1854/69 to 1861/65 . .	2.2	3.5	1.5	—	—	—
1861/65 to 1866/74 . .	4.0	6.1	5.3	—	5.0	—
1866/74 to 1874/83 . .	2.3	4.7	3.9	6.8	3.3	—
1874/83 to 1884/89 . .	1.7	2.3	3.5	6.7	4.7	3.3
1884/89 to 1890/99 . .	1.9	3.5	0.9	5.0	5.4	4.6
1890/99 to 1900/07 . .	1.9	2.2	1.9	7.7	5.8	5.4
1900/07 to 1908/13 . .	1.6	1.3	3.3	3.6	·3.1	3.9
1908/13 to 1914/20 . .	−0.1	−1.5	−0.8	5.1	−5.1	—
1914/20 to 1921/29 . .	−0.4	3.1	−1.8	4.4	+4.0	—
1921/29 to 1930/37 . .	+0.5	1.2	−2.2	−0.7	−1.3	4.3

15. From table XV, column 3.
16. From table XV, column 4.
17. From table XV, column 5.
18. From table XVI, column 12.
19. From table XVI, column 13.
20. From table XVI, column 14.

TABLE XVIII

U.S.A. Real Income Series. (*n*)

	% of National Product Saved	Annual Rates of Growth		
		Net Capital Formation	Net National Product	
	21	22	23	
1869/78 . .	13.7			
1874/83 . .	14.3	10.4	9.1	1869/78 to 1874/83
1879/88 . .	14.7	6.8	6.3	1874/83 to 1879/88
1884/93 . .	16.1	5.8	3.5	1879/88 to 1884/93
1889/98 . .	16.2	3.2	2.8	1884/93 to 1889/98
1894/03 . .	14.8	2.4	4.6	1889/98 to 1894/03
1899/08 . .	13.5	3.0	5.1	1894/03 to 1899/08
1904/13 . .	13.1	3.2	4.1	1899/08 to 1904/13
1909/18 . .	13.0	2.4	2.5	1904/13 to 1909/18
1914/23 . .	11.5	−0.1	2.6	1909/08 to 1914/23
1919/28 . .	10.2	1.4	4.1	1914/23 to 1919/28
1924/33 . .	6.0	−7.5	1.2	1919/28 to 1924/33
1929/38 . .	1.4	−15.2	−0.3	1924/33 to 1929/38

TABLE XIX

Annual Rate of Growth of Population

24 United States		25 Great Britain	
1820–30	3.35	1821–31	1.54
1830–40	3.27	1831–41	1.40
1840–50	3.59	1841–51	1.23
1850–60	3.56	1851–61	1.11
1860–70	2.26	1861–71	1.27
1870–80	3.01	1871–81	1.40
1880–90	2.55	1881–91	1.12
1890–00	2.07	1891–01	1.20
1900–10	2.10	1901–11	1.04
1910–20	1.49	1911–21	0.47
1920–30	1.61	1921–31	0.47
1930–40	0.72		

SOURCES

(*a*) This conversion to base 1913 has been made by Schlote, W., in his *Entwicklung und Strukturwandlungen des englischen Aussenhandels von 1700 bis zur Gegenwart*, p. 179.
(*b*) From the *Statistical Abstract of the United Kingdom*, and, for earlier years, from Warren, G. F. and Pearson, F.A., *Gold and Prices*.
(*c*) Up to 1929 the index compiled by Hoffman, W. in his article "Ein Index der industriellen Produktion für Grossbritannien seit dem 18 Jahrhundert," *Weltwirtschaftliches Archiv*, 1934.
(*d*) Calculated from Schlote, *op cit.*, p. 133.
(*e*) *Ibid.*, p. 133.
(*f*) *Ibid.*, p. 179.
(*g*) Up to 1920 the trade union rate; thereafter the insurance rate. Both taken from Beveridge, *Full Employment in a Free Society*.
(*h*) The index compiled by A.J. Cairncross, in his unpublished doctoral thesis, *Home Investment in Great Britain 1870–1913*. The figures relate to gross investment.
(*i*) Up to 1912, the figures of Hobson, C.K., in *The Export of Capital*. Thereafter, from the Board of Trade's Balance of Payments estimates.
(*j*) Calculated from A. J. Cairncross, *op. cit.* The capital export figures in this calculation are Cairncross's revision of Hobson's figures.
(*k*) Frickey's index as given in League of Nations *Industrialisation and Foreign Trade*. The missing years 1866–69 and 1914–19 are taken from the index used by Persons, W. M., in *Forecasting Business Cycles*.
(*l*) Up to 1929 the index compiled by Wagenfuhr, R., *Die Industrie-wirtschaft;* thereafter from League of Nations, *International Statistical Year Book*.
(*m*) League of Nations, *Industrialisation and Foreign Trade*.
(*n*) Estimates by Kuznets, S., in *National Product since* 1869.

NOTES

CHAPTER II

1. Manchester Guardian Commercial, *Reconstruction in Europe*, p. 489.
2. The League of Nations has published an excellent study, *Relief Deliveries and Relief Loans, 1919–1923*, on which the account given here is largely based.
3. For all these figures see *ibid.*, pp. 53–55.
4. The best account is in the League of Nations publication, *Economic Fluctuations in the United States and the United Kingdom, 1918–22.*
5. Quoted in League of Nations, *Europe's Overseas Needs 1919–20 and How They were Met*, p. 8.
6. Mitrany, D., *The Effects of the War on South Eastern Europe*, pp. 172–3.
7. The exhaustive study of the German inflation is Bresciani-Turroni, *The Economics of Inflation*, on which this account is based.
8. All figures in this section are from Prof. A. Baykov's admirable book, *The Development of the Soviet Economic System*, on which this account is based.
9. For discussion see Harris, S. E., *The Monetary Problems of the British Empire.*
10. League of Nations, *Urban and Rural Housing;* see also Bowley, M., *Housing and the State.*
11. Source: League of Nations, *Industrialisation and Foreign Trade*, p. 134.
12. League of Nations, *Agricultural Production in Continental Europe during the 1914–18 War and the Reconstruction Period.*

CHAPTER III

1. This and the figures in the next four paragraphs are computed from Burns, A. F., *Economic Research and the Keynesian Thinking of our Times*, which contains a most useful collection of American statistics for the period 1923 to 1929.
2. As calculated by Dr. J. Marschak; quoted in Clark, C. G., *The Conditions of Economic Progress*, p. 403. Investment here includes reparations and gold imports.
3. Report of the "Wiggin" Committee on *The Credit Situation of Germany*, published as a supplement to *The Economist*, 22nd August, 1931.
4. League of Nations, *Review of World Trade*, 1927–29.
5. Professor Bowley's index The earlier series based on 1913 has been recalculated and joined to the later series based on 1924: the recalculation is taken from Robbins, L. C., *The Great Depression*, p. 236.
6. Source: *Ministry of Labour Gazette*, January 1930. The wholesale price index is that published by *The Statist.* The index in the preceding chapter is the Board of Trade's.
7. U. S. Department of Agriculture, *Abstract of Agricultural Statistics*, 1945.
8. League of Nations, *Memorandum on Tariff Level Indices.*
9. League of Nations, *World Economic Survey, 1931/32*, pp. 39–40.
10. *Ibid.*, p. 176.

CHAPTER IV

1. It is particularly interesting now to read the reports of the Harvard Economic Society published in the *Bulletin of the London and Cambridge Economic Service* during 1929 and 1930.
2. League of Nations, *Statistical Year Book*, 1930–31.
3. For a summary of the American literature see Mason, E. S., "Price Inflexibility", *The Review of Economic Statistics*, May 1938. The position may have been different in Great Britain, where statistical analysis suggests some decrease in flexibility; see Singer, H. W., "The Inflexibility of the Price System", *Transactions of the Manchester Statistical Society*, 1938–39.
4. For some of the ablest expressions of this view see Robbins, L. C., *The Great Depression*, and the League of Nations publications, *The Course and Phases of the World Depression*, and *World Economic Survey, 1931–2*. The case against this view is marshalled in Wilson, T., *Fluctuations in Income and Employment*, and in Schumpeter, J. A., *Business Cycles*, Vol. II.
5. For discussion see Wilson, T., *op. cit.*
6. League of Nations, *Commercial Banks 1925–33*, p. 248.
7. The evidence is not clear, but this is the conclusion of Tucker, R. S., "The Distribution of Income among Income Taxpayers in the U.S., 1863–1935", *Quarterly Journal of Economics*, August 1938.
8. Consumption was a larger proportion of *net* national income in the decade 1919–28 (see series 21 in the Statistical Appendix), but it was about the same proportion of *gross* national income, 79·2 % in 1919–28 compared with an average of 79·6 % in 1889–1913.
9. See series 18 and 23 in the Statistical Appendix.
10. League of Nations, *Review of World Trade, 1933*.
11. League of Nations, *World Production and Prices, 1935/36*, p. 22.
12. United States Department of Commerce, *The United States in the World Economy*, p. 29.
13. *Ibid.*, p. 6.
14. League of Nations, *World Economic Survey, 1931/32*, p. 172.
15. Professor Schumpeter considers it to be the most important factor of all; see his *Business C cles*, Vol. II.
16. League of Nations, *Review of World Trade, 1938*.
17. League of Nations, *International Currency Experience*, p. 240.

CHAPTER V

1. Figures relating to British industry and trade are given in the Appendix.
2. Calculated from League of Nations, *Industrialisation and Foreign Trade*.
3. *Ibid.* All calculations in this chapter for world trade before 1913 are from the same source.
4. Imports calculated from Schlote, W., *Entwicklung und Strukturwandlungen des englischen Aussenhandels von 1700 bis zur Gegenwart;* national income from Clark, C., *National Income and Outlay*.
5. *Op. cit.*
6. *Der Deutsche Aussenhandel unter der Einwirkung weltwirtschaftlicher Strukturwandlungen*, compiled by Kiel University Institut für Weltwirtschaft; quoted here from Staley, E., *World Economic Development*, p. 150.
7. "*Ein Index der industriellen Produktion fur Grossbrittannien seit dem 18 Jahrhundert*", in *Weltwirtschaftliches Archiv*, 1934. This index estimates production in

1924 at only 1 per cent above 1907, whereas calculations based on the Censuses of Production put it at least 20 per cent higher. Hoffman's index does not give enough weight to new post-war industries. See Clark, C., "Statistical Studies relating to the Present Economic Condition of Great Britain", *Economic Journal*, 1931.

8. Balance of payments figures from League of Nations, *Balances of Payments, 1938.*

9. Quantum and price statistics from League of Nations, *Review of World Trade, 1938;* also the statistics for shares of world trade.

10. From League of Nations, *International Statistical Year Book.*

11. For discussion see Political and Economic Planning, *Report on International Trade*, and Benham, F. C., *Great Britain under Protection.*

12. From League of Nations, *International Trade Statistics.*

13. Taken from an article by Clay, H., "The Place of Exports in British Industry after the War", *Economic Journal*, 1942.

14. Calculated, using Colin Clark's estimates of national income for 1913 and 1929, in *National Income and Outlay*, and the official estimate for 1938.

15. Benham, F. C., *Great Britain under Protection*, p. 224. The source and the method of estimation are not given.

16. Clark, C., *National Income and Outlay*, Chapter XIII, relying especially on Jones, G. T., *Increasing Return.*

CHAPTER VI

1. The fullest discussion of Nazi economic policy is in Guillebaud, C. W., *The Economic Recovery of Germany 1933–38*, on which much of this account is based.

2. For full discussion see Royal Institute of International Affairs, *South Eastern Europe*, and Momtchiloff, N., *Ten Years of Controlled Trade in S.E. Europe.*

3. Guillebaud, *op. cit.*, p. 46.

CHAPTER VII

1. League of Nations, *Industrialisation and Foreign Trade.*
2. League of Nations, *Review of World Trade, 1938*, p. 76.
3. League of Nations, *Balances of Payments, 1938.*
4. League of Nations, *Statistical Year Book.*
5. Marjolin, R., "Reflections on the Blum Experiment", *Economica*, 1938.
6. League of Nations, *Statistical Year Book.*
7. *Ibid.*
8. Peel, G., *The Economic Policy of France*, p. 198.
9. Kalecki, M., "The Lesson of the Blum Experiment," *Economic Journal*, 1938.
10. *Ibid.*
11. This is the opinion of M. Marjolin, *loc. cit.*, on whose account this section is based.
12. Calculated from International Labour Office, *Year Book of Labour Statistics.*
13. League of Nations, *Statistical Year Book.*
14. These are the conclusions of Mr. Kalecki, *loc. cit.*

CHAPTER VIII

1. Calculated, using Kuznets's estimates of national income in *National Income and Its Composition 1919–1938*.
2. Hamilton, W. H., and Till, I. *Anti-Trust in Action*, Temporary National Economic Committee Monograph, No. 17.
3. This is one of the most disputed points of theory. A reduction in the "propensity to consume" diminishes consumption, and this discourages investment and employment. On the other hand an increase in profitability encourages investment. When the latter is secured only at the expense of the former the net result depends more than anything else, on psychological conditions at the moment. We are arguing here that in the U.S.A. in the summer of 1933 they were probably favourable to a cumulative upswing.
4. Arnold, T., *The Bottlenecks of Business*.
5. Barger, H., and Landsberg, H., *American Agriculture, 1899–1939*, p. 42.
6. Burns, A. F., *Economic Research and the Keynesian Thinking of our Times*.
7. *Ibid.*
8. *Ibid.*
9. League of Nations, *Statistical Year Book*.
10. Slichter, S. H., "The Downturn of 1937" in *The Review of Economic Statistics*, August 1938.
11. As defined and calculated by Villard, H. H., in *Deficit Spending and the National Income*.
12. All the figures in this paragraph are from Burns, A. F., *loc. cit.*

CHAPTER IX.

1. Calculated from League of Nations, *Industrialisation and Foreign Trade*.
2. Calculated from Allen, G. C., *A Short Economic History of Modern Japan*, p. 180. Professor Allen's writings on Japan are indispensable.
3. League of Nations, *Review of World Trade*.
4. Allen, G. C. *op. cit.*, pp. 104–5.
5. League of Nations, *Review of World Trade*.
6. League of Nations, *Balances of Payments;* also Schumpeter, E. B., ed., *The Industrialisation of Japan and Manchukuo*, 1930–1940.
7. League of Nations, *Statistical Year Book*.
8. National income figures in Schumpeter, E. B., *op. cit.*, p. 16.
9. *Ibid.*, p. 16.
10. *Ibid.*, p. 831.
11. Allen, G. C., *op. cit.*, p. 138.
12. This explanation is Professor Allen's, *op. cit.*, Chapter IX.

CHAPTER X

1. Baykov, A., *The Development of the Soviet Economic System*, p. 121. This is an invaluable book. Without it this chapter could not have been written.
2. *Ibid.*, p. 325.
3. Calculated from League of Nations, *Industrialisation and Foreign Trade*.
4. Baykov, A., *op. cit.*, pp. 154, 165.

5. Jasny, N., "Intricacies of Russian National Income Indices", *Journal of Political Economy*, 1947.

6. Lorimer, F., *The Population of the Soviet Union*, p. 106.

7. Clark, C. G., *Critique of Russian Statistics*, p. 52.

8. Baykov, A., *op. cit.*, p. 156.

9. Clark, C. G., *The Conditions of Economic Progress*, pp. 399–400. And for savings in other countries, see *ibid.*, p. 406.

10. There is some confusion in what we mean by "percentage of national income saved". The simplest way to express this confusion is to take an arbitrary example. Suppose that in a certain community 10 per cent of the physical resources of labour and property are devoted to increasing the stock of capital. Suppose, secondly, that these resources are remunerated at a much higher level than the rest, say at double the rate, so that they receive 18 per cent of the national income. And suppose, further, that they are highly inefficient, and produce only a very small quantity of capital goods, so that if their product and the product of the other resources are both revalued at British prices, it will amount only to 5 per cent of the national income. We then have three different measures of the amount of saving that the country is performing, each of them valid and useful. The first concept, according to which 10 per cent is saved, is that which we are normally seeking. The second concept, according to which 18 per cent is saved, is important if we are to understand the political repercussions of saving; e.g. it measures how much of their produce the peasants have to forego, for the benefit of persons engaged in producing capital goods. The second concept is also the one relevant to financial policy; it measures the inflationary potentialities of investment. The third concept, according to which only 5 per cent is saved, is valuable if one wishes to compare the effects on productivity of different levels of saving in different countries. This is Mr. Clark's purpose, and this is the concept he uses. But for understanding the internal repercussions of investment, it is the second concept that we need. On the basis of this concept, Russian saving was somewhere between 20 per cent and 30 per cent of the national income in the 1930's.

11. Baykov, A., *op. cit.*, p. 196.

12. *Ibid.*, p. 325.

13. This is the conclusion of a detailed comparison made by Professor A. Bergson, *The Structure of Soviet Wages*.

14. Baykov, A., *op. cit.*, p. 346.

15. *Ibid.*, p. 286.

16. Jasny, N., *op. cit.*

17. By Professor Paul Douglas; quoted in Clark, C. G., *The Conditions of Economic Progress*, p. 283.

18. Clark, C. G., *Critique of Russian Statistics*.

CHAPTER XI

1. Real wages did not rise in Germany or in Japan between 1929 and 1938 despite a great increase in industrial production because of the diversion of resources to war preparation.

2. Figures given in this and the following chapters for world manufacturing production are taken from League of Nations, *Industrialisation and Foreign Trade*. The world index given there becomes particularly doubtful in the 1930's. There are two important sources of error. The index for the U.S.S.R. exaggerates the growth of U.S.S.R. manufacturing, but on the other hand the weights used

underestimate the importance of U.S.S.R. output relatively to other countries, and this is actually the more significant. Thus, if the Russian figure for 1937 is reduced from 772.2 to 419.3 (see note 5 to Chapter X), and the weight increased from 4 per cent to 13 per cent of world output, the world index becomes 203 instead of 196. The world index given for the 1930's is therefore a little too low.

Figures for world trade are from League of Nations, *Review of World Trade*. Figures for the trade in primary products and in manufactures separately are from *Industrialisation and Foreign Trade*. Unfortunately the figures given in the latter for the 1920's and 1930's are not compatible with those given in the former, and are obviously too low. Value figures correspond, but price and quantum figures do not. The first reason for this is that the latter uses British prices for the 1920's, which are too high as British prices were out of line with world prices. Thus *Industrialisation and Foreign Trade* calculates prices for trade as a whole in 1926/29 as having risen by 48 per cent since 1913, whereas the *Review* estimate is 40 per cent, which is more likely and gives a greater quantum. Secondly, the prices used by *I. & F. T.* give an increase in manufacturing prices relatively to primary of about 13 per cent, which is too high. Comparison with other indices suggests about 10 per cent. The figures given in the text thus differ from those given by *I. & F. T.*, and the differences are as follows:

	Primary Products		Manufactures	
	Price	Quantum	Price	Quantum
1926/29				
Text . .	135.9	117.7	149.4	111.7
I. & F. T. .	142	112.7	160.0	104.3
1936/38				
Text . .	56.8	119.0	73.7	96.5
I. & F. T. .	58	116.6	77.2	92.1

3. Beveridge, *Full Employment in a Free Society*, p. 281.
4. Schumpeter, J. A., *Business Cycles*.
5. Garvy, G., "Kondratieff's Theory of Long Cycles", in *The Review of Economic Statistics*, November 1945.

CHAPTER XII

1. Quoted in League of Nations, *Industrialisation and Foreign Trade*, p. 19.
2. *Ibid.*, p. 18.
3. *Ibid.*, p. 157.
4. Liepmann, H., *Tariff Levels and the Economic Unity of Europe*. The author gives indices only for individual countries; the figures shown in the text are calculated from his indices, using import values as weights.
5. The figures for 1900 are from Carr-Saunders, A. M., *World Population*, and those for 1913 and 1929 from League of Nations, *Statistical Year Book*.
6. Notestein, F. W., *The Future Population of Europe and the Soviet Union*, p. 75.
7. Calculated from the appendices in League of Nations, *International Currency Experience*.
8. League of Nations, *The Network of World Trade*, pp. 73 *et seq*.
9. For discussion of the problems see Graham, B., *World Commodities and World Currency*.

NOTES

CHAPTER XIII

1. Snyder, C., "New Measures of Trade and of Economic Growth", in *Revue de l'Institut International de Statistique*, January 1934.
2. League of Nations, *Industrialisation and Foreign Trade*.
3. Hirschman, A. O., "The Commodity Structure of World Trade", in *The Quarterly Journal of Economics*, 1943.
4. Quoted in League of Nations, *Industrialisation and Foreign Trade*, p. 19.
5. Hirschman, A. O., *op. cit.*
6. There is a vigorous discussion of the relevance of U.S. data in Terborgh, G., *The Bogey of Economic Maturity*.
7. Clark, C., *National Income and Outlay*, p. 185.
8. Clark, C. *The Conditions of Economic Progress*, p. 406, and *The Economics of* 1960, facing p. 118.
9. *The Bogey of Economic Maturity*, Chapters III and IV.
10. From Kuznets's estimates we may calculate the average annual rate of growth of real income per head of population as follows:

1869/78	to	1874/83	5·1%	1894/03	to	1899/08	2·3%
74/83	„	79/88	2·5%	99/08	„	04/13	1·1%
79/88	„	84/93	0·2%	04/13	„	09/18	0·5%
84/93	„	89/98	0·5%	09/18	„	14/23	1·2%
89/98	„	94/03	2·2%	14/23	„	19/28	2·6 %

There is a marked wave, due to the choice of dates and the trade cycle. But the rate of growth in the 1920's is as high as that of the 1900's, and of the 1880's. The secular decline in the growth of total U.S. income is due not to falling growth per head, but to falling growth of total population .

11. *The Conditions of Economic Progress*, Chapter V, and *The Economics of* 1960, p. 29.
12. See the studies made by Burns, A. F., in his *Production Trends in the United States*.
13. See especially League of Nations, *Industrialisation and Foreign Trade*.
14. *Ibid.*, p. 100.
15. See Chapter XI, note 2. This is the uncorrected index; the four-fold increase for Russia in the preceding paragraph is the corrected estimate.
16. Clark, C., *The Conditions of Economic Progress*, Chapter VII.

BIBLIOGRAPHY

PART I, THE CYCLE

Arndt, H. W.: *The Economic Lessons of the Nineteen Thirties*, London, 1944.
Beveridge, Lord: *British Food Control*, London, 1928.
Bowley, A. L.: *Some Economic Consequences of the Great War*, London, 1930.
de Bordes, J. v. W.: *The Austrian Crown*, London, 1924.
Hodson, H. V.: *Slump and Recovery, 1929–1937*, Oxford, 1938.
Jack, D. T.: *The Restoration of European Currencies*, London, 1927.
League of Nations: *Agricultural Production in Continental Europe during the 1914–18 War and the Reconstruction Period*, Geneva, 1943.
Economic Fluctuations in the United States and the United Kingdom, 1918–1922, Geneva, 1942.
Europe's Overseas Needs, 1919–20, and How they were Met, Geneva, 1943.
Reconstruction Schemes in the inter-war Period, Geneva, 1945.
Relief Deliveries and Relief Loans, 1919–1923, Geneva, 1943.
The Course and Control of Inflation, Geneva, 1946.
The Course and Phases of the World Depression, Geneva, 1931.
World Economic Survey, Geneva, Annual from 1931–32.
Lloyd, E. M. H.: *Experiments in State Control*, Oxford, 1924.
Loveday, A. and others: *The World's Economic Future*, London, 1938.
Manchester Guardian Commercial: *Reconstruction in Europe Supplements*, Manchester, 1922–3.
Moulton, H. G. and Pasvolsky, L.: *War Debts and World Prosperity*, Washington, 1932.
National Industrial Conference Board: *A Picture of World Economic Conditions*, New York, 7 vols., 1928–32.
Pringle, W. H., ed.: *Economic Problems in Europe Today*, London, 1928.
Robbins, L. C.: *The Great Depression*, London, 1934.
Salter, Sir J. A.: *Recovery*, London, 1933.
Salter, Sir J. A. and others: *The World Economic Crisis*, London, 1932.
Schumpeter, J. A. *Business Cycles*, New York, 1939
U.K. Department of Overseas Trade: *Economic Survey of Certain Countries specially affected by the War at the close of the Year 1919*, London, 1920.
Wilson, T.: *Fluctuations in Income and Employment*, London, 1942.

PART II, NATIONAL POLICIES

The United Kingdom
Abrams, M. A.: *The Condition of the British People, 1911–45*, London, 1946.
Abrams, M. A., ed.: *Britain and her Export Trade*, London, 1946.
Anon: *Britain without Capitalists*, London, 1936.
Benham, F. C. C.: *British Monetary Policy*, London, 1932.
Great Britain under Protection, New York, 1941.
Beveridge, Lord: *Full Employment in a Free Society*, London, 1944.
Bowley, M.: *Housing and the State*, London, 1945.
British Association for the Advancement of Science: *Britain in Depression*, London, 1935. *Britain in Recovery*, London, 1938.

Burns, E. M.: *British Unemployment Programmes, 1920–38*, Washington, 1941.
Clark, C. G.: *National Income and Outlay*, London, 1937.
Clay, H.: *The Post-war Unemployment Problem*, London, 1929.
Cole, G. D. H.: *A Short History of the British Working Class Movement*, London, 1928. *British Trade and Industry*, London, 1932.
Cole, G. D. H. and M. I.: *The Condition of Britain*, London, 1937.
Francis, E. V.: *Britain's Economic Strategy*, London, 1939.
Harris, S. E.: *The Monetary Problems of the British Empire*, New York, 1931.
Hill, A. C. C. and Lubin, I.: *The British Attack on Unemployment*, Washington, 1937.
Hirst, F. W.: *The Consequences of the War to Great Britain*, Oxford, 1934.
Loveday, A.: *Britain and World Trade*, London, 1931.
Richardson, J. H.: *British Economic Foreign Policy*, London, 1936.
Schlote, W.: *Entwicklung und Strukturwandlungen des englischen Aussenhandels von 1700 bis zur Gegenwart*, Jena, 1938.

Germany

Angell, J. W.: *The Recovery of Germany*, New York, 1929.
Bresciani-Turroni, C.: *The Economics of Inflation*, London, 1937.
Einzig, P.: *Germany's Default*, London, 1934.
Graham, F. D.: *Exchange, Prices and Production in Hyper-inflation in Germany, 1920–23*, Princeton, 1930.
Guillebaud, C. W.: *The Economic Recovery of Germany, 1933–38*, London, 1939.
Levy, H.: *Industrial Germany*, Cambridge, 1935.
Moulton, H. G. and McGuire, E. E.: *Germany's Capacity to Pay*, New York, 1923.
Nathan, O.: *The Nazi Economic System*, Durham, 1944.
Schacht, H.: *The Stabilisation of the Mark*, London, 1926.
Schmidt, C. T.: *German Business Cycles*, 1924–33, New York, 1934.
Stolper, G.: *German Economy*, 1870–1940, London, 1940.
Trivanovitch, V.: *The Economic Development of Germany under National Socialism*, New York, 1937.
Wiggs, K. I.: *Unemployment in Germany since the War*, London, 1933.

France

Einzig, P.: *France's Crisis*, London, 1934.
Haight, F. A.: *French Import Quotas*, London, 1935. *A History of French Commercial Policies*, New York, 1941.
Ogburn, W. F. and Jaffe, W.: *The Economic Development of Post-war France*, New York, 1929.
Peel, G.: *The Economic Policy of France*, London, 1937.
Rogers, J. H.: *The Process of Inflation in France*, 1914–27, New York, 1929.

The United States of America

Arnold, T.: *The Bottlenecks of Business*, New York, 1940.
Bailey, S. K.: *Roosevelt and his New Deal, Fact No. 17*, London, 1938.
Barger, H. and Landsberg, H. A.: *American Agriculture, 1899–1939*, New York, 1942.
Barger, H., and Schurr, S. H.: *The Mining Industries, 1899–1939*, New York, 1944.
Baster, A. S. J.: *The Twilight of American Capitalism*, London, 1937.
Brookings Institution: *The Recovery Problem in the United States*, Washington, 1936.

Burns, A. F.: *Production Trends in the United States since 1870*, New York, 1934.
Fabricant, S.: *The Output of Manufacturing Industries, 1899–1937*, New York, 1940.
Employment in Manufacturing, 1899–1939, New York, 1942.
Hansen, A. H.: *Full Recovery or Stagnation*, New York, 1938.
Hugh-Jones, E. A. and Radice, E. M.: *An American Experiment*, London, 1936.
Kuznets, S. S.: *National Income and its Composition*, 1919–38, New York, 1941.
National Product since 1869, New York, 1946.
Lewis, C. and Schlotterbeck, K. T.: *America's Stake in International Investments*, Washington, 1938.
Lyon, L. S., ed.: *The National Recovery Administration*, Washington, 1935.
Mill, F. C.: *Economic Tendencies in the United States*, New York, 1932.
Nourse, E. G. and others: *Three Years of the Agricultural Adjustment Administration*, Washington, 1937.
Persons, W. M.: *Forecasting Business Cycles*, New York, 1931.
President's Conference on Unemployment: *Recent Economic Changes*, New York, 1929.
Roos, C. F.: *N.R.A. Economic Planning*, Bloomington, 1937.
Silberling, N. J.: *The Dynamics of Business*, New York, 1943.
Snyder, C.: *Capitalism the Creator*, New York, 1940.
Tasca, H. J.: *The Reciprocal Trade Policy of the United States*, Philadelphia, 1938.
U.S. Department of Commerce: *The United States in the World Economy*, Washington, 1942.

Japan

Allen, G. C.: *A Short Economic History of Modern Japan*, London, 1946.
Japanese Industry: Its Recent Development and Present Condition, London, 1939.
Moulton, H. G. and Ko, J.: *Japan, an Economic and Financial Appraisal*, Washington, 1931.
Schumpeter, E. B., ed.: *The Industrialisation of Japan and Manchukuo*, 1930–40, New York, 1940.
Takahashi, K.: *Factors in Japan's Recent Economic Development*, London, 1936.
Uyeda, T.: *The Recent Development of Japanese Foreign Trade*, London, 1936.
The Small Industries of Japan, Cambridge, 1938.

The U.S.S.R.

Baykov, A.: *The Development of the Soviet Economic System*, Cambridge, 1946.
Soviet Foreign Trade, Princetown, 1946.
Bergson, A.: *The Structure of Soviet Wages*, Cambridge, 1944.
Bienstock, G., and others: *Management in Russian Industry and Agriculture*, London, 1944.
Burns, E.: *Russia's Productive System*, London, 1930.
Citrine, Lord: *I Search for Truth in Russia*, London, 1936.
Clark, C. G.: *Critique of Russian Statistics*, London, 1939.
Cole, M. I. and others: *Twelve Studies in Soviet Russia*, London, 1933.
Dobb, M. H.: *Soviet Planning and Labour in Peace and War*, London, 1942.
Dobb, M. H. and Stevens, H. C.: *Russian Economic Development since the Revolution*, London, 1928.
Friedman, E. M.: *Russia in Transition*, London, 1932.
Haensel, P.: *The Economic Policy of Soviet Russia*, London, 1930.
Hoover, C. B.: *The Economic Life of Soviet Russia*, London, 1931.
Hubbard, L. E.: *Soviet Money and Finance*, London, 1936.
Soviet Trade and Distribution, London, 1938.
The Economics of Soviet Agriculture, London, 1939.

Littlepage, J. D., and Bess, D.: *In Search of Soviet Gold*, London, 1939.
Lorimer, F.: *The Population of the Soviet Union*, Geneva, 1946.
Maynard, Sir H. J.: *The Russian Peasant and Other Studies*, London, 1942.
Scott, J.: *Behind the Urals*, London, 1942.
The U.S.S.R. speaks for Itself, London, 1941.
Turin, S. P.: *The U.S.S.R., an Economic and Social Survey*, London, 1944.
Webb, S. and B.: *Soviet Communism*, London, 1935.

Miscellaneous.
Copland, D. B.: *Australia in the World Crisis, 1929–33*, Cambridge, 1934.
Ellis, H. S.: *Exchange Control in Central Europe*, Cambridge, 1939.
Mitrany, D.: *The Effect of the War in South-east Europe*, New Haven, 1936.
Momtchiloff, N.: *Ten Years of Controlled Trade in South-east Europe*, Cambridge, 1944.
Pasvolsky, L.: *The Economic Nationalism of the Danubian States*, London, 1928.
Phelps, D. M.: *The Migration of Industry to South America*, New York, 1936.
Royal Institute of International Affairs: *South Eastern Europe*, London, 1939.
Schacher, G.: *Central Europe and the Western World*, London, 1936.
Walker, E. R.: *Australia and the World Depression*, London, 1933.
Wythe, G.: *Industry in Latin America*, New York, 1945.

Part III. Trends

Bonn, M. J.: *The Crumbling of Empire*, London, 1938.
Brandt, K.: *The Reconstruction of World Agriculture*, London, 1945.
Brown, A. J.: *Industrialisation and Trade*, London, 1943.
Brown, W. A.: *The International Gold Standard Reinterpreted, 1914–34*, New York, 1940.
Clark, C. G.: *The Conditions of Economic Progress*, London, 1940.
The Economics of 1960, London, 1942.
Condliffe, J. B.: *The Reconstruction of World Trade*, London, 1941.
Feis, H.: *The Changing Pattern of International Economic Affairs*, New York, 1940.
Graham, B.: *World Commodities and World Currency*, New York, 1944.
Harris, S. E.: *Exchange Depreciation*, Cambridge, 1936.
Heuser, H.: *The Control of International Trade*, London, 1939.
Holland, W. L., ed.: *Commodity Control in the Pacific Area*, London, 1935.
International Chamber of Commerce and the Carnegie Endowment: *International Economic Reconstruction*, Paris, 1936.
Iversen, C.: *International Capital Movements*, Copenhagen, 1936.
League of Nations: *Commercial Policies in the Inter-war Period*, Geneva, 1942.
Commerical Policy in the Post-war Period, Geneva, 1945.
Enquiry into Clearing Agreements, Geneva, 1935.
Europe's Trade, Geneva, 1941.
Industrialisation and Foreign Trade, Geneva, 1946.
International Currency Experience, Geneva, 1944.
Quantitative Trade Controls, Geneva, 1943.
Raw Material Problems and Policies, Geneva, 1946.
Report on Exchange Control, Geneva, 1938.
The Conditions of Private Foreign Investment, Geneva, 1946.
The Network of World Trade, Geneva, 1942.
Urban and Rural Housing, Geneva, 1939.

Liepmann, H.: *Tariffs and the Economic Unity of Europe*, London, 1938.
Neisser, H.: *Some International Aspects of the Business Cycle*, Philadelphia, 1936.
Political and Economic Planning, *Report on International Trade*, London, 1937.
Richardson, J. H.: *Economic Disarmament*, London, 1931.
Rowe, J. W. F.: *Markets and Men*, Cambridge, 1936.
Royal Institute of International Affairs: *The Problem of International Investment*, Oxford, 1937.
World Agriculture, London, 1932.
Salter, Sir J. A.: *World Trade and its Future*, London, 1936.
Staley, E.: *World Economic Development*, Montreal, 1944.
World Economy in Transition, New York, 1939.
Tasca, H. J.: *World Trading Systems*, Geneva, 1939.
Terborgh, G.: *The Bogey of Economic Maturity*, Chicago, 1945.
Wilcox, W. F., ed.: *International Migrations*, New York.
Volume I, 1929, Volume II, 1931.
Yates, P. L.: *Commodity Control*, London, 1943.
Food Production in Western Europe, London, 1940.

League of Nations Annual Publications

Balances of Payments.
International Trade Statistics.
Money and Banking.
Review of World Trade.
Statistical Year Book.
World Economic Survey.
World Production and Prices.

AUTHORS CITED

INDEX

INDEX